ANNOTATED TEACHER'S EDITION

SADLIER

VOCABULARY WORKSHOP®

ACHIEVE

Level A

Jerome Shostak

Senior Series Consultant

Vicki A. Jacobs, Ed.D.
Lecturer on Education
Harvard Graduate School of Education
Cambridge, Massachusetts

Series Consultants

Louis P. De Angelo, Ed.D.
Superintendent of Schools
Diocese of Wilmington
Wilmington, Delaware

John Heath, Ph.D.
Professor of Classics
Santa Clara University
Santa Clara, California

**Sarah Ressler Wright,
  M.A. English Ed, NBCT**
Head Librarian
Rutherford B. Hayes High School
Delaware, Ohio

Carolyn E. Waters, J.D., Ed.S.
Georgia Dept. of Education (Ret.)
English Language Arts Consultant
Woodstock, Georgia

Ⓢ® Sadlier

Reviewers

The publisher wishes to thank for their comments and suggestions the following teachers and administrators, who read portions of the series prior to publication.

Ronald Apperson
Teacher
George Fox Middle School
Pasadena, MD

Rebecca Benjamin
English Teacher
Island Trees Memorial Middle School
Levittown, NY

Heidi Branch
8th Grade English Teacher,
  Department Chair
Belmont Ridge Middle School
Leesburg, VA

Lynne W. Jansen
ELA Instructor
Landrum Middle School
Ponte Vedra, FL

Kasandra Washington
School Counselor
Former ELA Instructor
Manor Middle School
Manor, TX

Cover: Concept/Art and Design: MK Advertising, Studio Montage and William H. Sadlier, Inc.
Cover pencil: Shutterstock.com/VikaSuh.
Photo Credits: iStockphoto.com/FatCamera: T17; fstop123: T18; kali9: T9. Getty Images/asiseeit: T6. Shutterstock.com/Tyler Olson: T21.

For additional online resources, go to SadlierConnect.com and enter the Teacher Access Code: VWA107ATN8WQ

CONTENTS

INTRODUCING
VOCABULARY WORKSHOP ACHIEVE

At each level of **VOCABULARY WORKSHOP ACHIEVE**, students are introduced to 300 carefully selected, high-utility words, many of them drawn from academic vocabulary word lists relevant to students' reading. Mastery of these words promotes word consciousness and, together with practice in vocabulary strategies, leads to improved reading and writing skills and improved performance on high-stakes standardized tests.

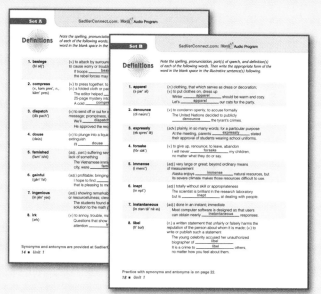

Fifteen Units of 20 words each are organized in two Sets, focusing student attention on 10 words at a time and facilitating classroom implementation. First in Set A and then in Set B, students are provided with instruction concentrated on 10 words each and practice with those words in a variety of contexts. Units conclude with synonym and antonym practice with all 20 words.

Two reading passages, related in theme or topic, begin and conclude each Unit. Students are introduced to taught words in context. Content-rich and engaging texts prompt student interest and provide examples of proper usage.

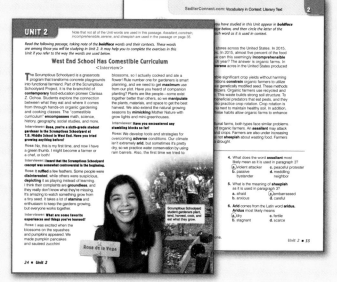

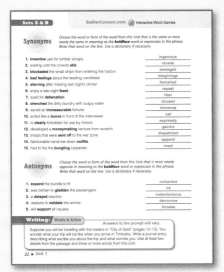

In every Unit, a writing activity prompts students to revisit the opening reading passage. In writing their responses to the prompt, students are asked to cite evidence from text and to demonstrate understanding of the meaning and proper usage of Unit words.

Practice in standardized-test formats helps students prepare for standards-aligned tests, and high-stakes state exams. Modeled on the reading sections of these tests, **Vocabulary for Comprehension** has students read single and paired passages and then answer questions associated with those passages, including questions that ask students to support their answers with details from the text.

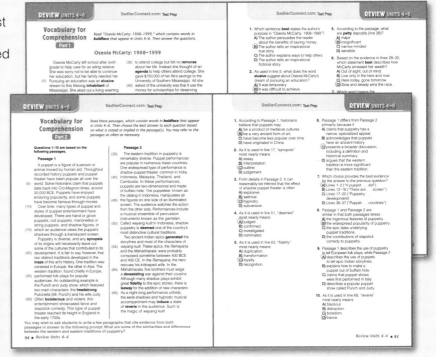

A variety of online resources and enrichment activities, including iWords audio, are available to students and teachers at **SadlierConnect.com**. Resources include interactive games, quizzes, and audio for taught words and reading passages—ideal support for English language learners and striving readers.

For more than five decades VOCABULARY WORKSHOP has helped millions of students increase their vocabularies, improve their reading, writing, and speaking skills, and prepare for standardized tests.

VOCABULARY WORKSHOP ACHIEVE continues the tradition in a redesigned format and with important new features. Standards-aligned and research-based, the program supports explicit instruction of high-utility words—ten words at a time—to expand and enrich students' vocabulary knowledge, provide skills that contribute to success on standardized tests, and complement a literature-based approach to vocabulary instruction.

VOCABULARY WORKSHOP ACHIEVE supplies instruction and practice with 300 words organized in 15 Units of 20 words each. Each of these Units is divided into two sets, focusing student attention on 10 words at a time and making classroom implementation more manageable.

All vocabulary words appear in one of the two related reading passages that begin and conclude the Units, providing students with multiple exposures to the words in the context of rich and engaging informational text, with examples of proper usage. These passages also serve as starting points for discussions of word meanings and semantic relationships.

The VOCABULARY WORKSHOP ACHIEVE word lists consist of high-utility, academic vocabulary relevant to students' classroom and independent reading. These are words that students will also encounter on standards-aligned exams.

Recognizing the importance of vocabulary to success on these tests, VOCABULARY WORKSHOP ACHIEVE includes practice with vocabulary and reading skills in standardized-test formats modeled on current standards-based exams.

Welcome to VOCABULARY WORKSHOP ACHIEVE. In the following pages, you will learn more about its instructional and assessment features, the program's print and online components, and implementation of the program.

INSTRUCTIONAL APPROACH

By Vicki A. Jacobs, Ed.D., Senior Series Consultant, Lecturer on Education, Harvard Graduate School of Education, Cambridge, MA

Vocabulary knowledge is at the heart of school learning. As early as kindergarten, it predicts later academic achievement. It is the largest contributing factor to reading comprehension, and it plays a critical role in the success that English language learners and struggling readers experience. Similarly, knowledge of academic vocabulary (words that are commonly used across academic disciplines and the specialized words characteristic of specific content areas) is at the core of student achievement.

Effective learning of academic vocabulary is a difficult, complex, and ongoing process. Research is clear that no one method or strategy is sufficient for deep word learning (for example, understanding a word well enough to use it appropriately in written and oral language). Research is also clear that direct instruction of academic vocabulary, the pedagogical foundation of VOCABULARY WORKSHOP ACHIEVE, plays a significant role in academic achievement. The requirements of effective, direct instruction of academic vocabulary are myriad. VOCABULARY WORKSHOP ACHIEVE meets these requirements, described below, through a range of approaches.

Effective direct instruction promotes word consciousness.

One purpose of direct vocabulary instruction, especially in the English classroom, where language itself is a focus of study, is the cultivation of students' word consciousness (their enthusiasm for, interest in, and ability to understand words as meaning-bearing entities). Effective teachers of word consciousness demonstrate their own curiosity about and fascination with academic language and develop students' self-consciousness about how to acquire deep knowledge of vocabulary independently.

Effective direct instruction of academic vocabulary treats word learning as an active, generative, integrative, and meaning-making process.

Over the grades, academic vocabulary becomes increasingly technical, abstract, and conceptual, and over time, the contribution of word knowledge to successful reading comprehension increases as well. From the upper elementary grades on, successful readers have self-knowledge about when, how, and why it is appropriate to apply specific word-learning skills, strategies, and processes, such as those introduced in VOCABULARY WORKSHOP ACHIEVE, to gain significant meaning from a text. They understand that vocabulary knowledge plays a significant role at all stages of the meaning-making process required for comprehension (for example, preparation for, guidance through, and the consolidation of learning from text). Through explicit instruction about the application of vocabulary skills, strategies, and processes introduced in VOCABULARY WORKSHOP ACHIEVE, teachers support students' reading comprehension as well as their ability to be independent and ongoing learners.

Effective direct instruction of academic vocabulary focuses on explicitly, purposefully, and systematically chosen words.

A common dilemma for teachers using content-area texts is choosing words for direct instruction. Teachers need to consider the words' utility across disciplines and within particular content areas, the depth of students' familiarity with the words, and the contribution that those words can make to disciplinary learning and achievement. The word lists for VOCABULARY WORKSHOP ACHIEVE meet these criteria and provide students with appropriate grade-level challenges.

Researchers agree that it is better to teach fewer academic words thoroughly than to teach more words in a cursory manner. In VOCABULARY WORKSHOP ACHIEVE, instruction and practice focus on 10 of the Unit's 20 words at a time, promoting deep knowledge of those words and contributing to the development of word consciousness.

Effective direct instruction of academic vocabulary provides students with multiple exposures to focal words in multiple contexts and offers them multiple opportunities to apply new vocabulary using a variety of strategies in oral and written language.

Multiple exposures to and varied practice with academic vocabulary contributes to students' understanding of and appreciation for the purposefulness with which writers and speakers choose their words. VOCABULARY WORKSHOP ACHIEVE exposes students to new words across a variety of exercises and contexts. Each Unit provides students with opportunities to understand words in text (receptively) and to apply that understanding through writing (expressively). Teachers can reinforce word learning by providing students with opportunities to investigate the nuanced meanings of each Unit word and how those meanings depend on the context of their use. Teachers can use writing prompts in class or as exit tickets that formatively assess how well students are synthesizing the meanings of new conceptual vocabulary words with their previous knowledge.

Effective direct instruction contributes to success on standardized tests.

Another purpose for direct instruction in academic language is to prepare students for standardized tests of verbal ability (including reading comprehension and essay writing). To perform well on standardized tests, students must have not only a wide range of vocabulary knowledge but also the ability to apply appropriate word learning strategies to determine the meaning of unfamiliar vocabulary.

Standards-aligned and state exams measure students' ability to use semantic and syntactic clues from illustrations and surrounding text in order to infer word meanings. VOCABULARY WORKSHOP ACHIEVE provides students with practice in using context to determine word meanings and nuances of meaning, as well as practice in reading skills assessed on standardized tests, including the ability to identify and cite textual evidence.

[Note: A full discussion of the research base supporting VOCABULARY WORKSHOP ACHIEVE, together with references to research sources, is available in the form of professional development papers by Vicki A. Jacobs at Professional Development in the Teacher Resources section at **SadlierConnect.com**.]

GRADE-LEVEL PLACEMENT

The chart below suggests grade placement for each level of VOCABULARY WORKSHOP ACHIEVE. These placements reflect teacher experience and recommendations but should not be taken too literally. Teachers should determine appropriate placement based on knowledge of their students' abilities, background knowledge, and reading levels, keeping in mind that differences in levels include not only the increasing difficulty of the words themselves but also syntactical complexity and the contexts in which those words appear. The program's online diagnostic materials can also help in determining appropriate placement.

Further guidance in placement is available at Professional Development in the Teacher Resources section at **SadlierConnect.com**.

Grade Placements	
Level	**Grade**
A	6
B	7
C	8

Word Lists

Each level of VOCABULARY WORKSHOP ACHIEVE presents 300 vocabulary words organized in 15 Units. Mastery of these words will increase students' comprehension, improve their writing, and enhance their oral communication skills.

Criteria for Selection: The selection of words for VOCABULARY WORKSHOP ACHIEVE is based on four criteria: currency in and usefulness for present-day American oral or written communication, frequency on recognized high-utility and academic vocabulary lists, applicability to standardized tests, and current grade-placement research.

General Sources: The word lists were developed from many sources in traditional, classic, and contemporary literature, including: novels, short stories, essays, newspaper and magazine articles, plays, and films. Spelling and vocabulary lists recognized as valid bases for teaching language skills at the middle and secondary levels were used, as well as current subject-area textbooks, glossaries, and ancillary materials (especially for general, nontechnical terms).

Dictionary and Reference Sources: The following are the primary dictionary resources used for word selection (and definitions):

- *Webster's Third International Dictionary of the English Language* (unabridged)
- *Merriam-Webster's Collegiate Dictionary* (10th, 11th, and online editions)
- *The American Heritage Dictionary of the English Language* (editions 1–4)
- *The Random House Dictionary of the English Language* (unabridged editions)
- *The Compact Edition of the Oxford English Dictionary*

Standard Word-Frequency Sources: Standard word-frequency studies were conducted to evaluate and revise the word list.

- **Primary**

  Dale-O'Rourke:

  The Living Word Vocabulary

  Carroll-Davies-Richman:

  The American Heritage Word Frequency Book

  Zeno-Ivens-Millard-Duvvuri:

  The Educator's Word Frequency Guide

- **Supplementary**

  Harris-Jacobsen:

  Basic Reading Vocabularies

  Thorndike-Lorge:

  The Teacher's Word Book of 30,000 Words

PROGRAM COMPONENTS

VOCABULARY WORKSHOP ACHIEVE offers an easily managed instructional model with print features and digital components that provide abundant practice and multiple exposures to each word in support of vocabulary building.

Print materials for each level include:

- Student Edition

- Annotated Teacher's Edition

- Unit Test Booklets, with Teacher Answer Key

- Test Prep for Standardized Exams, with Teacher Answer Key

For information about online resources available at SadlierConnect.com to support and enrich instruction, see page T17. Other digital options for each level of VOCABULARY WORKSHOP ACHIEVE include VOCABULARY WORKSHOP ACHIEVE INTERACTIVE EDITION (page T18) and VOCABULARY WORKSHOP ACHIEVE ONLINE ASSESSMENT (page T31).

Student Edition/Annotated Teacher's Edition

VOCABULARY WORKSHOP ACHIEVE features a consistent organization and instructional design that provides students with explicit, systematic instruction and practice with 300 high-utility words at each level.

The Student Edition is organized in 15 Units of 20 words each. A Review and a Word Study feature follow Units 3, 6, 9, 12, and 15. A Final Mastery Test follows the last Review.

Each Unit begins by introducing at least 15 of the Unit's 20 words in the context of a nonfiction reading passage. Those words not included in the opening passage always appear in the concluding passage.

Following the opening reading passage, instruction and practice with the 20 words is divided into two groups of 10, **Set A** and **Set B**, concentrating student attention on 10 words at a time and facilitating efficient classroom implementation. Each set includes **Definitions** and practice exercises that focus on 10 words, providing multiple exposures to the words in a variety of contexts.

The Units conclude with practice with the 20 words in aggregate, including synonyms and antonyms, a writing prompt, and a second reading passage, related in theme or topic to the first.

Reviews provide further exposures in different formats to the words taught in the three Units that precede them, and include preparation for the reading sections of standards-aligned exams.

Word Study sections provide instruction and practice with **Idioms**, **Denotation and Connotation**, and **Classical Roots**.

In the Annotated Teacher's Edition, teacher notes guide and support teachers in their instruction. Answers are shown for each student exercise page.

Units

Reading Passages (see pages 12–13)

Exposure to new or unfamiliar vocabulary in the context of reading passages helps students learn about the way these words are used as well as how to use context clues to help determine word meaning.

Each Unit in Vocabulary Workshop Achieve opens with a passage containing at least 15 of the 20 Unit words in context. These words appear in boldface to draw students' attention to the way they are used and the contexts in which they appear. Context clues embedded in the passages encourage students to figure out the meanings of words before they study their definitions.

The topics of the passages are grade-appropriate and of high-interest, and represent a variety of genres, including expository texts, informational essays, historical nonfiction, and biographies. Passages also provide exposure to figurative language such as idioms.

An iWords audio recording of each passage is available at **SadlierConnect.com**, in Student & Family Resources. Listening to audio recordings of the passages is particularly helpful to auditory learners, ELL students, and striving readers.

Instruction for the **Reading Passages** can be delivered in several ways, depending on students' reading proficiency levels and the implementation model used. Teachers may choose, during full class or small group instruction, to read aloud the passage to students to model fluent reading, have students read aloud the passages, or assign students to read the passage independently as homework prior to class.

Definitions (see pages 14–15)

One aspect of developing word consciousness in students involves providing them with definitional information about the word—the meaning or meanings denoted by it. The **Definitions** section introduces the Unit's 20 vocabulary words in two sets of 10 words each—**Set A** and **Set B**—making mastery of new words more manageable for students.

Definitions are clear, useful, and informal explanations, giving students each word's meaning without extensive detail or secondary connotations. Definitions often include synonyms to better situate the taught word in a semantic family of words closely related in meaning.

A simple abbreviation provides the part of speech with each definition. When a word functions as multiple parts of speech, the appropriate abbreviation appears before the corresponding definition.

A word's pronunciation is indicated by a simple set of diacritical marks. Only one pronunciation is given for each word, except when a word changes its pronunciation in accordance with its use as different parts of speech (for example, *ob' ject* for the noun form and *ob ject'* for the verb).

Concluding each **Definition** entry is an illustrative sentence. These sentences provide a context that clarifies the meaning of each word and provides students with an opportunity to practice writing and spelling each word in context so that they begin to see how the word can be used effectively in their own writing.

The iWords audio program is available online at **SadlierConnect.com** to support students' understanding of each Unit's words. With iWords students hear the correct pronunciation of each vocabulary word, its definition, and its use in an example sentence. iWords is a particularly valuable resource for auditory, striving, and ELL students.

Teachers should engage students in discussions about each word and its definition as well as its use in various contexts. Students should develop a meaningful explanation for each word. Visual images may be used to support understanding of a word and its meaning.

Using Context (see page 15)

Using Context is a transitional exercise that gives students the opportunity to determine whether a vocabulary word makes sense in the context of a sentence. In this exercise, students practice strategies for using context to determine whether a word is used correctly, given its meaning as provided in the **Definitions** section as well as its use in the **Reading Passage**.

Choosing the Right Word (see page 16)

Choosing the Right Word is a scaffolded exercise that appears in both **Set A** and **Set B** of each Unit. From a pair of words, students choose the word that better completes the sentence. Encourage students to refer to the definitions and example sentence in **Definitions**. Students' successful completion of this exercise supports their deepening understanding of word meanings.

Completing the Sentence (see page 17)

This activity provides a simple fill-in-the-blank exercise in which students choose and write the word from the 10-word **Set** that logically and meaningfully completes each sentence.

When using the exercise in the classroom, teachers should bear in mind the following:

- The sentences in this activity call for the literal or direct (as opposed to the metaphorical or extended) meaning of the words involved.

- The sentences are designed so that only one of the words fits in the given blank. Context clues have been embedded in each sentence to aid the student in choosing the right word from the word bank.

- Students might be reminded (not only at this point but whenever it seems appropriate to do so) of the three types of context clues described and illustrated on page 7 of the Student Edition.

- Note also that nouns introduced in the singular in the **Definitions** section may appear in plural form in the sentences; verbs given in the base form in **Definitions** may be used in any tense or form (including participial) required by the sentence.

Teachers may help students with this exercise by prompting them to choose a word that they think fits into the sentence and ask themselves, "Does that sound right? Does that make sense?" If they aren't sure, they should try another word and ask the same questions.

Synonyms (see page 22)

The **Synonyms** section further allows students to demonstrate their understanding of the new vocabulary words. This exercise, which draws 15 words from **Sets A & B** combined, reinforces meanings and provides students with examples of usage and context.

Teachers may wish to encourage students to use a thesaurus or dictionary to help them complete this exercise. Similarly, teachers might direct students to the Word Web graphic organizer found at **SadlierConnect.com** to help them visualize the relationship between the new vocabulary word and related words and synonyms.

Antonyms (see page 22)

Not all words have antonyms. For those that do, however, practice with antonyms reinforces meanings and provides students with further examples of usage and context. The **Antonyms** section asks students to draw from the Unit's 20 words the five most nearly opposite in meaning to highlighted antonyms presented in phrases.

As with **Synonyms**, teachers may wish to encourage students to use a thesaurus or dictionary to help them complete this exercise. Similarly, teachers might direct students to the Word Web graphic organizer found at **SadlierConnect.com** to help them visualize the relationship between the new vocabulary word and related words.

Students should consider how the antonym of a vocabulary word helps them understand that word's meaning as they continue to refine their mastery of the word.

All 20 of the Unit's words appear on the **Synonyms** and **Antonyms** page.

Writing: Words in Action (see page 22)

Writing: Words in Action provides practice with writing in response to a prompt that asks students to cite evidence from the introductory **Reading Passage** that begins the Unit to support their response. This exercise also gives students practice in using some of the Unit words in their own writing.

Teachers may provide students with a four-point rubric that will be used to score the exercise. It is best if the rubric aligns with those used on the assessments students most frequently take. Prior to assigning the writing exercise, teachers should model responding to text-based questions and how to cite details from the text to support responses.

Vocabulary in Context (see page 23)

All Units conclude with **Vocabulary in Context**, a second reading passage that provides further examples of selected Unit words in context and checks students' ability to use context within a passage to determine word meaning.

Vocabulary in Context is related in topic or theme to the introductory passage and includes all words that did not appear in that passage.

After students read the passage, they must use the knowledge they have gained of the Unit's words, as well as context clues, to answer questions about the meaning of those words as they appear in the context of the passage. This exercise gives students more practice analyzing words in context, a feature of standards-aligned and state exams.

Reviews

A Review follows every three Units and provides additional exposures, either as correct answers or as answer choices, to all 60 words taught in those three Units.

Vocabulary for Comprehension (see pages 48–51)

Reviews begin with a two-part **Vocabulary for Comprehension** feature designed to furnish students with practice in standardized-test formats modeled on the reading sections of standards-aligned and state exams.

In **Vocabulary for Comprehension: Part 1**, students are presented with a single nonfiction passage similar to those that appear in standardized exams. Based on their reading of that passage, students must answer questions assessing reading comprehension and vocabulary skills. These assessment items mirror those found in standardized exams and require students to refer to the passage, and occasionally to cite text evidence, in order to answer them.

In **Vocabulary for Comprehension: Part 2**, students are presented with either a single passage or paired passages, two texts related in subject matter or theme, and asked to answer questions about those texts, including questions requiring comparative analysis and evaluation. Again, both passages and assessment items are modeled on those that appear in standards-aligned and state exams.

Synonyms (see page 52)

Synonyms help students enrich and clarify their understanding of vocabulary. The **Synonyms** section of the Review reinforces meanings and provides students with further examples of usage and context. The synonyms appear in full sentences, and students must choose from a word bank of the Unit words that have the same or nearly the same meaning.

If students have difficulty with the **Synonyms** exercise, teachers might refer them to the **Definitions** section in which the Unit words first appeared.

Two-Word Completions

Students use their knowledge of the vocabulary words as well as context clues in the sentence to determine which pair of words should be used to fill in the blanks. Students' reading comprehension is supported as they are required to use information on either side of the blank to ascertain which vocabulary word should be used.

Teachers should assign this cloze exercise to provide ongoing practice with the vocabulary and to promote mastery.

Word Study (see page 54)

Following each of the five Reviews is a Word Study section that provides instruction and practice in either **Idioms** or **Denotation and Connotation**. All Word Study sections also provide instruction and practice in **Classical Roots**.

Since the literal meanings of the words that make up an idiom do not help a reader or listener to understand what the idiom is meant to express, idioms are especially problematic for students not well acquainted with the English language. Most languages possess idioms, but English is especially rich in them: "raining cats and dogs," "the apple of my eye," and "a dark-horse candidate" are just a few examples.

By developing a familiarity with and understanding of idioms and other forms of figurative language, students can better comprehend and respond to texts and other forms of written and oral communication.

Denotation and Connotation (see page 98)

In this part of the Word Study section, students investigate connotation—positive, negative, or neutral associations of a word—and denotation, the strict, dictionary definition of a word. Understanding the difference between denotation and connotation helps students better appreciate nuances of meaning and author's purpose or point of view, and helps them better express themselves in their own writing with more discriminating word choices.

Teachers may expand on the lesson by having students reflect on connotations associated with categories of words. Ask students to use the table heads provided on the **Denotation and Connotation** page—neutral, positive, and negative—to complete a table categorizing the words identified in brainstorming.

For example, teachers might prompt students to supply alternatives for the neutral word *dog*. Discuss whether each word has a negative or positive connotation. If the students are unable to give alternative words, provide examples such as *puppy*, *hound*, *mutt*, *pooch*, *canine*, *mongrel*. Ask students to explain why, in their opinion, each word has a negative or positive connotation.

Classical Roots (see page 55)

Instruction in classic roots will help students unlock the meanings of thousands of English words derived from Latin and Greek roots. Students will develop a useful and transferable strategy with which to make sense of a multitude of unfamiliar academic words.

Combined with an understanding of common affixes, familiarity with Latin and Greek roots can furnish students with a valuable tool in analyzing and decoding new vocabulary.

DIGITAL RESOURCES

Digital Resources for each Level are available to students and teachers at **SadlierConnect.com**. Students and families may use the resources without a username and password. Teachers may access answer keys and additional resources by creating an account under Teacher Resources at **SadlierConnect.com**. See the bottom of the copyright page (the back of the title page) in your Teacher's Edition for directions on registering for a teacher account at **SadlierConnect.com**.

Student and teacher digital resources include:

- **iWords** Audio program
- Audio of Reading Passages
- Interactive Vocabulary Games
- Vocabulary in Context: Literary Text
- Practice Worksheets
- Flash Cards
- Graphic Organizers

- Synonyms and Antonyms
- Greek and Latin Roots Reference Guide
- Pronunciation Key
- Diagnostic Tests and Cumulative Reviews
- Test Prep for Standardized Exams
- Interactive Quizzes

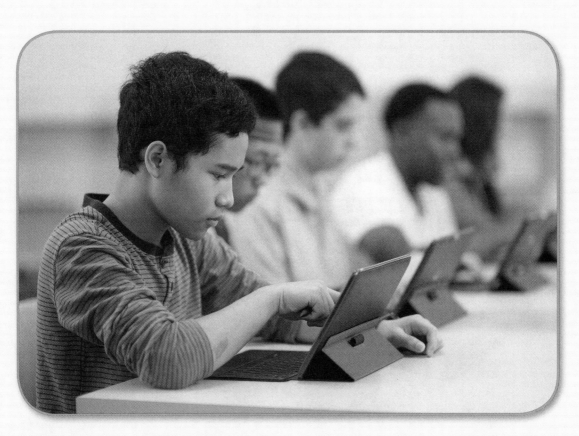

iWords Audio Program

The **VOCABULARY WORKSHOP ACHIEVE** iWords Audio Program provides students with pronunciations, definitions, and examples of usage for all taught vocabulary words.

The Audio Program is especially useful for English language learners. Students hear the recommended pronunciation of each word at least six times and are given two opportunities to pronounce each word themselves. Pronunciations are followed by brief definitions and examples of the word used in complete sentences.

Vocabulary Workshop Achieve Interactive Edition (optional purchase)

VOCABULARY WORKSHOP ACHIEVE INTERACTIVE EDITION provides all of the program's print components, including the program's ancillary components, (Unit Test Booklets and Test Prep booklets) in a fully interactive online format. **VOCABULARY WORKSHOP ACHIEVE INTERACTIVE EDITION** includes exercises that build academic vocabulary knowledge by using contextual and definitional information and ample practice of Unit words in multiple contexts, including responding to text-based questions.

VOCABULARY WORKSHOP ACHIEVE INTERACTIVE EDITION also provides personalized student learning by allowing teachers to build custom assessments to meet the varying needs of students as well as providing teachers the ability to adjust instruction and track student progress based on detailed real-time data reports.

IMPLEMENTING THE PROGRAM

The charts on pages T19–T21 offer an implementation model option to support consistent vocabulary instruction for middle and high school students. Both the Weekly Schedule chart and the Daily Activity charts reference the specific implementation guidance that can be found on the pages following the charts to assist teachers with integrating VOCABULARY WORKSHOP ACHIEVE into the English Language Arts classroom. Schedules and instructional needs among schools vary greatly, however, so the program methods and models suggested provide ideas that teachers can tailor to ensure success within their own classrooms. Additional implementation options, including best practices and further vocabulary exercises, can be found at Professional Development in Teacher Resources at **SadlierConnect.com**.

Prior to program implementation, teachers may wish to administer and score the **Beginning-of-Year Diagnostic Test** and use the resulting information, as well as their knowledge of the students in their class and student comprehension levels, to determine the most appropriate Level of VOCABULARY WORKSHOP ACHIEVE for their classroom or for small groups of students.

Weekly Schedule

Week(s)	Student Edition	Suggestions for Program Implementation
1 and 2	**Unit 1**	• Students read or listen to the initial Reading Passage prior to class. • Introduce the new vocabulary words in context—Reading Passage. • Focus study on two words each day. • Complete VOCABULARY WORKSHOP ACHIEVE exercises in the book or online. • Assessment Options: Assign Unit 1 test from Unit Test Booklet or from *Vocabulary Workshop Achieve Online Assessment*.
2 and 3	**Unit 2**	• Follow procedure for Unit 2 as shown in Unit 1. • Assessment Options: Assign Unit 2 test from Unit Test Booklet or from *Vocabulary Workshop Achieve Online Assessment*. • Review Unit 1 test to encourage deeper knowledge of the new vocabulary.
3 and 4	**Unit 3**	• Follow procedure for Unit 3 as shown in Unit 1. • Assessment Options: Assign Unit 3 test from Unit Test Booklet or from Vocabulary Workshop Achieve Online Assessment. • Review Units 1 and 2 tests to encourage deeper knowledge of the new vocabulary.
5	**Review Units 1–3** **Word Study** **Test Prep for Standardized Exams**	• Complete Review Units 1–3 exercises, and ensure knowledge of all 60 vocabulary words. • Assessment Options: Assign Cumulative Test 1 from Unit Test Booklet or from *Vocabulary Workshop Online Assessment*. • Teach mini-lessons on Idioms, Classical Roots, and Denotation and Connotation to develop students' word learning strategies. • Complete Word Study exercises. • Assign Test Prep 1 or 2 for Units 1–3.

Daily Activity

How to use VOCABULARY WORKSHOP ACHIEVE exercises and online exercises with 10 sessions/periods

Note: Review completed exercises as appropriate and differentiate instruction and assignments based on results. See Professional Development in Teacher Resources at **SadlierConnect.com** for more information on "focus on two words" and for additional exercises and implementation options.

Assignment	Day 1	Day 2	Day 3	Day 4	Day 5
Classwork	**1.** Read the Unit's Reading Passage aloud. **2.** Review word meanings and usage in context in the Unit's Reading Passage (for Set A words). **3.** Focus on two words (Set A).	**1.** Focus on two additional words (Set A). **2.** Have students find synonyms and antonyms for Set A words at **SadlierConnect.com**.	**1.** Assign Set A Completing the Sentence. **2.** Focus on two additional words (Set A).	**1.** Have students play online Unit games. **2.** Focus on two additional words (Set A).	**1.** Assign Vocabulary Race online at **SadlierConnect.com**. **2.** Focus on two additional words (Set A).
Homework	**1.** Review words from previous Unit and study Set A words. **2.** Assign Set A Using Context.	**1.** Assign Set A Choosing the Right Word.	**1.** Study Set A words using online Flash Cards at **SadlierConnect.com**.	**1.** Assign Set B Using Context. **2.** Have students play online Unit games.	**1.** Assign Set B Choosing the Right Word.

Assignment	Day 6	Day 7	Day 8	Day 9	Day 10
Classwork	**1.** Review word meanings and usage in context in the Unit's Reading Passage (for Set B words). **2.** Focus on two words (Set B).	**1.** Focus on three additional words (Set B). **2.** Have students find the synonyms and antonyms for Set B words at **SadlierConnect.com**.	**1.** Assign Sets A & B Writing: Words in Action. **2.** Focus on three additional words (Set B).	**1.** Assign Vocabulary in Context: Literary Text at **SadlierConnect.com**. **2.** Focus on two additional words (Set B).	**1.** Assign online Unit Self Check and/or Unit 1 test from Unit Test Booklet or from **SadlierConnect.com** *Vocabulary Workshop Online Assessment.*
Homework	**1.** Review Set A words and study Set B. **2.** Assign Set B Completing the Sentence.	**1.** Study Set B words using online Flash Cards. **2.** Assign Sets A & B Synonyms and Antonyms.	**1.** Assign Vocabulary Race online at **SadlierConnect.com**.	**1.** Assign Sets A & B Vocabulary in Context.	**1.** Read or listen to the Reading Passage for the next Unit.

Review and Word Study Exercises

How to use VOCABULARY WORKSHOP ACHIEVE **Review, Word Study, and online resources with 5 sessions or periods**

Note: Review completed exercises and assessments as appropriate and differentiate instruction and assignments based on results. See Professional Development in Teacher Resources at **SadlierConnect.com** for more information and implementation options.

Assignment	Day 1	Day 2	Day 3	Day 4	Day 5
Classwork	**1.** Assign Vocabulary for Comprehension: Part 1.	**1.** Assign Synonyms.	**1.** Present Idioms or Denotation and Connotation. **2.** Present Classical Roots.	**1.** Assign Test Prep 1 or 2 for Units 1–3.	**1.** Assign Cumulative Test 1.
Homework	**1.** Assign Vocabulary for Comprehension Part 2.	**1.** Assign Two-Word Completions.	**1.** Assign Idioms or present Denotation and Connotation. **2.** Assign Classical Roots.	**1.** Have students play online Review and Word Study games at **SadlierConnect.com**.	**1.** Read or listen to the Reading Passage for the next Unit.

BEST PRACTICES FOR USING
VOCABULARY WORKSHOP ACHIEVE IN THE CLASSROOM

By Sarah Ressler Wright, Series Consultant,
Head Librarian, Rutherford B. Hayes High School, Delaware, OH

Classroom Environment

Classroom experience and research have shown that repeated exposure to and varied application of vocabulary words embed meanings in students' minds. The more teachers and students utilize vocabulary in the Language Arts class period, the more likely students are to understand and use new vocabulary themselves.

To encourage students' use of vocabulary, teachers may post vocabulary words in the classroom—on bulletin boards, walls, or chalkboards and whiteboards. Students and teachers may bring in examples of vocabulary from print sources to be displayed in the classroom. Additionally, students may create visual representations or drawings of vocabulary words that can be posted in the classroom. Discuss which visual representations are the most appropriate and accurate representations of the vocabulary words.

Differentiation may be achieved through choice. Create a vocabulary choice menu of extension exercises, such as using vocabulary words to write a poem, or create an interactive presentation that appeals to different learning modalities.

Students may share experiences in which they hear or use vocabulary outside of the classroom. Whether it is another teacher who has used a vocabulary word, a television show or movie that incorporated vocabulary, or the students themselves who embedded words in their assignments, it is important to recognize the use of academic vocabulary.

Daily Discussion and Review

Teachers may model vocabulary usage by including vocabulary words in their instructions or conversations with students. The more frequently the teacher uses a word, the easier it becomes for students to understand its meaning and usage.

Teachers can have "Words of the Day" that students must incorporate into classroom exercises. Whoever correctly uses the words the most might receive a reward.

During debates, discussions, or at other times when students are conversing, teachers should require them to use the learned vocabulary words. A set minimum number of words can be established, and students who go above the minimum should be recognized for their efforts.

When there is extra time, the class may review vocabulary words. See the following "Vocabulary Projects and Games" section for suggested exercises.

Writing with Vocabulary

Students should incorporate at least one or two vocabulary words into their daily writing prompts, reading journals, or other forms of informal communication. Use pictures or photographs from magazines as inspiration for writing.

Whenever students write formally for class (essays, stories, etc.), teachers may require a set minimum number of vocabulary words to be used, check to make sure that the usage is appropriate, and provide feedback. Students should highlight the vocabulary words in the writing. Read aloud essays and review the use of vocabulary for correct usage. Point out instances where the forms of the words have been changed or a secondary meaning is used. Suggest ways for students to check their usage, such as replacing the vocabulary word in the sentence with its definition to see if it makes sense.

Teachers may also:

- Ask students to write poems for individual words. Example: "There once was a word called _____."

- Ask students to write a "Where I'm From" poem that explains both a word's origins and use and that also traces its relationship to words in the same family.

- Have students write myths about the origins of individual words or groups of words.

Vocabulary Projects and Games

Students may create advertisements for a word to "sell" its uses. For example: "Race to your local dictionary and pick up the word _____. Whether frustrated with your social life or unhappy with a school assignment, this word can be used in a variety of ways." Alternatively, teachers may have students sell a product by using as many vocabulary words as possible to describe the item's attributes.

Students often learn words best when setting them to music. Students may write lyrics incorporating all (or most) of a Unit's vocabulary words and definitions and then perform, videotape, or record their songs. Create a library of the videos and recordings for future classes to use.

Do a review of the words and their definitions. This activity can be teacher-directed or student-led. To begin, a student names a vocabulary word, a second student defines it, then another gives the kinesthetic gesture the class has given the word, and a fourth student puts the definition in his or her own words or provides a synonym or antonym. Another student uses the word in a sentence, and then another student finishes the activity by giving feedback on how the word was used in the sentence. Allow time after the activity for follow-up questions.

Create a "deck" of review cards, consisting of the word, the definition, a sentence with a blank where the vocabulary word would go, and the image for the word selected by the class. Have teams go head-to-head to see who can complete the sentence with the correct vocabulary word first.

Groups of students can act in skits or pantomimes that demonstrate a word's meaning; the rest of the class must guess the word being acted out.

Student groups may tell stories using vocabulary words. Create groups according to the students' abilities and levels.

ADDRESSING DIFFERENT LEARNERS

Depending on the needs of their students, teachers may differentiate and/or scaffold instruction to accommodate individual or small-group learning differences.

Students who are on or above grade level often already have a basic understanding of many of the vocabulary words. The goal for these students should not just be to recognize the words, but rather to incorporate them into their personal lexicon for writing and speaking.

Differentiating Daily Instruction for Striving and ELL Students

Begin with audio: Beginning each vocabulary unit by playing the audio of the introductory **Reading Passage** and the iWords audio of each word being spoken, defined, and used in example sentences can help all learners—especially striving and ELL students—understand how vocabulary words are used in multiple contexts.

Repeat use of iWords: Having students download and repeatedly listen to the iWords audio can deepen their understanding of word pronunciations and meanings.

Show examples of correct use in varied contexts: Providing students with opportunities to encounter words repeatedly and in more than one context helps students place these words in their long-term memories and improves word consciousness.

Provide opportunities for oral practice: Engaging students in actively using the new vocabulary in classroom discussions and conversations allows them to enrich their understanding of the words' meanings and to make connections between words while building their vocabularies.

Focus on context clues: Having students underline context clues in the **Using Context**, **Choosing the Right Word**, and **Completing the Sentence** exercises helps them understand how context provides clues to deciphering word meaning.

Utilize **SadlierConnect.com** graphic organizers: Using graphic organizers is especially important for striving readers and ELL students as they help learners visualize their words and come to a richer recognition of word meanings.

Differentiating Assignments for Striving Readers and ELL Students

Work together: Pair striving and/or ELL students together to complete the Unit's exercises. They should work at a similar pace and clarify word meaning through discussions over answers.

Focus on **Set A** or **Set B**: In each Unit of 20 words, have striving and ELL students spend all of their time learning one set of 10 words, rather than both sets, and assess accordingly.

Practice with online exercises at **SadlierConnect.com**: There are a variety of exercises online that help students gauge for themselves their level of understanding.

Play online games at **SadlierConnect.com**: Striving and ELL students especially will enjoy the Test Your Vocabulary and Hangman games, as they make word retention fun and include an audio component to aid in word recognition.

Differentiating Assessment for Striving Readers and ELL Students

Modify assessments: Reducing the number of incorrect answer choices in test items makes the assessment more accessible and does not harm the psychometric properties of the test.

Use word banks: Often, giving students a word bank, as in the Synonym activity in the Review sections, allows students to recall words and meanings more easily on tests.

Create an alternative test: Have students demonstrate their knowledge of words through the real-world medium of their choice. Whether in song lyrics, stories, or artwork, student success should be determined based on correct usage with context and/or an explanation to show understanding.

Recognize context clues: Consider giving partial credit to students who can underline the context clues correctly in the **Completing the Sentence**, **Vocabulary in Context**, and/or **Vocabulary for Comprehension** exercises when used as assessments.

Differentiating Exercises and Assignments for Above Grade-Level Students

Use words in conversations: During discussions of current events or literature, teachers can require students to use vocabulary words when making claims and expressing ideas.

Categorize vocabulary: Have students not only learn word meanings but also categorize words as they relate to general labels such as "travel words," "food words," or "compliments versus insults," for example.

Get to the root of it: The **Classical Roots** Word Study activity and the **SadlierConnect.com Greek and Latin Roots Matching Challenge** help students move beyond individual word meaning to understanding the roots of words and etymological concepts, and to build their own vocabularies.

Utilize Vocab Gal's resources: The Vocab Gal blog (**Sadlier.com/school/vocab-gal**) has more than 100 games and exercises designed to help students of all abilities learn and retain vocabulary in fun and engaging ways.

Differentiating Assessment for Above Grade-Level Students

Pre-assess: The **Using Context** and **Choosing the Right Word** exercises can be used as pre-assessments for students. Based on their scores, students can opt out of completing the workbook exercises and go straight to the **Writing: Words in Action**. Students should include in their writing the words they did not get correct on the pretest.

Assign a written test: Consider using the **Writing: Words in Action** activity as a Unit assessment, with students required to use several of the vocabulary words in their responses. Alternatively, have students write on topics of their (or your) choice.

Practice for standardized tests: The **Vocabulary for Comprehension** exercises in the Review sections provide other ways to assess students not only on their vocabulary knowledge but also on literary analysis questions crucial to success on standardized tests.

STUDENT STUDY GUIDES

When students employ a review system for their vocabularies, they tend to learn the words and their meanings more thoroughly. Students may create flash cards or vocabulary charts as two simple review methods. What students write down on their flash cards or charts may vary among learning styles.

For Basic Vocabulary Learners: Students should write the vocabulary word on one side of a flash card (or in the first chart box), a mnemonic device that helps them recall the word's meaning, and a synonym or brief definition of the word. On the back of the flash card (or in chart boxes two, three, and four), have students write a short student-created phrase incorporating the word. Students should then review by looking only at the word side of the flash card (or at the first column of the chart, folding the paper so the other information is behind the first column) and by seeing if they can remember the mnemonic device or phrase that enables them to recall the word's meaning.

For Kinesthetic Learners: Students may create a motion that goes with a vocabulary word definition when possible. Students should then write the word on one side of a flash card (or in the first chart box), then the motion and a synonym or brief definition on the back of the flash card (or in the second and third chart boxes). Students may review by looking only at the word side of the flashcard (or at the first column of the chart, folding the paper so the other information is behind the first column) and seeing if they can recall first the motion and then the word's meaning.

For Visual/Artistic Learners: Students should draw a picture that goes with each vocabulary word definition. They may write the word on one side of a flash card (or in the first chart box) and then draw the associated picture and write the synonym or brief definition on the back of the flash card (or in the second and third chart boxes). Students should then review by looking only at the word side of the flash card (or at the first column of the chart, folding the paper so the other information is behind the first column) and seeing if they can recall first the drawing and then the word's meaning.

For Auditory Learners: In addition to the Basic Vocabulary Learner review sheet, teachers may strongly encourage these learners to review iWords on a daily basis to recall definitions.

Vocabulary Workshop Achieve AND LITERATURE

Though it is first and foremost a program of direct and explicit instruction, VOCABULARY WORKSHOP ACHIEVE can also be used to complement and support a literature-based approach to vocabulary study.

The word lists for VOCABULARY WORKSHOP ACHIEVE are rich in the language of literature. Many of the words selected for instruction are drawn from classic and contemporary fiction and nonfiction and commonly appear in the texts and anthologies that students encounter in their classroom reading.

A list of excerpts from such literature appears below and on page T28. These **Vocabulary in Context: Literary Text** excerpts, available for all levels on **SadlierConnect.com**, show students how Unit words in Levels A–C of VOCABULARY WORKSHOP ACHIEVE have been used in classical literary contexts.

The VOCABULARY WORKSHOP ACHIEVE word lists are also well stocked with vocabulary employed in analyzing, discussing, and writing about literature. With mastery of these words, students will be better able to contribute to classroom discourse about the texts they read and to express their thinking about literature with more precise and fluent writing.

Words singled out for instruction in the texts that students are reading can be compared with the words in VOCABULARY WORKSHOP ACHIEVE to explore semantic families, nuances of meaning, diction, etymology, and many other features of language and the art of writing.

Level A

Unit 1	Johann David Wyss	*The Swiss Family Robinson*
Unit 2	Walt Whitman	*Leaves of Grass*
Unit 3	Jules Verne	*Twenty Thousand Leagues Under the Sea*
Unit 4	Edgar Rice Burroughs	*A Princess of Mars*
Unit 5	H.G. Wells	*The First Men in the Moon*
Unit 6	Mark Twain	*The Prince and The Pauper* and "The Celebrated Jumping Frog of Calaveras County"
Unit 7	Charles Dickens	*Oliver Twist*
Unit 8	Sir Arthur Conan Doyle	*The Adventures of Sherlock Holmes*
Unit 9	L.M. Montgomery	*Anne of the Island*
Unit 10	Edgar Allan Poe	"The Gold Bug," "The Unparalleled Adventure of One Hans Pfaall," "MS. Found in a Bottle," and "The Murders in The Rue Morgue"
Unit 11	Jack London	*White Fang*
Unit 12	Sir Arthur Conan Doyle	*Tales of Terror and Mystery*
Unit 13	L.M. Montgomery	*Anne of Green Gables*
Unit 14	Charles Dickens	*The Life and Adventures of Nicholas Nickelby*
Unit 15	Washington Irving	"The Legend of Sleepy Hollow"

Level B

Unit 1	Edgar Allan Poe	"The Balloon Hoax," "The Mystery of Marie Roget," "MS. Found in a Bottle," and "The Gold-Bug"
Unit 2	O. Henry	"The Cop and the Anthem," "The Coming-out of Maggie," "The Green Door," "Springtime á la Carte," and "Man About Town"
Unit 3	Sir Arthur Conan Doyle	*The Lost World*
Unit 4	Jack London	*The Sea-Wolf*
Unit 5	Charles Dickens	*Oliver Twist*
Unit 6	Sir Arthur Conan Doyle	*The Adventures of Sherlock Holmes*
Unit 7	Mark Twain	*A Connecticut Yankee in King Arthur's Court*
Unit 8	Jules Verne	*A Journey to the Center of the Earth*
Unit 9	Bram Stoker	*Dracula*
Unit 10	Victor Hugo	*The Hunchback of Notre Dame*
Unit 11	Mary Wollstonecraft Shelley	*Frankenstein*
Unit 12	Victor Hugo	*Les Misérables*
Unit 13	Jules Verne	*Around the World in 80 Days*
Unit 14	Hans Christian Andersen	*Andersen's Fairy Tales*
Unit 15	Sir Arthur Conan Doyle	*The Adventures of Sherlock Holmes* and *The Hound of the Baskervilles*

Level C

Unit 1	Baroness Orczy	*The Scarlet Pimpernel*
Unit 2	O. Henry	"Brickdust Road," "Two Thanksgiving Day Gentlemen," "The Trimmed Lamp"
Unit 3	Henry David Thoreau	*Walden*
Unit 4	Edgar Allan Poe	"A Descent into the Maelström," "The Premature Burial," "The Pit and the Pendulum," "William Wilson"
Unit 5	Charles Dickens	*A Christmas Carol*
Unit 6	Jack London	*The Call of the Wild* and *White Fang*
Unit 7	Louisa May Alcott	*Little Women*
Unit 8	Stephen Crane	*The Monster and Other Stories* and *The Red Badge of Courage*
Unit 9	Mark Twain	*Life on the Mississippi*
Unit 10	Edgar Rice Burroughs	*Tarzan of the Apes*
Unit 11	E.M. Forster	*Where Angels Fear to Tread*
Unit 12	Sir Arthur Conan Doyle	*The Lost World*
Unit 13	George Eliot	*Silas Marner* and *The Mill on the Floss*
Unit 14	Robert Louis Stevenson	*Strange Case of Dr. Jekyll and Mr. Hyde*
Unit 15	Henry James	*The Turn of the Screw*

ASSESSMENT OPTIONS

VOCABULARY WORKSHOP ACHIEVE's comprehensive assessment plan includes diagnostic, formative, and summative assessment options—in print and digital formats—to measure students' vocabulary development. Teachers may choose from among these assessments to monitor and track mastery throughout the school year.

VOCABULARY WORKSHOP ACHIEVE Comprehensive Assessment Plan				
Assessment	**Assessment Type**	**What Is Assessed**	**Where Found**	**When to Administer**
Beginning-of-Year Diagnostic Test	Diagnostic	Sampling of words from the Level	• Online Digital Resources	At the start of the school year
Beginning-of-Year Pre-Test	Diagnostic	All vocabulary words from the Level	• Online Assessments	At the start of the school year
Unit Practice Test	Formative	Unit vocabulary words	• Online Assessments	At the end of each Unit
Unit Test	Summative	Unit vocabulary words	• Unit Test Booklet • Online Assessments • Online Digital Resources	At the end of each Unit
Reviews	Formative	60 vocabulary words	• Student Edition	After every 3 Units
Cumulative Test 1–5	Summative	Select words from every 3 Units	• Unit Test Booklet • Online Assessments	After every 3 Units
Test Prep for Standardized Exams	Formative	Select words from every 3 Units	• Test Prep booklet • Online Digital Resources • Online Assessments	After every 3 Units
Test Prep for Standardized Exams Cumulative Test	Formative	Select words from the Level	• Test Prep booklet • Online Digital Resources • Online Assessments	At the completion of the program
Final Mastery Test	Summative	Select words from the Level	• Student Edition • Online Assessments	At the completion of the program
Post Test	Summative	Sampling of grade-level words	• Online Assessments	At the completion of the program

Assessment in the Student Editions

Reviews Each Student Edition includes five Review sections, one after every three Units. These Reviews reinforce the application of word knowledge of the 60 vocabulary words introduced in the previous three Units. The Reviews expose students to the types of questions they will experience on standardized state exams.

Final Mastery Test This practice assessment, which covers taught words from throughout the Student Edition, is meant to give students and teachers insight into how much progress has been made during the year and what kind of additional work, if any, is in order. It can also serve as preparation for more formal and secure mastery tests available at **SadlierConnect.com** and/or in the Unit Test and Test Prep booklets.

Unit Test Booklets, Grades 6–8 (optional purchase)

Fifteen Unit Tests may be used to assess student knowledge of all 20 of each Unit's vocabulary words, with exercises that include **Vocabulary in Context**, **Definitions**, **Synonyms**, **Antonyms**, and **Completing the Sentence**.

Five Cumulative Tests, to be administered after the completion of every three Units, serve as continuous assessments of students' retention of previously studied words. Cumulative Test 5, meant to be administered at the completion of the program, is designed to determine the students' degree of mastery of the Level's word list.

Assessments in the Test Prep Booklets, Grades 6–8 (optional purchase)

At Levels A–C, VOCABULARY WORKSHOP Test Prep provides practice for the reading sections of standards-aligned and state exams.

Each Test Prep booklet provides:

- Ten Test Prep assessments with a reading passage and 10 assessment items mirroring those found in the two exams, including both vocabulary and reading comprehension questions

- Two Cumulative Test Prep tests, featuring paired passages and assessment items

- Reading passages excerpted from published texts and adapted to include words from the corresponding Review sections in VOCABULARY WORKSHOP ACHIEVE

- Passages in the fields of History and Social Studies that are approximately the same length and contain the same number of questions as appear on standards-aligned and state exams.

Students respond to a range of multiple-choice questions based on a passage or a pair of passages. Question types include items that ask students to find evidence in a passage that best supports the answer to questions or serves as the basis for a reasonable conclusion.

The practice tests are meant to be administered at the end of every three Units, and the Cumulative Test Prep Tests to be administered after the completion of all Units in the VOCABULARY WORKSHOP ACHIEVE Student Edition.

A Teacher Answer Key provides answers for all tests in the VOCABULARY WORKSHOP Test Prep student booklets.

Assessments at SadlierConnect.com

The following assessments are available in Digital Resources at **SadlierConnect.com**.

Beginning-of-Year Diagnostic Test: This interactive diagnostic assessment uses a sampling of the grade level's 300 taught words and is meant to be administered at the start of the school year to assess students' prior knowledge of that grade level's words.

Unit Tests: Each **Unit Test** assesses students' understanding of the Unit's vocabulary words through Vocabulary in Context passages, Definitions, Synonyms, and Antonyms. Have students complete the **Unit Test** at the end of every Unit to check their understanding of the Unit's words.

Test Prep for Standardized Exams: These interactive assessments (see page T30) may be administered after every three Units to help students master the critical reading skills measured in the reading sections of standards-aligned exams.

Cumulative Tests: Using select words from all previous Units, these assessments include Vocabulary in Context, Definitions, Synonyms, Antonyms, Completing the Sentences, and Framing Sentences. Have students complete each of the five Cumulative Tests after every three Units.

Vocabulary Workshop Achieve Online Assessments (optional purchase)

VOCABULARY WORKSHOP ACHIEVE ONLINE ASSESSMENTS is a secure, web-based assessment program that includes all VOCABULARY WORKSHOP ACHIEVE program assessments in an interactive format, plus Pre- and Post-Tests to measure annual vocabulary acquisition and growth.

Interactive assessments include:

- Pre- and Post-Tests
- Unit Tests
- Practice Unit Tests
- Test Prep for Standardized Exams

- Test Prep for Standardized Exams Cumulative Tests
- Cumulative Tests
- Final Mastery Test
- End-of-Year Post-Test

VOCABULARY WORKSHOP ACHIEVE ONLINE ASSESSMENT features auto-scoring formative and summative assessments in an interactive format. A **Build an Assessment** feature personalizes student learning with the option of customizing assignments.

The program also offers flexible administration of assessments to individual students, small groups, or an entire class, either online or in print for a more traditional test-taking environment.

VOCABULARY WORKSHOP ACHIEVE ONLINE ASSESSMENT is equipped with tools to monitor student progress and to adjust instruction using real-time, standards-based data and a variety of class and student reports to help drive instruction and look at data from a standards and trend perspective.

NOTES

SADLIER
VOCABULARY WORKSHOP®
ACHIEVE

Level A

Jerome Shostak

Senior Series Consultant

Vicki A. Jacobs, Ed.D.
Lecturer on Education
Harvard Graduate School of Education
Cambridge, Massachusetts

Series Consultants

Louis P. De Angelo, Ed.D.
Superintendent of Schools
Diocese of Wilmington
Wilmington, Delaware

John Heath, Ph.D.
Professor of Classics
Santa Clara University
Santa Clara, California

Sarah Ressler Wright,
   M.A. English Ed, NBCT
Head Librarian
Rutherford B. Hayes High School
Delaware, Ohio

Carolyn E. Waters, J.D., Ed.S.
Georgia Dept. of Education (Ret.)
English Language Arts Consultant
Woodstock, Georgia

Reviewers

The publisher wishes to thank for their comments and suggestions the following teachers and administrators, who read portions of the series prior to publication.

Ronald Apperson
Teacher
George Fox Middle School
Pasadena, MD

Rebecca Benjamin
English Teacher
Island Trees Memorial Middle School
Levittown, NY

Heidi Branch
8th Grade English Teacher,
    Department Chair
Belmont Ridge Middle School
Leesburg, VA

Lynne W. Jansen
ELA Instructor
Landrum Middle School
Ponte Vedra, FL

Kasandra Washington
School Counselor
Former ELA Instructor
Manor Middle School
Manor, TX

Cover: Concept/Art and Design: MK Advertising, Studio Montage and William H. Sadlier, Inc. Cover pencil: Shutterstock.com/VikaSuh.
Photo Credits: A'Lelia Bundles/Madam Walker Family Archives: 200, 201. akg-images/British Library: 120; Collection Jean-Pierre Verney, Paris: 81 *bottom*; Universal Images Group: 37 *bottom right*, 36, 37 *top*. Alamy Stock Photo/Archive Images: 164; Everett Collection Inc.: 104, 192; INTERFOTO: 16; LatitudeStock: 28; Lebrecht Music and Arts Photo Library: 88, 208; National Geographic Image Collection/Edward Herbert Miner: 212; Pictorial Press Ltd: 145 *top*; Picture Press/Detlev van Ravenswaay: 69 *top*; Wild Places Photography/Chris Howes: 60; Edward Krupa: 76; Igorr Norman: 132; Aurora Photos: 84; dpa picture alliance archive: 204; Hero Images Inc.: 32; Lebrecht Music and Arts Photo Library: 40; robertharding/Angelo Cavalli: 216; Wild Places Photography/Chris Howes: 148; WILDLIFE GmbH: 160. Art Resource, NY/Alinari: 57 *bottom*; HIP: 113; Van Gogh Museum, Amsterdam: 196. Associated Press/Wilfredo Lee: 172. Bridgeman Images/'I Want You for the U.S. Army', 1917 (colour litho) by James Montgomery Flagg (1877–1960) Private Collection/Peter Newark Pictures: 81 *top*; Medicine man of the Mandan tribe in the costume of the Dog Dance, 1834 (colour litho) by Karl Bodmer (1809–93) Private Collection/Peter Newark American Pictures: 56. Digital Vision: 68–69. Everett Collection, Inc.: 64. Fotolia/highwaystarz: 10. Getty Images: 69 *bottom*; Aminart: 116; De Agostini/DEA/F. Galardi: 157; Dorling Kindersley: 188; Michael Ochs Archives: 144; Paramount Pictures: 101 *top*; NY Daily News Archive/Jim Mooney: 201; Science Source: 44; Tim Flach: 213; Time & Life Pictures: 128, 176; Archive Photos: 189; Bettmann: 152, 220; Ileximage: 20; NASA: 68 *top*; VCG/Corbis/Tim Davis: 189. Granger, NYC/ullstein bild: 124. The Image Works, Inc./Mary Evans Picture Library: 57 *top*. Lebrecht Music & Arts/'A Christmas Carol' by Charles Dickens/Illustration by Harold Copping: 72. Mary Evans Picture Library/ONSLOW AUCTIONS LIMITED: 80. Masterfile/Science Faction/Steven Kazlowski: 188. Media Bakery/Frans Lanting: 213. NASA: 101 *bottom*, 125 *bottom*. National Portrait Gallery: 112. NativeStock Pictures/Marilyn Angel Wynn: 100. Photodisc: 201. PhotoEdit/Michelle D. Bridwell: 108. Punchstock/Blend Images: 24. Science & Society Picture Library/SSPL/Pastpix: 37 *bottom*. Shutterstock.com/ alphaspirit: 68, 69; emo_O: 113 *inset*; Fotokor77: 124, 125; Ice-Storm: 36–37; Iwona Grodzka: 144; Jeff Metzger: 112 *background*; Kompaniets Taras: 169, 170; Lina_S: 169, 170 *background*; Marc Dietrich: 57 *background*; MaxyM: 80–81 *background*; More Trendy Design Here: 68, 69; Olivier Le Moal: 25 *inset*; Pola36: 145 *top*; Valentyn Volkov: 100–101 *background*. Superstock: 145 *bottom*; All Canada Photos/Wayne Lynch: 156; Ambient Images, Inc.: 24–25; Stockbroker/Purestock: 25. Wikipedia: 125 *top*, 156.

Illustration Credits: Sally Wern Comport: 12–13. Britt Spencer: 168–169.

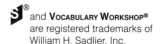 and **Vocabulary Workshop®** are registered trademarks of William H. Sadlier, Inc.

Printed in the United States of America.
ISBN: 978-1-4217-8506-6
1 2 3 4 5 6 7 8 9 10 EB 21 20 19 18 17

For additional online resources, go to SadlierConnect.com.

CONTENTS

iWords Audio Program is available at **SadlierConnect.com**.

PROGRAM FEATURES

For more than five decades, VOCABULARY WORKSHOP has proven to be a highly successful tool for vocabulary growth and the development of vocabulary skills. It has also been shown to help students prepare for standardized tests. VOCABULARY WORKSHOP ACHIEVE maintains that tradition in a newly designed format.

Each of VOCABULARY WORKSHOP ACHIEVE's 15 Units introduces 20 words in two 10-word lists—**Set A** and **Set B**. Both Set A and Set B contain exercises to help you develop deeper understanding of the 10 words in each set. Combined Sets A and B then provide practice with all 20 of the words in the Unit. Review and Word Study activities follow Units 3, 6, 9, 12, and 15 and offer practice with the 60 vocabulary words in the preceding three Units.

Each level of VOCABULARY WORKSHOP ACHIEVE introduces and provides practice with 300 vocabulary words and contains features such as reading passages, writing prompts, vocabulary in context, evidence-based questions, and word study that will help you to master these new vocabulary words and succeed in using skills to comprehend unfamiliar words.

Each Unit in VOCABULARY WORKSHOP ACHIEVE consists of the following sections for **Set A** and **Set B**: an introductory **Reading Passage** that shows how vocabulary words are used in context, **Definitions** that include sentences that give examples of how to use the words, **Using Context, Choosing the Right Word**, and **Completing the Sentence**—activities that provide practice with the vocabulary words. Each introductory **Reading Passage** is a nonfiction text that includes most of the vocabulary words from the Unit to which it belongs. In addition, **Synonyms**, **Antonyms**, and **Vocabulary in Context** in combined Sets A and B round out each Unit with practice with all 20 Unit words.

The five Review sections cover all 60 words from their corresponding Units. **Vocabulary for Comprehension** is modeled on the reading sections of college entrance exams. It presents reading comprehension questions, including vocabulary-related items and evidence-based items that are based on the reading passages.

Word Study sections that contain activities on **Idioms**, **Denotation and Connotation**, and **Classical Roots** follow the Review. These sections will help you develop your understanding of figurative language and practice skills that will help you to determine the meaning of new and unfamiliar vocabulary.

The Final Mastery Test assesses a selection of words from the year and allows you to see the growth you have made in acquiring new vocabulary words and in mastering the comprehension skills you need to understand unfamiliar words.

ONLINE RESOURCES
SadlierConnect.com

Go to **SadlierConnect.com** to find iWords, an audio program that provides pronunciations, definitions, and examples of usage for all of the vocabulary words presented in this level of VOCABULARY WORKSHOP ACHIEVE. You can listen to the entire **Reading Passage** and the 20 Unit vocabulary words one word at a time, or download all of the words in any given Unit.

At **SadlierConnect.com** you will also find interactive vocabulary quizzes, flash cards, and interactive games and puzzles that will help reinforce and enrich your understanding of the vocabulary words in this level of VOCABULARY WORKSHOP ACHIEVE.

VOCABULARY IN CONTEXT

The context of a word is the printed text of which that word is part. By studying a word's context, we may find clues to its meaning. We might find a clue in the immediate or adjoining sentence or phrase in which the word appears; in the topic or subject matter of the passage; or in the physical features—such as photographs, illustrations, charts, graphs, captions, and headings—of a page itself.

The **Reading Passages** as well as the **Using Context**, **Choosing the Right Word**, **Vocabulary in Context**, and **Vocabulary for Comprehension** exercises that appear in the Units, the Reviews, and the Final Mastery Test provide practice in using context to decode and to determine the meaning of unfamiliar words.

Three types of context clues appear in the exercises in this book.

A **restatement clue** consists of a synonym for or a definition of the missing word. For example:

Faithfully reading a weekly newsmagazine not only broadens my knowledge of current events and world or national affairs but also _____ my vocabulary.

a. decreases   **b.** fragments   **c.** increases   **d.** contains

In this sentence, *broadens* is a synonym of the missing word, *increases*, and acts as a restatement clue for it.

A **contrast clue** consists of an antonym for or a phase that means the opposite of the missing word. For example:

"My view of the situation may be far too rosy," I admitted. "On the other hand, yours may be a bit (**optimistic, bleak**)."

In this sentence, *rosy* is an antonym of the missing word, *bleak*. This is confirmed by the presence of the phrase *on the other hand*, which indicates that the answer must be the opposite of *rosy*.

An **inference clue** implies but does not directly state the meaning of the missing word or words. For example:

"A treat for all ages," the review read, "this wonderful novel combines the _____ of a scholar with the skill and artistry of an expert _____."

a. ignorance . . . painter   **c.** wealth . . . surgeon

b. wisdom . . . beginner   **d.** knowledge . . . storyteller

In this sentence, there are several inference clues: (a) the word *scholar* suggests knowledge; (b) the words *novel*, *artistry*, and *skill* suggests the word *storyteller*. These words are inference clues because they suggest or imply, but do not directly state, the missing word or words.

VOCABULARY AND READING

There is a strong connection between vocabulary knowledge and reading comprehension. Although comprehension is much more than recognizing words and knowing their meanings, comprehension is nearly impossible if you do not know an adequate number of words in the text you are reading or have the vocabulary skills to figure out their meaning.

The **Reading Passages** in this level provide extra practice with vocabulary words. Vocabulary words are in boldface to draw your attention to their uses and contexts. Context clues embedded in the passages encourage you to figure out the meanings of words before you read the definitions provided on the pages directly following the passages.

Test Prep

Your knowledge of word meanings and your ability to think carefully about what you read will help you succeed in school and on standards-aligned and state exams.

The **Vocabulary for Comprehension** exercises in each Review consist of a reading passage followed by comprehension questions. The passages and questions are similar to those that you are likely to find on standards-aligned and state exams.

Types of Questions

You are likely to encounter the following types of questions in VOCABULARY WORKSHOP ACHIEVE and on standards-aligned and state exams.

Main Idea Questions generally ask what the passage as a whole is about. Often, but not always, the main idea is stated in the first paragraph of the passage. You may also be asked the main idea of a specific paragraph. Questions about the main idea may begin like this:

- The primary or main purpose of the passage is . . .

- The author's primary or main purpose in the passage is to . . .

- Which of the following statements most nearly paraphrases the author's main idea in the ninth paragraph (lines 77–88)?

- The main purpose of the fourth paragraph (lines 16–25) is to . . .

Detail Questions focus on important information that is explicitly stated in the passage. Often, however, the correct answer choices do not use the exact language of the passage. They are instead restatements, or paraphrases, of the text.

Vocabulary in Context Questions check your ability to use context to identify a word's meaning. For example:

- As it is used in paragraph 2, "adherents" most nearly means . . .

Use the word's context in a passage to select the best answer, particularly when the vocabulary word has more than one meaning. The answer choices may contain two (or more) correct meanings of the word in question. Choose the meaning that best fits the context.

Inference Questions ask you to make inferences or draw conclusions from the passage. These questions often begin like this:

- It can be most reasonably inferred from the information in the fifth paragraph (lines 53–69) that . . .

- The passage clearly implies that . . .

The inferences you make and the conclusions you draw must be based on the information in the passage. Using the facts you learn from the passage in addition to the knowledge and reasoning you already have helps you understand what is implied and reach conclusions that are logical.

Evidence-Based Questions ask you to provide evidence from the passage that will support the answer you provided to a previous question. These questions often begin like this:

- Which choice provides the best evidence for the answer to the previous question?

- Which statement is the best evidence for the answer to the previous question?

Questions About Tone show your understanding of the author's attitude toward the topic of the passage. To determine the tone, pay attention to the author's word choice. The author's attitude may be positive (respectful), negative (scornful), or neutral (distant). These are typical questions:

- The author's primary purpose in the passage is to . . .

- Which word best describes the author's tone?

Questions About Author's Technique focus on the way a text is organized and the language the author uses. These questions ask you to think about structure and function. For example:

- In the context of the passage, the primary function of the fourth paragraph (lines 30–37) is to . . .

- The organizational structure of the passage is best described as . . .

To answer the questions, you must demonstrate an understanding of the way the author presents information and develops ideas.

VOCABULARY AND WRITING

The **Writing: Words in Action** prompt provides you with an opportunity to practice using text evidence to respond to a prompt about the introductory **Reading Passage**. You will have the opportunity to demonstrate your understanding of the Unit words by incorporating the new vocabulary you have learned into your own writing.

WORD STUDY

Word Study helps build word knowledge with strategies to help you look closely at words for meanings. Word Study instruction and practice include **Idioms**, **Denotation and Connotation**, and **Classical Roots**.

Idioms

Three Word Study sections feature instruction on and practice with idioms. An idiom is an informal expression whose literal meaning does not help the reader or listener understand what the expression means, such as "raining cats and dogs," "the apple of my eye," or "a dark horse." While every language has its own idioms, English is particularly rich in idioms and idiomatic expressions. Developing a clear understanding of idioms will help you better understand the figurative language that authors use in their writing.

Denotation and Connotation

Instruction in **Denotation and Connotation** and practice with connotations is included in two of the Word Study sections. Understanding a word's connotation will develop your skills as a reader, writer, and speaker.

Understanding the difference between denotation and connotation is important to understanding definitions and how concepts are used, as well as in choosing the right word. In these exercises, practice choosing the correct word by determining the emotional association of the word.

Classical Roots

Each Word Study includes a **Classical Roots** exercise that provides instruction in and practice with Greek and Latin roots. Developing a useful, transferable technique to make sense out of unfamiliar words through Greek and Latin roots will help you unlock the meanings of thousands of words. An example word drawn from the vocabulary words in the previous Units is referenced at the top of the page and serves as a guide to help you complete the exercise.

PRONUNCIATION KEY

The pronunciation is indicated for every basic word in this book. The pronunciation symbols used are similar to those used in most recent standard dictionaries. The author has primarily consulted *Webster's Third New International Dictionary* and *The Random House Dictionary of the English Language* (*Unabridged*). Many English words have multiple accepted pronunciations. The author has given one pronunciation when such words occur in this book except when the pronunciation changes according to the part of speech. For example, the verb *project* is pronounced **prə jekt'**, and the noun form is pronounced **präj' ekt**.

Vowels	ā	lake	e	stress	ü	loot, new
	a	mat	ī	knife	u̇	foot, pull
	â	care	i	sit	ə	jump, broken
	ä	bark, bottle	ō	flow	ər	bird, better
	au̇	doubt	ô	all, cord		
	ē	beat, wordy	oi	oil		

Consonants	ch	child, lecture	s	cellar	wh	what
	g	give	sh	shun	y	yearn
	j	gentle, bridge	th	thank	z	is
	ŋ	sing	t̶h̶	those	zh	measure

All other consonants are sounded as in the alphabet.

Stress	The accent mark follows the syllable receiving the major stress: en rich'.

Abbreviations	*adj.*	adjective	*n.*	noun	*prep.*	preposition
	adv.	adverb	*part.*	participle	*v.*	verb
	int.	interjection	*pl.*	plural		

UNIT 1

Note that not all of the Unit words are used in this passage. *Compress, denounce, forsake,* and *libel* are used in the passage on page 23.

*Read the following passage, taking note of the **boldface** words and their contexts. These words are among those you will be studying in Unit 1. It may help you to complete the exercises in this Unit if you refer to the way the words are used below.*

City of Gold
<First-Person Narrative>

L ong ago in western Africa, bands of traders traveled to the city of Timbuktu to buy goods in exchange for gold. The following account is given by a boy describing his first trip to the famous city. He is with a group of friends in the year 1450.

My father has been carrying gold from our land to sell in Timbuktu since he was young. His father was a gold trader before him, and now I've joined him and my brothers. We joined other travelers with their goods and camels in a caravan. We brought gold to Timbuktu to sell, and now I've come home. I'll tell you about that city of gold, because soon you'll be old enough to go there with your fathers, too. I'm **famished**—I haven't eaten since morning. Let's enjoy this small **repast** together while I talk.

I'll start at the end: What a **gainful** expedition! You saw the great load of goods we brought home. **Immense** packages of salt, some **expressly** for our own use, but most for trade here and to the south. We brought back kola nuts to chew on, some palm oil for cooking, and fine cloth for clothing. We profited more than usual, because the buyers of gold wanted more than was available. One man even offered to lend my father gold at interest so we could trade more before having to leave. Father refused, saying, "Lend your money and lose a friend."

Before the journey, I had imagined that we would take our bags to Timbuktu and trade a handful here and there. What an **inept** trader I would become, if not for the wisdom of my father! My father is an **ingenious** man who knows his way around the world. Before we even entered the city, we stopped to rest by the river.

We washed and set up a cooking fire. My father left and returned with a wealthy merchant and his men. They brought us much salt in exchange for our gold. My father and this merchant, who's a big man in Taghaza up north, chewed kola nuts and spoke like old friends. Then, the merchant **dispatched** his men, ordering them back to their camp. Their compliance was **instantaneous**, and I watched them **recede** into the distance, carrying gold this time instead of salt. **Irked** by my idling, my father told me to stop gawking like an **oaf** and start packing the salt.

We ate a quick meal and **doused** the fires. At last, I entered the city of Timbuktu. There are people in Timbuktu of every shape, size, and color; and they come from everywhere, wearing all sorts of **apparel** and speaking many languages. Many speak Arabic, and many speak Mande, like us. There are thousands of people in that city. It's a busy place, but exciting, with massive mosques and palaces and markets.

We exchanged the rest of our gold in the marketplaces. Because there was so much happening, our time in the city went quickly. Now that I am home, I confess that I had some **misgivings** before I went. I feared thieves would attack our caravan. I wondered if the city might be raided or **besieged** while we were there. But everything went smoothly on my first visit. What a place, that busy city—I can hardly wait till we return!

Definitions

Note the spelling, pronunciation, part(s) of speech, and definition(s) of each of the following words. Then write the appropriate form of the word in the blank space in the illustrative sentence(s) following.

1. besiege
(bi sēj')

(*v.*) to attack by surrounding with military forces; to cause worry or trouble

If troops _____ **besiege** _____ their stronghold, the rebel forces may be forced to surrender.

2. compress
(*v.,* kəm pres', *n.,* käm' pres)

(*v.*) to press together; to reduce in size or volume; (*n.*) a folded cloth or pad applied to an injury

The editor helped _____ **compress** _____ my rambling 25-page mystery into an 8-page thriller.

A cold _____ **compress** _____ may soothe headache pain.

3. dispatch
(dis pach')

(*v.*) to send off or out for a purpose; to kill; (*n.*) an official message; promptness, speed; the act of killing

We'll _____ **dispatch** _____ a repair crew right away.

He approved the request with _____ **dispatch** _____.

4. douse
(daủs)

(*v.*) to plunge into a liquid, drench; to put out quickly, extinguish

I'll _____ **douse** _____ the flames with the hose.

5. famished
(fam' isht)

(*adj., part.*) suffering severely from hunger or from a lack of something

The Vietnamese immigrants, new to a strange American city, were _____ **famished** _____ for news of home.

6. gainful
(gān' fəl)

(*adj.*) profitable; bringing in money or some special advantage

I hope to find _____ **gainful** _____ employment that is pleasing to me.

7. ingenious
(in jēn' yəs)

(*adj.*) showing remarkable originality, inventiveness, or resourcefulness; clever

The students found an _____ **ingenious** _____ solution to the math problem.

8. irk
(ərk)

(*v.*) to annoy, trouble, make weary

Questions that show a student's lack of attention _____ **irk** _____ the teacher.

Synonyms and antonyms are provided at SadlierConnect.com.

9. **oaf**
   (ōf)

(*n.*) a stupid person; a big, clumsy, slow individual

He generally moved like an _____ **oaf** _____, so I was surprised to see how graceful he was on the dance floor.

10. **recede**
    (ri sēd′)

(*v.*) to go or move backward; to become more distant

The town residents must wait for the flood waters to _____ **recede** _____ before they can deal with the terrible mess left behind.

Using Context

*For each item, determine whether the **boldface** word from pages 14–15 makes sense in the context of the sentence. Circle the item numbers next to the six sentences in which the words are used correctly.*

1. A cup of warm cocoa and a crossword puzzle always **besiege** me when I have trouble falling asleep.

2. If you suspect a gas leak, you should call this number; the operator will then **dispatch** an emergency crew to your address.

3. The guests at the small, expensive hotel were **famished** by the rude behavior of the staff.

4. Volunteer work may not be **gainful** experience, but it can be rewarding in ways that don't involve money.

5. Because it has no bones, an octopus can **compress** its body and squeeze into small spaces.

6. The mystery novel is cleverly written, with an **ingenious** and slightly shocking twist at the end.

7. Firefighters **douse** oil fires with a chemical foam rather than water.

8. The coach always finds exactly the right words to **irk** the players to go out on the field and do their best.

9. We sat on the dock and watched the fleet of tall ships **recede** into the horizon as they sailed away.

10. At the beginning of the fairy tale, a tiny **oaf** meets a traveller and offers to grant him three wishes.

Choosing the Right Word

*Select the **boldface** word that better completes each sentence. You might refer to the passage on pages 12–13 to see how most of these words are used in context. Note that the choices might be related forms of the Unit words.*

1. His notebooks show that Leonardo da Vinci was not only a masterful artist but a(n) (**famished, ingenious**) inventor as well.

2. Instead of feeling (**doused, irked**) because you did poorly on the exam, why don't you make up your mind to study harder in the future?

3. Hold the (**dispatch, compress**) on your ankle until the swelling goes down.

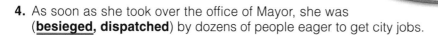

4. As soon as she took over the office of Mayor, she was (**besieged, dispatched**) by dozens of people eager to get city jobs.

5. Tom may not be as polished and clever as some of the other boys, but I think it is unfair of you to call him a(n) (**compress, oaf**).

6. My sister is learning French, taking cooking classes, and participating in other (**ingenious, gainful**) pursuits that will allow her to become a master chef.

7. We can (**compress, besiege**) the message of the sermon into one short sentence: "Do unto others as you would have others do unto you."

8. (**Famished, Compressed**) for a chance to see her work in print, the young writer begged the magazine editor to publish her story.

9. When I realized that I was thoroughly prepared for the final exams, my fears quickly (**receded, irked**).

10. Which job would you take—one that is more (**ingenious, gainful**) right now or one that pays a small salary but offers a chance for valuable training?

11. As soon as he began his long, boring speech, our excitement died down, as though we had been (**receded, doused**) with cold water.

12. We were pleasantly surprised to see that she completed the difficult task we had given her with neatness and (**irk, dispatch**).

You may wish to provide students with an explanation and example of a related form.

Completing the Sentence

Choose the word from the word bank that best completes each of the following sentences. Write the correct word or form of the word in the space provided.

besiege	dispatch	famished	ingenious	oaf
compress	douse	gainful	irk	recede

1. Far away on the horizon, we saw the tiny figures of a lonely traveler and his mule _____**recede**_____ into the sunset.

2. You will be able to get everything into a single suitcase if you _____**compress**_____ all the items as much as possible.

3. You had no right to call me a clumsy _____**oaf**_____ just because I spilled some water on you.

4. A(n) _____**dispatch**_____ will be sent to all our representatives in South America advising them how to handle the problem.

5. Don't allow yourself to be _____**irked**_____ by every small trouble that may arise during the day.

6. Because I have reached an age at which I am unwilling to depend on my parents, I am out to find a(n) _____**gainful**_____ occupation.

7. None of us could figure out how the _____**ingenious**_____ magician had managed to escape from the trunk submerged in the tank of water.

8. How can we hope to _____**besiege**_____ a city that is surrounded by such strong walls and has ample supplies of everything it needs?

9. Let's make certain to _____**douse**_____ the fire before leaving camp.

10. As it was well past their lunchtime by the time we arrived home, the children were _____**famished**_____ and demanding food.

Encourage students to look for context clues. See page 7.

End Set A

Definitions

Note the spelling, pronunciation, part(s) of speech, and definition(s) of each of the following words. Then write the appropriate form of the word in the blank space in the illustrative sentence(s) following.

1. **apparel**
   (ə par' əl)

   (*n.*) clothing, that which serves as dress or decoration;
   (*v.*) to put clothes on, dress up
   Winter _____**apparel**_____ should be warm and cozy.
   Let's _____**apparel**_____ our cats for the party.

2. **denounce**
   (di naủns')

   (*v.*) to condemn openly; to accuse formally
   The United Nations decided to publicly
   _____**denounce**_____ the tyrant's crimes.

3. **expressly**
   (ek spres' lē)

   (*adv.*) plainly, in so many words; for a particular purpose
   At the meeting, parents _____**expressly**_____ stated
   their approval of students wearing school uniforms.

4. **forsake**
   (fôr sāk')

   (*v.*) to give up, renounce; to leave, abandon
   I will never _____**forsake**_____ my children,
   no matter what they do or say.

5. **immense**
   (i mens')

   (*adj.*) very large or great; beyond ordinary means
   of measurement
   Alaska enjoys _____**immense**_____ natural resources, but
   its severe climate makes those resources difficult to use.

6. **inept**
   (in ept')

   (*adj.*) totally without skill or appropriateness
   The scientist is brilliant in the research laboratory
   but is _____**inept**_____ at dealing with people.

7. **instantaneous**
   (in stən tā' nē əs)

   (*adj.*) done in an instant; immediate
   Most computer software is designed so that users
   can obtain nearly _____**instantaneous**_____ responses.

8. **libel**
   (lī' bəl)

   (*n.*) a written statement that unfairly or falsely harms the
   reputation of the person about whom it is made; (*v.*) to
   write or publish such a statement
   The young celebrity accused her unauthorized
   biographer of _____**libel**_____.
   It is a crime to _____**libel**_____ others,
   no matter how you feel about them.

Practice with synonyms and antonyms is on page 22.

9. **misgiving**
(mis giv′ iŋ)

(*n.*) a feeling of fear, doubt, or uncertainty
They had _____ **misgivings** _____ about joining the chorus because of its demanding schedule.

10. **repast**
(ri past′)

(*n.*) a meal, food
Let's get together after the show at Callie's Café for a late-night _____ **repast** _____.

Using Context

*For each item, determine whether the **boldface** word from pages 18–19 makes sense in the context of the sentence. Circle the item numbers next to the six sentences in which the words are used correctly.*

(**1.**) In an age when **instantaneous** answers to our questions can be found online, it seems strange that people once had to slog through encyclopedias or archives to find information.

2. The photographer was known for her close-up images, which captured the tiniest, most **immense** details of nature.

(**3.**) I admire your ability to find **apparel** that is fashionable but still expresses your unique taste and style.

4. As valedictorian, I plan on delivering a **repast** at graduation that will make my classmates grateful for their past experiences and excited for the future.

(**5.**) The school guidelines **expressly** forbid using cell phones on school property, but some students still ask if there is any way around that rule.

6. Many professional teams wanted to recruit the skillful hockey player because he was so **inept** at shooting the puck into the net while evading the goalie.

(**7.**) The mayor was quick to **denounce** the message of the protesters, although some people thought she should first hear them out.

(**8.**) The biographer was careful to fact-check every story about his subjects because he never wanted to be accused of **libel**.

9. In such a close race, it is impossible to **forsake** who the winner might be.

(**10.**) When the hiring manager mentioned the "difficult personalities" I would be working with, I had yet another **misgiving** about accepting the job.

Choosing the Right Word

*Select the **boldface** word that better completes each sentence. You might refer to the passage on pages 12–13 to see how most of these words are used in context. Note that the choices might be related forms of the Unit words.*

1. The beauty of the Grand Canyon is so (**immense, instantaneous**) that it is absolutely impossible to capture its grandeur on film.

2. You may criticize the roads and the lights, but the fact is that (**inept, immense**) drivers are the cause of most car accidents.

3. We are working hard to improve conditions in our community, but we cannot expect (**inept, instantaneous**) results.

4. He may claim that we have (**libeled, denounced**) him, but we have facts to back up every statement made in the column about him.

5. I will never (**libel, forsake**) the people who helped me in my hour of need!

6. The story I am reading features an (**inept, immense**) detective who cannot solve a case and continually loses things.

7. Where did he ever get the curious idea that we set up this volleyball court (**expressly, instantaneously**) for him and his friends?

8. Each day, after she finishes her homework, she enjoys a light (**repast, misgiving**) of the detective stories she loves so well.

9. His conceit is so (**immense, instantaneous**) that he cannot imagine anyone voting against him in the election for class president.

10. Her conscience forced her to (**denounce, libel**) the conspirators to the authorities.

11. I always feel sad at the end of the autumn, when the trees lose their beautiful (**repast, apparel**) of leaves.

12. After all the bad things he has done, I feel no (**repast, misgivings**) about telling him that I don't want him to be my "friend" anymore.

You may wish to provide students with an explanation and example of a related form.

Completing the Sentence

Choose the word from the word bank that best completes each of the following sentences. Write the correct word or form of the word in the space provided.

apparel	expressly	immense	instantaneous	misgiving
denounce	forsake	inept	libel	repast

1. The laws of this land do not shield public figures from just criticism, but they do protect them against _____**libel**_____.

2. Some people hailed the man as a genius; others _____**denounced**_____ him as a quack.

3. As an inexperienced sailor, I had more than a few _____**misgivings**_____ about taking out the small boat in such rough weather.

4. On my first baby-sitting job, I found that one must have _____**immense**_____ patience to take care of young children.

5. The terms of our agreement _____**expressly**_____ forbade us to take any of the goods for our own use.

6. Your _____**apparel**_____ can be neat and attractive without being expensive.

7. Some of life's rewards are _____**instantaneous**_____; others are a long time in coming.

8. When you play tennis for the first time, you are going to find that your attempts to hit the ball are very _____**inept**_____.

9. While all true vegetarians _____**forsake**_____ animal meats, some do eat dairy products, such as milk and yogurt.

10. When you are really hungry, even the simplest foods, such as a slice of buttered bread, will be a delicious _____**repast**_____.

Encourage students to look for context clues. See page 7.

Synonyms

*Choose the word or form of the word from this Unit that is the same or most nearly the same in meaning as the **boldface** word or expression in the phrase. Write that word on the line. Use a dictionary if necessary.*

1. **inventive** use for lumber scraps   ingenious
2. waiting until the crowds **ebb**   recede
3. **blockaded** the small ships from entering the harbor   besieged
4. **bad feelings** about the leading candidate   misgivings
5. **starving** after missing last night's dinner   famished
6. enjoy a late-night **feast**   repast
7. sued for **defamation**   libel
8. **drenched** the dirty laundry with soapy water   doused
9. saved an **immeasurable** fortune   immense
10. acted like a **dunce** in front of the interviewer   oaf
11. is **clearly** forbidden for use by minors   expressly
12. developed a **moneymaking** venture from scratch   gainful
13. troops that were **sent off** to the war zone   dispatched
14. fashionable hand-me-down **outfits**   apparel
15. had to fire the **bungling** carpenter   inept

Antonyms

*Choose the word or form of the word from this Unit that is most nearly opposite in meaning to the **boldface** word or expression in the phrase. Write that word on the line. Use a dictionary if necessary.*

1. **expand** the bundle to fit   compress
2. was certain to **gladden** the passengers   irk
3. a **delayed** reaction   instantaneous
4. reasons to **validate** the winner   denounce
5. will **support** all causes   forsake

Writing: Words in Action

Answers to the prompt will vary.

Suppose you will be traveling with the traders in "City of Gold" (pages 12–13). You wonder what your trip will be like when you arrive in Timbuktu. Write a journal entry, describing what excites you about the trip and what worries you. Use at least two details from the passage and three or more words from this Unit.

Vocabulary in Context

*Some of the words you have studied in this Unit appear in **boldface** type. Read the passage below, and then circle the letter of the correct answer for each word as it is used in context.*

Believe it or not, camels once roamed the Wild West. Just before the Civil War, the U.S. Army imported 75 Bactrian camels (which have two humps) and dromedaries (which have one) from the Middle East. The camels' purpose? To transport soldiers and supplies between military settlements on the vast desert region of the southwestern frontier.

Military leaders calculated that a rugged camel caravan could replace weaker mule trains. This plan was met with anger by mule owners who had more than one **misgiving**. They considered the army's assertion that their traditional pack animals were weak to be **libel**, almost treason. But in fact, the hardy camels, who were able to adapt to extremes in temperature and could go for long periods without water, performed very well under tough conditions. The soldiers' travel time was cut in half. To the weary men, the thousands of miles they had to travel seemed to **compress**, and their hardships **recede**.

The roving U.S. Army Camel Corps was declared a success, and more camels were exported from their native lands. In the meantime, the mule lobby in Washington, D.C., protested angrily to **denounce** the use of the camels. But after 10 years, the Civil War started, many camel stations and camels were seized by the Confederate Army, and the camel experiment ground to a halt. Some of the creatures were sold to zoos and circuses, or to ranchers and farmers for use as working animals. Others were left to fend for themselves when the government had no choice but to **forsake** them. For decades after, sightings of wild camels were reported all over the West.

---

1. What is the meaning of **misgiving** as it is used in paragraph 2?
   a. question   **c.** fear
   b. assurance   **d.** misunderstanding

2. Which word means the same as **libel** as it is used in paragraph 2?
   a. a false impression   **c.** a generalization
   b. a slur   **d.** an attitude

3. What is the meaning of **compress** as it is used in paragraph 2?
   a. widen   **c.** ease
   b. shorten   **d.** increase

4. **Recede** comes from the Latin word **recedere**. **Recedere** most likely means
   a. to move backward   **c.** to move quickly
   b. to lengthen   **d.** to endure

5. The word **denounce** means about the same as
   a. criticize   **c.** warn
   b. reject   **d.** embrace

6. What does **forsake** most likely mean as it is used in paragraph 3?
   a. train   **c.** abandon
   b. export   **d.** adopt

See pages T29–T31 for assessment options.

UNIT 2

Note that not all of the Unit words are used in this passage. *Assailant, constrain, incomprehensible, serene,* and *sheepish* are used in the passage on page 35.

*Read the following passage, taking note of the **boldface** words and their contexts. These words are among those you will be studying in Unit 2. It may help you to complete the exercises in this Unit if you refer to the way the words are used below.*

West End School Has Comestible Curriculum
<Interview>

The Scrumptious Schoolyard is a grassroots program that transforms concrete playgrounds into functional farmland. Part of the Scrumptious Schoolyard Project, it is the brainchild of **contemporary** food-education pioneer Clarissa Z. Ochoa. Students explore the connection between what they eat and where it comes from through hands-on organic gardening and cooking classes. The "comestible curriculum" **encompasses** math, science, history, geography, social studies, and more.

Interviewer: Rosa, you're a sixth-grade student gardener in the Scrumptious Schoolyard at T.R. Middle School in West End. Have you tried growing anything before?

Rosa: No, this is my first time, and now I have a green thumb. I might become a farmer or a chef, or both!

Interviewer: I heard that the Scrumptious Schoolyard concept was somewhat controversial in the beginning.

Rosa: It **ruffled** a few feathers. Some people were **disinterested**, while others were suspicious, **depicting** it as playing instead of learning. I think their complaints are **groundless**, and they really don't know what they're missing. It's amazing to watch something grow from a tiny seed. It takes a lot of **stamina** and enthusiasm to keep the gardens growing, but everyone works together.

Interviewer: What are some favorite experiences and things you've learned?

Rosa: I was excited when the blossoms on the squashes and pumpkins appeared. We made pumpkin pancakes and sauteed zucchini blossoms, so I actually cooked and ate a flower! Rule number one for gardeners is smart planning, and we need to get **maximum** use from our plot. Have you heard of companion planting? Plants are like people—some exist together better than others, so we **manipulate** the plants, materials, and space to get the best harvest. We also extend the natural growing seasons by **mimicking** Mother Nature with grow lights and mini-greenhouses.

Interviewer: Have you encountered any stumbling blocks so far?

Rosa: We develop tools and strategies for overcoming **adverse** conditions. Our climate isn't extremely **arid**, but sometimes it's pretty dry, so we practice water conservation by using rain barrels. Also, the first time we tried to

Scrumptious Schoolyard student gardeners plant, tend, harvest, cook, and eat what they grow.

Rosa de la Vega

make compost, it was unbelievably smelly. You have to get the ingredients and layers right. The second time, it turned out great. One of our teachers calls compost "black gold."

Interviewer: Do you have a secret for attracting butterflies and bees to the garden?

Rosa: We grow flowers that draw beneficial insects. Honeybees pollinate our plants,

One of the best parts of the Scrumptious Schoolyard program is eating what you've grown.

but the bees are in trouble because of Colony Collapse Disorder, so we try to do our part. Since our gardens are organic, we would be **hypocrites** if we used pesticides, so we're studying all-natural pest control. One raised bed has a *koinobori*, a Japanese fish kite that **billows** in the breeze and scares off scavengers.

Interviewer: What would you say to other schools or kids interested in the program?

Rosa: Confront obstacles and go for it! You may think one kid can't do much to help the environment or change how people eat, but working in the Scrumptious Schoolyard has made me believe we *can* make a big difference.

Interviewer: Finally, I have to ask–do you really eat all the vegetables you're growing? I thought kids were supposed to hate vegetables.

Rosa: There's no way I'm going to eat turnips. But it's good to try new things, according to my science teacher. We're still waiting to see *him* try turnips!

Audio

For iWords and audio passages, go to SadlierConnect.com.

Definitions

Note the spelling, pronunciation, part(s) of speech, and definition(s) of each of the following words. Then write the appropriate form of the word in the blank space in the illustrative sentence(s) following.

1. adverse
(ad vərs')

(*adj.*) unfavorable, negative; working against, hostile
Some people suffer an _____**adverse**_____ reaction if they eat peanut butter or anything with peanuts.

2. assailant
(ə sa' lənt)

(*n.*) a person who attacks violently (with blows or words)
The jogger was injured by an unknown _____**assailant**_____, who left him immobile at the side of the road.

3. confront
(kən frənt')

(*v.*) to meet face-to-face, especially as a challenge; come to grips with
In court, defendants can _____**confront**_____ their accusers in a controlled setting.

4. contemporary
(kən tem' pə rer ē)

(*adj.*) belonging to the same period of time as oneself; (*n.*) a person of the same time
His novel used a _____**contemporary**_____ style but had a historical setting.
Rather than ask parents for help, teens often turn to a _____**contemporary**_____ for advice.

5. depict
(di pikt')

(*v.*) to portray; to represent or show in the form of a picture
The painter chose to _____**depict**_____ a plain prairie landscape using bold colors and shadows.

6. groundless
(graund' ləs)

(*adj.*) without any good reason or cause, unjustified
Kate's _____**groundless**_____ fear of hurting herself during exercise has left her weak and out of shape.

7. hypocrite
(hip' ə krit)

(*n.*) a person who pretends to be what he or she is not or better than he or she really is; a two-faced person
The speaker who said one thing but did something else entirely was regarded as a _____**hypocrite**_____.

8. mimic
(mim' ik)

(*n.*) a person who does imitations; (*v.*) to imitate; to make fun of
The comedy troupe needs to hire a _____**mimic**_____.
Troy can _____**mimic**_____ any accent he hears.

Synonyms and antonyms are provided at SadlierConnect.com.

9. **serene**
(sə rēn')

(*adj.*) peaceful, calm; free of emotional upset; clear and free of storm; majestic, grand

She stayed _____**serene**_____ in the face of chaos.

10. **sheepish**
(shēp' ish)

(*adj.*) embarrassed; resembling a sheep in meekness, timid

His _____**sheepish**_____ grin made the crowds cheer all the more for his unlikely victory.

Using Context

*For each item, determine whether the **boldface** word from pages 26–27 makes sense in the context of the sentence. Circle the item numbers next to the six sentences in which the words are used correctly.*

(**1.**) The lawyer insisted that the charges were **groundless** and that they should be dropped immediately.

(**2.**) The students discussed ways to **confront** a bully as well as ways to avoid an argument with one.

3. The advertisements for the detergent promised that it could **depict** even the most stubborn stains.

(**4.**) Experienced mountain climbers are used to dealing with all sorts of **adverse** conditions, but the odds of surviving an avalanche are slim for even the most skilled climber.

(**5.**) The soft, **serene** music that plays in the dentist's waiting room helps patients relax before their appointments.

(**6.**) The police officers took off after the **assailant** and chased him for ten blocks before finally capturing him.

7. Every year, the university's department of physics honors a top **hypocrite** in the field.

8. The interior decorator can **mimic** a room and completely change its look in just a day or two.

(**9.**) Our theater group performs both classic and **contemporary** plays.

10. I tried to stay up until midnight on New Year's Eve, but by 11:30 p.m., I was feeling so **sheepish** that I could hardly keep my eyes open.

Choosing the Right Word

*Select the **boldface** word that better completes each sentence. You might refer to the passage on pages 24–25 to see how most of these words are used in context. Note that the choices might be related forms of the Unit words.*

1. After many stormy years in the service of his country, George Washington retired to the (**serene**, **adverse**) life of his beloved Mount Vernon.

2. The (**adverse**, **sheepish**) publicity that he received during the investigation was probably the cause of his defeat in the next election.

3. She has gained success as a writer who knows how to (**confront**, **depict**) in a lifelike way the hopes, fears, and problems of young people today.

4. Despite the fact that she was in shock, the victim gave a clear description of her (**hypocrite**, **assailant**).

5. While some find her smile comical, I have always found the Mona Lisa's smile to be (**serene**, **sheepish**) and mysterious.

6. The man was trying to (**depict**, **mimic**) the young woman as a troublemaker, simply because she had dyed her hair purple and dressed in an unusual manner.

7. If you (**depict**, **confront**) your problems honestly and openly, instead of trying to hide them, you will have a better chance of solving them.

8. What a relief to learn that my parents had been delayed by a storm, and that all my fears about an accident were (**groundless**, **contemporary**)!

9. Instead of working so hard to (**mimic**, **confront**) popular TV stars, why don't you try to develop an acting style of your own?

10. My idea of a(n) (**assailant**, **hypocrite**) is a person who gives advice that he or she is not willing to follow.

11. Martin Luther King, Jr. and Robert F. Kennedy were (**contemporaries**, **mimics**), born within a few years of each other.

12. After giving a few (**sheepish**, **serene**) excuses, the swimmers packed up and left the private beach.

You may wish to provide students with an explanation and example of a related form.

Completing the Sentence

Choose the word from the word bank that best completes each of the following sentences. Write the correct word or form of the word in the space provided.

adverse	confront	depict	hypocrite	serene
assailant	contemporary	groundless	mimic	sheepish

1. Held back by _____ **adverse** _____ winds, the plane arrived at the airport two hours late.

2. You and Lucy will never settle your quarrel unless you _____ **confront** _____ each other directly and listen to what the other person has to say.

3. The skyscraper is one of the best-known and widely admired forms of _____ **contemporary** _____ architecture.

4. Fortunately, I was able to fight off my _____ **assailant** _____, even though his attack took me by complete surprise.

5. The _____ **serene** _____ expression on her face showed that she was totally undisturbed by the confusion and turmoil around her.

6. For a long time, I thought that he was a good and sincere person, but I finally saw that he was no more than a(n) _____ **hypocrite** _____.

7. The jury found the defendant "not guilty" because they were convinced that the charges against her were _____ **groundless** _____.

8. Using the entire east wall of the new post office building, the painter tried to _____ **depict** _____ the founding of our city.

9. Parrots and a few other kinds of birds can _____ **mimic** _____ sounds, particularly human speech.

10. I was so embarrassed by my blunder that I could do nothing but grin in a(n) _____ **sheepish** _____ and self-conscious way.

Encourage students to look for context clues. See page 7.

Definitions

Note the spelling, pronunciation, part(s) of speech, and definition(s) of each of the following words. Then write the appropriate form of the word in the blank space in the illustrative sentence(s) following.

1. **arid**
   (ar′ id)

   (*adj.*) extremely dry; uninteresting, dull
   Although California leads the nation in farming, crops won't grow in its most _____**arid**_____ regions.

2. **billow**
   (bil′ o)

   (*n.*) a large wave; (*v.*) to rise or swell like a wave
   The ocean _____**billows**_____ rose and fell, attracting the most daring surfers.
   Fans cheered enthusiastically when they saw their team's flags _____**billow**_____ over the stadium.

3. **constrain**
   (kən strān′)

   (*v.*) to force, compel; to restrain, hold back
   You can't _____**constrain**_____ me against my will.

4. **disinterested**
   (dis in′ trəst id)

   (*adj.*) fair-minded, free from selfish motives; indifferent
   A judge must remain _____**disinterested**_____ in order to render an evenhanded and logical decision.

5. **encompass**
   (en kəm′ pəs)

   (*v.*) to encircle, go or reach around; to enclose; to include with a certain group or class
   Oceans _____**encompass**_____ about three-fourths of the surface of our planet.

6. **incomprehensible**
   (in käm pri hen′ sə bəl)

   (*adj.*) impossible to understand
   Our school's intercom system is so old that this morning's announcements were almost _____**incomprehensible**_____.

7. **manipulate**
   (mə nip′ yə lāt)

   (*v.*) to handle or use skillfully; to manage or control for personal gain or advantage
   Scientists should not _____**manipulate**_____ data.

8. **maximum**
   (mak′ sə məm)

   (*n.*) the greatest possible amount or degree; (*adj.*) reaching the greatest possible amount or degree
   This postage scale can weigh a _____**maximum**_____ of only five pounds.
   To ease the patient's suffering, the doctor prescribed the _____**maximum**_____ dosage of painkillers.

Practice with synonyms and antonyms is on page 34.

9. ruffle
(rəf′ əl)

(*v.*) to wrinkle, make uneven; to annoy, upset; to flip through; (*n.*) material used for trimming edges; a ripple; a low drumbeat

His wisecracks always _____**ruffle**_____ my feelings.

My favorite pillow has a velvet _____**ruffle**_____.

10. stamina
(stam′ ə nə)

(*n.*) the strength needed to keep going or overcome physical or mental strain; staying power

Marathon runners need a great deal of _____**stamina**_____ to cover the many miles.

Using Context

*For each item, determine whether the **boldface** word from pages 30–31 makes sense in the context of the sentence. Circle the item numbers next to the six sentences in which the words are used correctly.*

1. I like stretching exercises because they help me to **constrain** any tension from my muscles that might be caused by stress.

2. As soon as I opened the refrigerator, an **arid** smell reached my nostrils, and I suspected that someone had forgotten about some expired food.

(**3.**) The **maximum** number of people allowed in the school auditorium is 500, so we won't be able to sell any more tickets than that for each performance of the play.

(**4.**) The opposing team jeered at us while we walked onto the field, but we did not let their comments **ruffle** our confidence.

(**5.**) The lawyers told the witness that, as the defendant's mother, she could not testify on his behalf as no one would describe her as being **disinterested**.

6. The **stamina** she displayed when she found out she did not get the promotion shows just how unqualified she is to be a leader.

(**7.**) The literature we study in this class will **encompass** everything from works by ancient philosophers to contemporary fiction.

(**8.**) *Finnegan's Wake* by James Joyce is considered a great novel, but its irregular language, difficult storyline, and unconventional style make it **incomprehensible** to many readers.

9. The boy looked dejected as his balloon began to lose air and **billow** to the ground.

(**10.**) As I watched the carpenter precisely **manipulate** each floorboard into its space, I knew I could not have done this project alone.

Choosing the Right Word

*Select the **boldface** word that better completes each sentence. You might refer to the passage on pages 24–25 to see how most of these words are used in context. Note that the choices might be related forms of the Unit words.*

1. A good scientist must have a keen mind, an unquenchable curiosity, and a(n) (**incomprehensible, <u>disinterested</u>**) desire to discover the truth.

2. The big-league shortstop (**<u>manipulates</u>, constrains**) his glove like a magician, snaring every ball hit within reach.

3. His decision not to accept our sincere offer of assistance is completely (**disinterested, <u>incomprehensible</u>**) to me.

4. The science program in our school (**manipulates, <u>encompasses</u>**) biology, chemistry, physics, earth science, and other related courses.

5. Anyone who has ever sailed a small boat knows how thrilling it is to feel the spray in your face while the sails (**<u>billow</u>, encompass**) overhead.

6. Do you think it would be a good idea to set a (**<u>maximum</u>, disinterested**) figure for the amount of homework any teacher is allowed to assign?

7. I didn't want to (**<u>ruffle</u>, manipulate**) the feelings of the hotel manager, but I felt that I had to complain about the miserable service.

8. It was (**disinterested, <u>incomprehensible</u>**) to think that our grandparents had to spend sweltering summers without air-conditioning.

9. She has many interesting ideas, but she seems to lack the physical and mental (**<u>stamina</u>, billow**) to make good use of them.

10. After the storm, residents were (**<u>constrained</u>, ruffled**) to stay in their homes, as all roads were impassable.

11. We expected the lecture on the energy crisis to be exciting, but it turned out to be a(n) (**ruffled, <u>arid</u>**) rundown of well-known facts and figures.

12. After living for many years in that roomy old farmhouse, I felt awfully (**arid, <u>constrained</u>**) in that small apartment.

You may wish to provide students with an explanation and example of a related form.

Completing the Sentence

Choose the word from the word bank that best completes each of the following sentences. Write the correct word or form of the word in the space provided.

arid	constrain	encompass	manipulate	ruffle
billow	disinterested	incomprehensible	maximum	stamina

1. Although I may hurt your feelings, my conscience __**constrained**__ me to tell you exactly what is on my mind.

2. Very few starting pitchers have the __**stamina**__ to pitch consistently well for nine innings.

3. Under the law, the __**maximum**__ number of people who may ride in this bus is seventy-five.

4. Since Tom is both smart and __**disinterested**__, I think he is just the person to decide which of us is right in this long and bitter quarrel.

5. As you become a more skillful driver, you will be able to __**manipulate**__ all the controls of the car while keeping your eyes on the road.

6. You talk so fast and in such a low tone of voice that you are going to be completely __**incomprehensible**__ to most people.

7. The hot, __**arid**__ climate of Arizona is favorable for many people suffering from various diseases, such as arthritis.

8. This basic textbook __**encompasses**__ all the information you will have to master for the entrance examination.

9. A breeze sprang up and began to __**ruffle**__ the smooth and tranquil surface of the water.

10. The brisk breeze caused the sheets on the line to __**billow**__ like the sails on a yacht that is running with the wind.

Encourage students to look for context clues. See page 7.

Synonyms

Choose the word or form of the word from this Unit that is the same or most nearly the same in meaning as the **boldface** *word or expression in the phrase. Write that word on the line. Use a dictionary if necessary.*

1. remembered the **attacker**'s voice   assailant

2. able to **replicate** a bird's call   mimic

3. to serve as a **neutral** witness   disinterested

4. **disturbed** by the sound of the horn   ruffled

5. a park that **envelops** a playground and an open field   encompasses

6. shirts on the clothesline that **swell out** from the wind   billow

7. untruths that **influenced** the voters   manipulated

8. a painting **illustrating** the life of a settler   depicting

9. the **largest** number of occupants   maximum

10. dismissed the **baseless** accusations   groundless

11. not able to **face** their fears   confront

12. spent their youth in a **boring** town   arid

13. looked for advice from a **peer**   contemporary

14. mistrustful of that **impostor**   hypocrite

15. demonstrates **endurance** in the walkathon   stamina

Antonyms

Choose the word or form of the word from this Unit that is most nearly opposite in meaning to the **boldface** *word or expression in the phrase. Write that word on the line. Use a dictionary if necessary.*

1. hopes to **release** the prisoner   constrain

2. rules that are quite **clear**   incomprehensible

3. expected a **favorable** reaction from the audience   adverse

4. trying to control his **stormy** emotions   serene

5. exhibits a **confident** attitude   sheepish

Writing: Words in Action

Answers to the prompt will vary.

Can healthful foods be tasty? Do you think a healthful diet requires too much effort? Write a brief essay in which you support your opinion with specific examples, personal experience, and the reading (pages 24–25). Write at least three paragraphs, and use three or more words from this Unit.

Vocabulary in Context

*Some of the words you have studied in this Unit appear in **boldface** type. Read the passage below, and then circle the letter of the correct answer for each word as it is used in context.*

Organic items are abundant in grocery stores across the United States. In 2015, organic food recorded $37.9 billion in sales. In 2015, almost five percent of the food sold in the United States was organic. How can this seemingly **incomprehensible** amount of organic food get produced each year? The answer is organic farms. In 2014, 14,093 organic farms on 3.7 million **serene** acres in the United States produced this staggering amount of food.

Organic farmers use techniques that enable significant crop yields without harming the natural environment. Government regulations **constrain** organic farmers to utilize agricultural production systems that do not use genetically modified seed. These methods cannot include synthetic pesticides or fertilizers. Organic farmers use recycled and composted crop waste and animal manure. This waste builds strong soil structure. To control pests, organic farmers encourage beneficial predators that eat pests, and they use natural pesticides. Organic farmers also practice crop rotation. Crop rotation is rotating plant families from one season to the next to maintain healthy soil. In addition, organic farmers use water carefully. All of these habits allow organic farms to enhance the ecosystem rather than harming it.

Though organic farms differ from conventional farms, both types face similar problems. Farm crime is a problem for conventional and organic farmers. An **assailant** may attack farms to steal irrigation systems, livestock, and crops. Farmers are also under increasing pressure to feed a growing population that is not **sheepish** about wasting food. Farmers also have to worry about **arid** land during a drought.

---

1. The word **incomprehensible** means about the same as
  a. baffling
  b. dangerous
  c. interesting
  d. insignificant

2. Which word means the same as **serene** as it is used in paragraph 1?
  a. lush
  b. rural
  c. sprawling
  d. peaceful

3. What is the meaning of **constrain** as it is used in paragraph 2?
  a. to suggest
  b. to compel
  c. to reason
  d. to permit

4. What does the word **assailant** most likely mean as it is used in paragraph 3?
  a. violent attacker
  b. passive bystander
  c. peaceful protester
  d. meddling neighbor

5. What is the meaning of **sheepish** as it is used in paragraph 3?
  a. afraid
  b. anxious
  c. embarrassed
  d. careful

6. **Arid** comes from the Latin word **aridus.** **Aridus** most likely means
  a. dry
  b. stagnant
  c. fertile
  d. scarce

See pages T29–T31 for assessment options.

Note that not all of the Unit words are used in this passage. *Bigot, designate, global, pacifist,* and *terrain* are used in the passage on page 47.

Read the following passage, taking note of the **boldface** *words and their contexts. These words are among those you will be studying in Unit 3. It may help you to complete the exercises in this Unit if you refer to the way the words are used below.*

This Day in 1923: The *Olympic*'s the Thing!
<Archived Newspaper Article>

Before planes whisked people around the world in a day, travelers sailed to their destinations on large ocean liners. Shipping companies such as the Cunard Line and the White Star Line competed with each other to build the largest, most luxurious ships. Today the *Times* archives presents a 1923 feature article about one of the most glamorous of all sea-going vessels, the *Olympic*.

London, June 24, 1923—As the White Star Liner *Olympic* shoved off from New York last Monday, I stood on its giant deck and gazed at the open sea. I've traveled on big ships before, but never one quite so big. I felt small on its sprawling decks and a bit in awe of the vessel's size. I stood quietly. The **enigma** of the ocean and the equally mysterious grandeur of this gigantic boat surrounded me.

For a time the *Olympic* was the largest ocean liner in the world. She was matched once by her sister ship, the doomed *Titanic*. The *Olympic* has been plying the seas since her maiden voyage in 1910. In World War I she entered military service. She transported troops about the Atlantic. Incredibly, the *Olympic* was the only merchant vessel to sink an enemy warship during the war. She rammed a German submarine, the U-103, and sent it underwater for good. That was five years ago, in the spring of 1918.

Today on the *Olympic*, the war is ancient history. Happy passengers wander the ship. Linger in one spot, and you might be **waylaid** by a passenger who wants a partner for a game of that great racquet sport, squash, or for shuffleboard. And the dining rooms are full of good eating. There's a great **diversity** of food, with English, French, and American cuisine on the menu. A variety of beverages is also available for guests to **slake**

Tug boats push the *Olympic* out of the New York Harbour in 1912.

their summer thirsts. Open-air settings provide the **illusion** of relaxing at a Mediterranean café. At every turn, there's another surprise, another lounge, another entertainment. I've made several trips between the library and the swimming pool. And I've **vowed** to visit the gym before we get to England. I'm sure I will—just as soon as that **infuriating** fellow with the squash racquet stops irritating me and sits down for a bite to eat. Perhaps he'll trot off somewhere to **gloat** about his latest score.

The Turkish baths are a favorite stop for many guests. This area has rooms of the most fantastic decoration. They are decked out from top to

The fabulous promenade deck

Passengers enjoy the open air on deck.

look forward to the return trip to New York. Then it's back to the usual routine. For the time being, I'm happy to report, the sun is setting, the squash racquets are tucked away, and all's well on the *Olympic*.

bottom. The floors and walls are dressed in colorful tiles. The decoration is so fine and abundant that any more would have been gilding the lily. What **sage** was it who knew to stop at this perfection? Each day I am **motivated** to return to the baths. All cares seem to **wither** away under the **barrage** of care and attention the attendants shower upon visitors there.

If I could make it my **vocation** to wander the earth on ships like this, I'd **queue** up for the job without a moment's hesitation. But obligation **restricts** the choices we make. My life's work lies ashore. Tomorrow we'll arrive in Southampton, England. I'll attend to my business there and

Famous Ladies who use

The Hon. Mrs. Alfred Lyttelton

The Hon. Mrs. Alfred Lyttelton writes: "I always keep a bottle of Formamint Tablets in the house, as I think them quite excellent for Sore Throat."

Photo by Lafayette

The Marchioness of Sligo

"The Most Hon. the Marchioness of Sligo finds Formamint Tablets very useful for Sore Throats, and always has a bottle of it in the house."

All Chemists sell W
genuine Wulfing's F
to A. Wulfing & C
of Sanatogen. Ple

Audio

For iWords and audio passages, go to SadlierConnect.com.

Definitions

Note the spelling, pronunciation, part(s) of speech, and definition(s) of each of the following words. Then write the appropriate form of the word in the blank space in the illustrative sentence(s) following.

---

1. bigot
(big' ət)

(*n.*) an intolerant, prejudiced, or biased person
When you speak in that narrow-minded way, you sound like a _____ **bigot** _____.

---

2. diversity
(di vər' sə tē)

(*n.*) difference, variety; a condition of having many different types or forms
Our science teacher has a _____ **diversity** _____ of interests, including an appreciation of Russian literature.

---

3. gloat
(glōt)

(*v.*) to look at or think about with great intensity and satisfaction; to take great personal joy in
I will try not to _____ **gloat** _____ about winning a scholarship to music camp.

---

4. global
(glō' bəl)

(*adj.*) of, relating to, or involving the entire world; comprehensive
E-mail and the Internet have linked the entire world into a _____ **global** _____ village.

---

5. illusion
(i lü' zhən)

(*n.*) a false idea; something that one seems to see or to be aware of that really does not exist
Magicians use optical _____ **illusions** _____ to amaze their audiences.

---

6. motivate
(mō' tə vāt)

(*v.*) to provide with a reason for doing; to push on to some goal
How can we _____ **motivate** _____ the students to undertake more challenging work?

---

7. restrict
(ri strikt')

(*v.*) to keep within set limits; to confine
Doctors often advise patients to _____ **restrict** _____ their intake of fatty or salty foods.

---

8. sage
(sāj)

(*adj.*) wise; (*n.*) a very wise person
My aunt always gives me _____ **sage** _____ advice.
Let's ask the _____ **sage** _____ for guidance.

Synonyms and antonyms are provided at SadlierConnect.com.

9. vocation
(vō kā′ shən)

(*n.*) any trade, profession, or occupation; a sense of fitness or special calling for one's work

After many years of searching, she found her true _____**vocation**_____ as a horse trainer.

10. wither
(with′ ər)

(*v.*) to dry up, wilt, sag; to cause someone to feel ashamed, humiliated, or very small

Despite people's best efforts to remain young looking, skin will eventually _____**wither**_____ with age.

Using Context

*For each item, determine whether the **boldface** word from pages 38–39 makes sense in the context of the sentence. Circle the item numbers next to the six sentences in which the words are used correctly.*

(**1.**) Every two years, the world's best athletes compete on a **global** scale at either the summer or the winter Olympics.

(**2.**) Her discriminatory treatment of people and intolerant remarks about them revealed that she was, in fact, a **bigot**.

(**3.**) The **diversity** of plant life in this region is stunning; so far, scientists have identified thousands of different species.

4. The shy cat would immediately **gloat** whenever visitors came to the house.

5. Some take a guided tour of a museum, while others just like to **wither** around on their own.

(**6.**) Is that television commercial merely entertaining, or does it actually **motivate** people to buy the product?

7. We spent a **sage** and relaxing afternoon rowing and just drifting on the clear, blue lake.

(**8.**) He feels that teaching is his true **vocation**, and he cannot imagine himself doing anything else.

9. Lightning is an **illusion** that occurs when an electrical discharge jumps from a cloud to the ground.

(**10.**) We promised to **restrict** our recreational screen time to just one or two hours per day.

Choosing the Right Word

*Select the **boldface** word that better completes each sentence. You might refer to the passage on pages 36–37 to see how most of these words are used in context. Note that the choices might be related forms of the Unit words.*

1. Many view Shakespeare as the timeless (**illusion, sage**) and constantly use his words to give advice.

2. Has it ever occurred to you that your belief that you are a superior person and a natural leader may be no more than a(n) (**vocation, illusion**)?

3. The United States has laws that (**restrict, gloat**) the numbers and kinds of immigrants allowed to enter this country.

4. By the time you are old enough to enter the workforce, many (**sages, vocations**) that are important today may not even exist anymore.

5. With the other team ten points ahead and only a few minutes left to play, our hopes of victory began to (**gloat, wither**).

6. She is never bored because she has a great (**vocation, diversity**) of interests, ranging from folk dancing to mathematics.

7. World War II was a truly (**global, sage**) struggle, fought in all parts of the world by people of every race and background.

8. Lilies are delicate and will (**wither, gloat**) quickly if not protected from the hot sun.

9. Her analysis of what is wrong with our city government seems to me remarkably (**sage, global**) and helpful.

10. A good loser doesn't sulk over defeat; a good winner doesn't (**gloat, wither**) after victory.

11. A great teacher not only makes the material of the course understandable but also (**restricts, motivates**) the students to want to learn more.

12. As you have so many prejudices of your own, you should think twice before you accuse other people of being (**sages, bigots**).

You may wish to provide students with an explanation and example of a related form.

Completing the Sentence

Choose the word from the word bank that best completes each of the following sentences. Write the correct word or form of the word in the space provided.

bigot	gloat	illusion	restrict	vocation
diversity	global	motivate	sage	wither

1. I came to regard my grandmother as a(n) _____**sage**_____ whose wisdom helped solve many family problems.

2. For better or for worse, as you become older and more experienced, you will lose many of the comforting _____**illusions**_____ of youth.

3. The pollution problem, far from being limited to the United States, is truly _____**global**_____ in scope.

4. How sad it is to see such beautiful flowers _____**wither**_____ and die!

5. As he greatly enjoys woodworking and also makes a living from it, his hobby and his _____**vocation**_____ are one and the same.

6. The desire to be the world's top tennis player _____**motivated**_____ the young woman to spend hours every day improving her game.

7. Because the show is scheduled to end after midnight, the management will _____**restrict**_____ admission to people over sixteen years old.

8. Like a typical _____**bigot**_____, he believes that any customs different from his own are "wrong" and "uncivilized."

9. The rich _____**diversity**_____ of plant and animal life in a tropical rain forest never ceases to amaze me.

10. No decent or kind person will _____**gloat**_____ over someone else's failures or misfortunes.

Encourage students to look for context clues. See page 7.

Definitions

Note the spelling, pronunciation, part(s) of speech, and definition(s) of each of the following words. Then write the appropriate form of the word in the blank space in the illustrative sentence(s) following.

1. barrage
(bə räzh')

(*n.*) a rapid, large-scale outpouring of something
The governor faced a _____**barrage**_____ of questions about possible budget cuts.

2. designate
(dez' ig nāt)

(*v.*) to indicate, point out; to appoint; (*adj.*) selected but not yet installed
Will you please tell me when the coach will _____**designate**_____ a team leader?
The new student council _____**designate**_____ is looking forward to making many changes to the student government.

3. enigma
(i nig' mə)

(*n.*) someone or something that is extremely puzzling; that which cannot be understood or explained
Critics complained that the plot twists in the new mystery movie make it an _____**enigma**_____.

4. infuriate
(in fyu̇r' ē āt)

(*v.*) to make very angry, enrage
It _____**infuriates**_____ most parents when their children refuse to listen to them and treat them with disrespect.

5. pacifist
(pas' ə fist)

(*n.*) one who is against war or the use of violence; (*adj.*) opposing war or violence
Martin Luther King, Jr., was a _____**pacifist**_____ who influenced the civil rights movement.
_____**Pacifist**_____ students protested the war.

6. queue
(kyü)

(*n.*) a line of people waiting for something (such as a bus); (*v.*) to form such a line
A long _____**queue**_____ formed at the bus stop.
Eager fans _____**queue**_____ up for the best seats.

7. slake
(slāk)

(*v.*) to satisfy, relieve, or bring to an end
Nothing can _____**slake**_____ thirst better than water.

8. terrain
(tə rān')

(*n.*) the landscape, especially its physical features or fitness for some use; a field of knowledge
Mountain bikes are designed to withstand even the most rugged _____**terrain**_____.

Practice with synonyms and antonyms is on page 46.

9. vow
(vaủ)

(*n.*) a solemn or sacred promise or pledge; (*v.*) to declare or promise in a solemn way

Prince Hamlet made a solemn ____**vow**____ to avenge his father's murder.

A bride and groom ____**vow**____ to love each other throughout their marriage.

10. waylay
(wā′ lā)

(*v.*) to lie in wait for and attack, ambush

Thugs will often choose to ____**waylay**____ weary travelers as they make their way home.

Using Context

*For each item, determine whether the **boldface** word from pages 42–43 makes sense in the context of the sentence. Circle the item numbers next to the six sentences in which the words are used correctly.*

(**1.**) Although some people aren't bothered by spelling mistakes in books or advertisements, such oversights really **infuriate** me.

(**2.**) After driving on the rough **terrain** in the mountains, I was grateful to return to the smooth roads of the highway.

(**3.**) If you have such **pacifist** beliefs, why are you always embroiled in conflicts and heated arguments?

4. The orchestra knew when to start playing based on the **queue** given by the conductor.

5. It's often satisfying to **waylay** the day by sitting on the couch and watching television.

(**6.**) When our group decided to split up, I insisted that we **designate** a specific meeting time and place to ensure that we all returned safely.

(**7.**) Although the fast food will tide me over for a few hours, it won't be able to **slake** my need for a nutritious and balanced meal.

8. Meteorologists have proposed a simple scientific **enigma** to explain why ships and aircraft have gone missing in the area called the Bermuda Triangle.

(**9.**) I made a **vow** to myself long ago that I will stand up for what I believe, and I will never break such a promise.

10. The dog attempted to escape the yard to chase a squirrel, but the fence turned out to be too great a **barrage** for him to scale.

Choosing the Right Word

*Select the **boldface** word that better completes each sentence. You might refer to the passage on pages 36–37 to see how most of these words are used in context. Note that the choices might be related forms of the Unit words.*

1. Jane Addams was an outspoken (**pacifist**, **enigma**), yet her views about war were not embraced by everyone.

2. To (**slake**, **infuriate**) our curiosity, you will have to tell us everything that happened during that strange trip.

3. As the defense attorney left the courtroom, he was (**waylaid**, **designated**) by a group of eager reporters trying to get a statement from him.

4. The applicants for the job will have to (**queue**, **slake**) up in an orderly way and wait their turns to be interviewed.

5. When the speaker asked for opinions from the audience, he was greeted with a (**terrain**, **barrage**) of critical remarks and angry questions.

6. Because Sam is so good at stealing bases, he has become the (**slake**, **designated**) runner for our baseball team.

7. No matter what it may cost me to carry out, I will never break my sacred (**vow**, **terrain**).

8. President Jefferson sent Lewis and Clark to survey water routes, animals, plant life, and the (**terrain**, **waylay**) of the Louisiana Territory.

9. Entangled in the trapper's net, the (**infuriated**, **pacifist**) lion thrashed at the ropes and roared in helpless anger.

10. Just how and why two people fall in love is a(n) (**queue**, **enigma**) that no scientist has ever been able to explain.

11. Because I am convinced that violence always creates more problems than it solves, I have become a(n) (**pacifist**, **enigma**).

12. The children who are admitted free to the ball game will be allowed to sit only in certain (**slaked**, **designated**) parts of the stands.

You may wish to provide students with an explanation and example of a related form.

Completing the Sentence

Choose the word from the word bank that best completes each of the following sentences. Write the correct word or form of the word in the space provided.

barrage	enigma	pacifist	slake	vow
designate	infuriate	queue	terrain	waylay

1. The animals in the drought area traveled for many miles to reach a body of water where they could _____**slake**_____ their thirst.

2. The police now believe that the mugger _____**waylaid**_____ the victim as she entered the elevator of her apartment house.

3. Our hike was not very long, but the _____**terrain**_____ was so rocky and hilly that we were exhausted by the time we reached our goal.

4. The deadly _____**barrage**_____ of shells from our guns pinned down the enemy troops on the narrow beach where they had landed.

5. Even before the new president took office, he _____**designated**_____ the men and women who were to serve in his cabinet.

6. I don't understand what he is aiming at or why he behaves as he does; in fact, his whole personality is a(n) _____**enigma**_____ to me.

7. A person can usually tell how popular a new movie is by the length of the _____**queue**_____ in front of the box office.

8. As she was sworn in, she made a(n) _____**vow**_____ that she would never use the powers of her office for selfish or unworthy purposes.

9. Is it possible to be a(n) _____**pacifist**_____ in a world where so many people are using force to take unfair advantage of others?

10. Nothing _____**infuriates**_____ my boss more than an employee who is late for work and then offers a foolish excuse for not arriving on time.

Encourage students to look for context clues. See page 7.

Synonyms

Choose the word or form of the word from this Unit that is the same or most nearly the same in meaning as the **boldface** *word or expression in the phrase. Write that word on the line. Use a dictionary if necessary.*

1. close-ups of the **land** of Mars _____ terrain
2. the magician's most unique **delusion** _____ illusion
3. **encourage** citizens to vote in the election _____ motivate
4. one of the great **mysteries** of the universe _____ enigmas
5. **named** as the union representative _____ designated
6. her **calling** as a nurse _____ vocation
7. a plot to **entrap** unsuspecting victims _____ waylay
8. the long **line** of cars _____ queue
9. followed the **philosopher's** teachings _____ sage's
10. **shrivel** from lack of water _____ wither
11. must **pledge** to tell the truth _____ vow
12. told to **limit** strenuous activity _____ restrict
13. **quench** their cravings for a refreshing drink _____ slake
14. surprised by the **bombardment** of criticism _____ barrage
15. conducting trade in the **international** markets _____ global

Antonyms

Choose the word or form of the word from this Unit that is most nearly opposite in meaning to the **boldface** *word or expression in the phrase. Write that word on the line. Use a dictionary if necessary.*

1. the actions of a **fair-minded person** _____ bigot
2. speeches given by a notable **warmonger** _____ pacifist
3. **feeling chagrin** after receiving the news _____ gloating (about)
4. the cultural **similarity** of the citizens _____ diversity
5. a call that **pleased** the coach _____ infuriated

Writing: Words in Action

Answers to the prompt will vary.

Read this quotation from Euripides: *Experience, travel—these are an education in themselves.* Do you agree with this outlook? In what ways can experience and travel be educational? Write an essay supporting your opinion. Use personal experience and the reading (pages 36–37). Include three or more words from this Unit.

Vocabulary in Context

*Some of the words you have studied in this Unit appear in **boldface** type. Read the passage below, and then circle the letter of the correct answer for each word as it is used in context.*

Before Albert Ballin (1857–1918), ocean voyages were an ordeal. The Atlantic Ocean was dangerous, unpredictable, and vast. In 1891, Ballin invented the pleasure cruise and transformed the ocean voyage into an experience to be savored.

Born in Hamburg, Germany, at age 17 Ballin inherited his father's modest passenger booking agency. His success was phenomenal—he knew his **terrain**. During the 1880s, shipping lines entered into a lethal price war to sell tickets to the rising tide of passengers emigrating to America. When Ballin was hired in 1886 to save Hapag, the largest shipping line in Germany, he found his true **vocation**.

He rescued Hapag by turning its ocean liners into sea-going luxury hotels. There was space for plenty of immigrants in steerage, while life on the upper decks was a dream of gracious living. Passenger accommodations were palatial, chefs were hired from the finest restaurants, and the entertainment was splendid.

Ballin's strategy was a **global** success. Hapag liners were soon touring the Mediterranean, the Caribbean, and the world. In 1900, Hapag launched the world's first **designated** pleasure cruiser—the *Prinzessin Viktoria Luise*, named for the daughter of Kaiser Wilhelm. Despite his modest origins and background, Ballin became the Kaiser's trusted envoy to London when relations with Britain became tense.

When the First World War broke out in 1914, **bigots** attacked Ballin as a **pacifist**. Later, when Germany was headed toward defeat, even Kaiser Wilhelm turned against him. Ballin died in 1918, a broken man. His legacy lives on, however, on every ocean and in ports throughout the world.

---

1. What is the meaning of **terrain** as it is used in paragraph 2?
  a. terra firma
  b. area of expertise
  c. limitations
  d. earth

2. In paragraph 2, what does the use of the word **vocation** suggest about Ballin?
  a. He knew his worth.
  b. He had a mission.
  c. He was of the elite.
  d. He knew his fate.

3. **Global** comes from the Latin word **globus. Globus** most likely means
  a. sphere
  b. universe
  c. world
  d. orbit

4. The word **designated** means about the same as
  a. specific
  b. special
  c. notable
  d. specified

5. Which word means the same as **bigots** as it is used in paragraph 5?
  a. fanatics
  b. nationalists
  c. sailors
  d. soldiers

6. What does the word **pacifist** most likely mean as it is used in paragraph 5?
  a. comforter
  b. philanthropist
  c. peacemaker
  d. west-coaster

See pages T29–T31 for assessment options.

Vocabulary for Comprehension
Part 1

*Read "A Winter Playground," which contains words in **boldface** that appear in Units 1–3. Then answer the questions.*

A Winter Playground

Picture a vast castle, or imagine an oversized cartoon figure. Now try to imagine each of them made of snow and ice. That sight is what you might see if

(5) you attend the Sapporo Snow Festival, a weeklong event held each year in northern Japan, on the island of Hokkaido.

Sapporo is the capital of Hokkaido. Unlike other cities in Japan, Sapporo is

(10) fairly young. It has no ancient temples. Its streets are unusually wide and straight. Sapporo is known for its cold winters and heavy snowfall. The average annual snowfall in the city is around 19 feet.

(15) The climate of Sapporo makes it an ideal place for winter festivities and a popular destination for winter sports. In fact, the city hosted the 1972 Winter Olympic Games. Skiing is even part

(20) of the school curriculum for many children in Sapporo.

The Sapporo Snow Festival takes place every February. The event draws both young and old into its wintry wonderland

(25) fantasies. Most people familiar with winter festivals **designate** the Sapporo Snow Festival as the most famous of its kind. The city plans ahead for months. It is impossible for visitors to get hotel rooms

(30) without **expressly** reserving them far in advance.

The Sapporo Snow Festival had modest beginnings. In 1950, high school students made six snow sculptures in a **serene**

(35) park in the center of town. What began as fun for creative teenagers has grown into an event that has **global** appeal. Odori Park, the location of those first snow sculptures, continues to be one

(40) of the three main festival sites.

Since the early days, much of the work to mount the festival has been done by the Self-Defense Forces. This branch of the Japanese military **dispatches** hundreds

(45) of soldiers in army trucks to haul snow from nearby mountains into the city. This peacetime work serves the public and keeps festival costs down.

Visitors to the Snow Festival today

(50) might see gigantic sculptures that **depict** prehistoric animals, Viking warriors, famous people, and even cartoon characters! Bands play music from atop huge sound stages built of snow.

(55) Daredevils can zoom down elaborate ice and snow slides at a sports venue called the Tsudome, one of the festival sites. Here, a snow rafting attraction also treats visitors to rides on rafts towed by

(60) snowmobiles. Every year at the Sapporo Snow Festival, one young woman is crowned "Queen of the Ice." Nightly fireworks, colored lights, and other special sound and lighting effects add

(65) extra excitement. The festival has earned a worldwide reputation as a winter playground.

1. Part A
Based on the evidence in the passage, what is **most likely** the author's purpose in "A Winter Playground"?
A) to entertain the reader with amusing anecdotes
B) to praise the Japanese Self-Defense Forces
C) to describe traditional Japanese customs
D) to inform the reader about the Sapporo Snow Festival

Part B
Which line from the text **best** supports the answer to Part A?
A) "Picture a vast castle, or imagine an oversized cartoon figure." (lines 1–2)
B) "the Sapporo Snow Festival, a weeklong event held each year in northern Japan" (lines 5–7)
C) "Sapporo is the capital of Hokkaido." (line 8)
D) "known for its cold winters and heavy snowfall" (lines 12–13)

2. What does the word **designate** mean as it is used in line 26?
A) name
B) deny
C) attend
D) avoid

3. Which word means the opposite of **expressly** in line 30?
A) explicitly
B) unintentionally
C) purposely
D) pointedly

4. What is the author's **most likely** reason for including lines 35–37 in "A Winter Playground"?
A) to explain the Sapporo Snow Festival's rules
B) to describe the history of the festival
C) to introduce the festival's artists
D) to demonstrate the festival's popularity

5. What does the word **serene** mean as it is used in line 34?
A) pretty
B) popular
C) tranquil
D) enormous

6. As used in line 37, what does the word **global** suggest about the festival?
A) Its popularity is widespread.
B) It is a mysterious event.
C) It has regional appeal.
D) It is held in many different countries.

7. What does the word **dispatches** most likely mean as it is used in line 44?
A) trains
B) joins with
C) recruits
D) sends out

8. According to line 50, what does it mean to **depict** something in a snow or ice sculpture?
A) restore it
B) analyze it
C) replace it
D) represent it

9. Why does the author **most likely** refer to the sights and sounds of the festival in lines 50–65?
A) to provide statistics about the festival
B) to use sensory details to make the festival come alive
C) to describe the festival through exaggerations
D) to make generalizations about the festival

10. What is **most likely** the purpose of the last two paragraphs?
A) to promote attendance at the festival
B) to analyze athletic events in Japan
C) to suggest festival improvements
D) to caution visitors about dangers

Vocabulary for Comprehension
Part 2

*Read this passage, which contains words in **boldface** that appear in Units 1–3. Then choose the best answer to each question based on what is stated or implied in the passage. You may refer to the passage as often as necessary.*

Questions 1–10 are based on the following passage.

Among the most famous words of the American Revolution is the exclamation, "Give me liberty or give me death!" This was the **vow** of Patrick Henry
(5) in his address to the Second Virginia Convention in March of 1775. As a member of the House of Burgesses, the lower house of the legislature, Henry was well known as a brilliant orator and a
(10) radical opponent of the British government. In 1765, for example, he had spoken out vehemently against the Stamp Act. Some of his adversaries branded Henry's views as treason.
(15)   In 1775, Henry's goal was to persuade the convention to raise a militia. He felt that war with Britain was inevitable. His opponents, to whom he refers ironically in his speech as "very worthy gentlemen,"
(20) advocated caution and patience. Early in the speech, Henry **ingeniously** turns the accusation of treason on its head. He defiantly declares, "Should I keep back my opinions at such a time, through fear of
(25) giving offence, I should consider myself as guilty of treason towards my country. . . ." Henry solemnly warns his fellow legislators that the issue they are debating is "nothing less than a question of freedom or slavery."
(30)   Two arguments lie at the heart of the speech. In the first, Henry invokes the "lamp of experience" to show that the conduct of the British over the past ten years has been both treacherous and
(35) menacing. The buildup in British forces, he says, can have only one objective: to **douse** resistance and force the colonists into submission. Every petition, argument,

and entreaty the colonists have presented
(40) has been rejected or has **withered** away. Addressing the presiding officer of the convention, Henry declares, "Let us not, I beseech you sir, deceive ourselves. . . . There is no longer any room for hope. If we
(45) wish to be free . . . we must fight! I repeat it, sir, we must fight!" Plainly, Henry found his opponents' hesitation **incomprehensible.** For Henry, serene coexistence with Britain had proved impossible. Any other view
(50) amounted to an **illusion.** Henry implied, in fact, that the British were **gloating** over the prospect of reducing the colonies to servitude to the Crown.
    In his second major argument, Patrick
(55) Henry refutes the claim that the colonists are weak. On the contrary, Henry argues, the passage of time will only allow the British to diminish the colonists' strength. In a remarkably accurate prediction,
(60) Henry proudly emphasizes the size of the American population and the geographical advantages of the colonists' **terrain**. "Three millions of people, armed in the holy cause of liberty, and in such
(65) a country as that which we possess, are invincible by any force which our enemy can send against us."
    Henry concludes with **maximum** emotional force in his call to arms.
(70) "Our brethren are already in the field. Why stand we here idle? What is it that gentlemen wish? . . . Is life so dear, or peace so sweet, as to be purchased at the price of chains and slavery? . . . I
(75) know not what course others may take, but as for me, give me liberty or give me death!" Barely four weeks later, the first shots of the Revolution were fired at Lexington and Concord, Massachusetts.

1. According to the passage, Patrick
Henry was well known in Virginia for his
A) wealth and influence.
B) brilliant public speaking.
C) tact and diplomacy.
D) writing ability.

2. Which choice provides the best evidence
for the answer to the previous question?
A) Lines 1–3 ("Among the . . . death!'")
B) Lines 4–6 ("This was . . . 1775")
C) Lines 6–10 ("As a member . . .
government")
D) Lines 15–17 ("In 1775 . . . inevitable")

3. As it is used in line 4, "vow"
most nearly means
A) hint.
B) pledge.
C) threat.
D) distress.

4. The author includes Henry's description
of his opponents as "very worthy
gentleman" (line 19) in order to
A) show the Henry was loyal to England.
B) show that Henry was scornful
and unafraid.
C) give an example of a speech
that is rambling and incoherent.
D) give an example of how subtle
and sensitive Henry was.

5. As it is used in line 21, "ingeniously"
most nearly means
A) proudly
B) arrogantly
C) resourcefully
D) hopelessly

6. As it is used in line 37, "douse"
most nearly means
A) maintain.
B) fortify.
C) sacrifice.
D) extinguish.

7. According to the passage, Patrick
Henry warned his fellow Americans
that the British planned to
A) increase taxes on the colonies.
B) forbid colonial expansion to the West.
C) reduce the colonies to slavery.
D) expand the power of colonial
governors.

8. In his speech, Patrick Henry emphasizes
which of the following ideas?
A) The colonists are stronger
that they realize.
B) The passage of time will make
the colonists stronger.
C) British strength is an illusion.
D) The colonial population is
growing at a slow rate.

9. As it is used in line 63, "terrain"
most nearly means
A) coastline.
B) ground.
C) road network.
D) mountain ranges.

10. Which of the following best identifies
the primary purpose of the passage?
A) to provide a brief biographical
sketch of Patrick Henry
B) to explain how Patrick Henry
became a prominent politician
C) to offer a brief survey of Patrick
Henry's most famous speech
D) to refute the claim that Patrick
Henry was guilty of treason

Synonyms

*From the word bank below, choose the word that has the same or nearly the same meaning as the **boldface** word in each sentence and write it on the line. You will not use all of the words.*

bigot	designate	global	restrict
compress	expressly	instantaneous	sage
contemporary	forsake	irk	sheepish
depict	gainful	recede	slake

1. Whenever I have a question about a pressing matter, I always appreciate a **prompt** reply.

   instantaneous

2. He acts confident around his peers, but if an authority figure scolds him, he immediately assumes a **meek** demeanor.

   sheepish

3. Hunger and poverty are **universal** problems that we all must work together to solve.

   global

4. Hearing someone mispronounce a word can **irritate** me as much as the sound of nails scratching a chalkboard.

   irk

5. I don't know how I can **condense** my extensive thoughts on the subject into a one-page article, but I know many people would have no interest in reading something much longer than that.

   compress

6. She usually prefers to read classic novels, but there are some **current** authors whose work interests her.

   contemporary

7. I try to **limit** the amount of television I watch to one hour per day, although I often end up watching more on the weekends.

   restrict

8. When the manager said she would **name** him as her successor, he was shocked and thrilled to receive such an honor.

   designate

9. When I announced my get-rich-quick scheme, my friend **pointedly** explained how irresponsible and dangerous it could be.

   expressly

10. After hiking for hours in the hot sun, I didn't think there was enough water on earth to **sate** my dehydration.

    slake

11. The historians were thrilled to find drawings that seemed to **illustrate** what daily life was like for the ancient people.

    depict

12. The climax of the novel occurs when the main character's mother threatens to **disown** her for her actions.

    forsake

Two-Word Completions

Select the pair of words that best completes the meaning of each of the following sentences.

1. Two ruffians _____ the weary traveler on a lonely stretch of road, but the man was able to beat off his _____ with the help of his stout staff.
   a. confronted … hypocrites
   b. constrained … pacifists
   c. waylaid … assailants
   d. dispatched … oafs

2. Running a marathon leaves athletes feeling _____, but months of training provide them with the incentive to reach the finish line before heading off to a satisfying _____.
   a. famished … repast
   b. groundless … vocation
   c. adverse … terrain
   d. inept … barrage

3. It took a great deal of _____ to keep up with the rest of the pack as they sped across the broken and hilly _____ that separated them from the finish line in the cross-country race.
   a. diversity … barrage
   b. stamina … terrain
   c. dispatch … apparel
   d. misgiving … repast

4. As the travelers crossed the hot and _____ wasteland known as the Sahara Desert, their eyes were deceived more than once by mirages and other optical _____.
   a. immense … vocations
   b. adverse … mimics
   c. arid … illusions
   d. groundless … enigmas

5. Though other people have been moved to action by high ideals, Thomas Alva Edison, one of the most _____ inventors ever to be produced by this country, seems in part to have been _____ simply by the love of a challenge.
   a. ingenious … motivated
   b. disinterested … manipulated
   c. immense … dispatched
   d. inept … infuriated

6. The demand for tickets to the play-offs was so heavy that for days the box office was _____ like some embattled fortress by mobs of people waiting more or less impatiently in long _____ that snaked endlessly around the whole block.
   a. confronted … ruffles
   b. encompassed … billows
   c. denounced … enigmas
   d. besieged … queues

7. Despite the _____ of vigorous insults coming from the other gubernatorial candidate, she refused to retaliate and _____ her competition.
   a. billow … infuriate
   b. illusion … libel
   c. barrage … denounce
   d. apparel … besiege

WORD STUDY

Idioms

In the passage about the luxury liner, the *Olympic* (see pages 36–37), the narrator describes the decorations in the Turkish baths and mentions that adding more would have been "gilding the lily."

"Gilding the lily" is an idiom that means "adding extra adornments to something that is already beautiful." An **idiom** is a figure of speech or an informal expression that is not meant literally. When you say that someone is "gilding the lily," you are saying that the person is adding additional and probably unnecessary decoration to something that does not need it. You learn idioms by hearing them used in daily conversation. Idioms can be fun to use in writing and in conversations, but you should use them sparingly and in informal situations.

Choosing the Right Idiom

*Read each sentence. Use context clues to figure out the meaning of each idiom in **boldface** print. Then write the letter of the definition for the idiom in the sentence.*

1. The suspect, exhausted from the reporters' constant questioning at the courthouse, begged them to **call off the dogs**. ____i____

2. I always have to **ride shotgun**; I get carsick when I sit in the backseat. ____b____

3. After yelling and cheering at last night's football game, I woke up with **a frog in my throat**. ____c____

4. Evan should stop the **monkey business** and just finish his project. ____h____

5. My brother always has to **put in his two cents' worth** when it comes to my choice of music. ____a____

6. It sure seems as if **time is flying** when we get together and play games. ____e____

7. We spent all afternoon praising Mom's great apple pie, so her **ears must be burning**. ____d____

8. That hot chocolate sure **hit the spot** after a long hike in the snow! ____f____

9. The amount of money she paid for that smartphone is **small potatoes** compared to what her fancy computer cost. ____j____

10. Don't you think Mark is a little **long in the tooth** to be taking on the role of a young superhero? ____g____

a. make a comment or give an opinion

b. sit in the front seat of a car

c. a feeling of hoarseness in the throat

d. awareness that one is being talked about

e. a certain period passes quickly

f. was refreshing and satisfying

g. old

h. fooling around

i. stop criticizing or harassing

j. not very big in comparison

Classical Roots

de—down; away from; completely; not

The Latin root *de* appears in **denounce** (page 18), **depict** (page 26), and **designate** (page 42). The root signifies separation or undoing. Some other words based on the same root are listed below.

debunk	default	demerit	desperate
decapitate	defraud	depression	devolve

From the list of words above, choose the one that corresponds to each of the brief definitions below. Write the word in the blank space in the illustrative sentence below the definition. Use a dictionary if necessary.

1. driven to take any risk; hopeless; extreme
Lack of water led homesteaders to take _____**desperate**_____ measures.

2. a mark against, usually involving the loss of some privilege or right; a fault, defect
Bad behavior at school earned him many _____**demerits**_____.

3. an area that is sunk below its surroundings; a period of severe economic decline; a mood of dejection or sadness.
Slapstick comedy films were popular during the Great _____**Depression**_____ of the 1930s.

4. to fail to perform a task or fulfill an obligation; the failure to do something required by law or duty
Because the challenger failed to show up, the defender won the match by _____**default**_____.

5. to cheat, take away from, or deprive of by deceit or trickery
The corrupt attorney tried to _____**defraud**_____ the heirs of their rightful inheritance and fortune.

6. to cut off the head, behead
Experienced chefs know how to gut, scale, and _____**decapitate**_____ a fish before cooking it.

7. to expose the falseness of unsound or exaggerated claims
New evidence allows us to _____**debunk**_____ a time-honored legend.

8. to pass on (*"a duty or task"*) to someone else; to be passed on to; to be conferred on
When the mayor's powers _____**devolve**_____ upon her successor, little will change at City Hall.

UNIT 4

Note that not all of the Unit words are used in this passage. *Ingratitude, ovation, repent, revocation,* and *strife* are used in the passage on page 67.

*Read the following passage, taking note of the **boldface** words and their contexts. These words are among those you will be studying in Unit 4. It may help you to complete the exercises in this Unit if you refer to the way the words are used below.*

The Art and Science of Traditional Healing
<Expository Essay>

Advances in science provide modern man with cures and treatments undreamed of by his prehistoric counterparts. But how did early humans deal with disease? Serious illnesses could **devastate** whole families or clans. What remedies were available? In olden times, folk medicine **generated** relief or cures. A thorough **scan** of the long history of medicine reveals some similar **strands** woven throughout the history of healing.

Plants were one source of medicine for early humans. Some vegetables or herbs were **deemed** especially effective for minor illnesses, and botanics are the source of many modern medicines. In ancient times, though, major disorders were likely to have **mortal** results. These deadly diseases needed more intensive treatment than the herbal remedies offered.

To fight these killer illnesses, early medicine men turned to magic and ritual. In many parts of the world, healers were called shamans. Although precise definitions of shamanism are **elusive**, it is likely that these shamans resembled what other societies called magicians or sorcerers. It is easy now, from a modern perspective, to dismiss them as quacks. But most shamans seem to have **acquitted** themselves honorably. Indeed, the specialized knowledge of shamans often caused society to **idolize** and revere them.

Shamans lived in different societies around the world and can still be found today. Some North American Indian nations and people in areas such as modern Siberia, Mongolia, and South America practiced shamanism. Wherever they were found, shamans revealed some common qualities. They often experienced periods of deep trance. Trances were not just **reveries** or daydreams; they were altered states of consciousness. The shaman's soul was believed to roam on journeys through the upper and lower worlds. A shaman's contact with spirits, both

A Mandan Indian medicine man during ceremonial dance

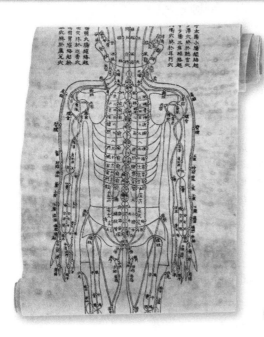

The Chinese practice of acupuncture is based on the idea that stimulating certain pressure points in the body can correct imbalances.

Despite their successes, early healers could not have hoped to cure all the sick. As the Arabic saying goes, "When fate arrives, the physician becomes a fool." If a healer lived in ancient Babylon, the price of failure could be steep. In the Law Code of Hammurabi around 1750 BCE, for example, doctors were warned that their hands would be cut off if a patient died from certain treatments.

In early Greek medicine, the outstanding figure was Hippocrates. Born around 460 BCE, probably on the island of Cos, he insisted that disease was a natural rather than a supernatural phenomenon. His written works began to **topple** magic from its commanding position in medicine. Perhaps his most enduring **keepsake** for the modern world is the Hippocratic Oath; this solemn promise "to do no harm" is still subscribed to by physicians today.

good and evil, was no **petty** talent. On the contrary, it was a key element in the healer's ability to rescue ailing patients from their wretched **plights**.

The early historical period had many medical traditions. In China, a typical healer's goal was to control the proportions of various elements in the body. Water therapy and acupuncture came from the Chinese tradition. Such treatments are still practiced today. In India, the classic writings on disease and treatment date back several thousand years. In both India and China, though, religious beliefs hindered efforts to learn more about anatomy. Cutting the bodies of the dead was considered a breach of the law and a source of **discredit**.

Hippocrates is known as the father of Western medicine.

Audio

For iWords and audio passages, go to SadlierConnect.com.

Definitions

Note the spelling, pronunciation, part(s) of speech, and definition(s) of each of the following words. Then write the appropriate form of the word in the blank space in the illustrative sentence(s) following.

1. **acquit**
(ə kwit′)

(*v.*) to declare not guilty, free from blame, discharge completely; to conduct or behave oneself

Now that we have proof of their innocence, we can _____ **acquit** _____ them of all charges.

2. **discredit**
(dis kred′ it)

(*v.*) to throw doubt upon, cause to be distrusted; to damage in reputation; (*n.*) a loss or lack of belief, confidence, or reputation

Evidence was gathered to _____ **discredit** _____ her story.

Both parents and students felt strongly that the cheating scandal was a _____ **discredit** _____ to the school.

3. **generate**
(jen′ ə rāt)

(*v.*) to bring into existence; to be the cause of

The energy of the sun _____ **generates** _____ electricity.

4. **ingratitude**
(in grat′ ə tüd)

(*n.*) a lack of thankfulness

Hosts who make every effort to please their guests are apt to be hurt by _____ **ingratitude** _____.

5. **ovation**
(ō vā′ shən)

(*n.*) an enthusiastic public welcome, an outburst of applause

The audience gave the dancer a standing _____ **ovation** _____ after his impressive performance.

6. **plight**
(plīt)

(*n.*) a sorry condition or state; (*v.*) to pledge, promise solemnly

The _____ **plight** _____ of the homeless upsets many.

The bride and groom _____ **plight** _____ their love.

7. **reverie**
(rev′ ə rē)

(*n.*) a daydream; the condition of being lost in thought

My happy _____ **reverie** _____ was interrupted by the shrill of the class bell.

8. **scan**
(skan)

(*v.*) to examine closely; to look over quickly but thoroughly; to analyze the rhythm of a poem; (*n.*) an examination

Let's _____ **scan** _____ the list to see the finishing times of each marathon runner.

The doctor did a bone _____ **scan** _____ to discover the location of each fracture.

Synonyms and antonyms are provided at SadlierConnect.com.

9. strife
(strīf)

(*n.*) bitter disagreement; fighting, struggle
The experienced senator from South Carolina
was a veteran of political _____**strife**_____.

10. topple
(tăp' əl)

(*v.*) to fall forward; to overturn, bring about the downfall of
The trains that rumble past our apartment often cause
books to _____**topple**_____ from the shelves.

Using Context

*For each item, determine whether the **boldface** word from pages 58–59 makes sense in the context of the sentence. Circle the item numbers next to the six sentences in which the words are used correctly.*

1. It will take months for the residents of the neighborhood to recover from the **reverie** caused by the fire.

(2.) The knights vowed to never behave in any way that would **discredit** the honorable reputation of their king.

(3.) Before you read a chapter in a textbook, do you **scan** the headings and look at the pictures to see what it will be about?

(4.) The purpose of the meeting is to **generate** ideas for this year's fundraiser and decide which ones we like best.

5. After many years of **ovation**, the artist's work has been rediscovered and is suddenly soaring in value.

6. Everyone admired the **plight** that the team showed as it came from behind in the last minutes of the game and managed to win by three points.

(7.) We never thought you were guilty of **ingratitude**; we simply assumed that you were too busy to write a thank-you note while you were traveling.

(8.) In bowling, your objective is to **topple** as many pins as you can during each turn.

(9.) Did the jury **acquit** the defendant or find her guilty?

10. Now that the long weekend is here, we are looking forward to three days of **strife** and relaxation.

Choosing the Right Word

*Select the **boldface** word that better completes each sentence. You might refer to the passage on pages 56–57 to see how most of these words are used in context. Note that the choices might be related forms of the Unit words.*

1. During several of Heracles's labors, Athena noticed the (**ovation, plight**) the hero was in and offered her assistance.

2. What a(n) (**ovation, reverie**) he received when he trotted back to the bench after scoring the winning touchdown!

3. Imagine his (**plight, ingratitude**)—penniless, unemployed, and with a large family to support!

4. Our business is barely managing to pay its bills; one bad break will be enough to (**acquit, topple**) it into bankruptcy.

5. I knew that she was wrapped up in herself, but I never dreamed that even she could be guilty of such (**reverie, ingratitude**).

6. At times we all enjoy a(n) (**ovation, reverie**) about "what might have been," but before long we must return to "the way things are."

7. By reelecting him to Congress, the court of public opinion has forever (**generated, acquitted**) him of the charges of neglecting his duties.

8. At times it is quite natural to feel afraid, and it is certainly no (**discredit, strife**) to anyone to admit it.

9. After so many years of (**strife, ovation**)—in business, politics, and the family— he wants only to retire to the peace and quiet of his ranch.

10. Our supervisor (**topples, scans**) the newspaper each morning for items that may serve as leads for the sales force.

11. We will never allow such vicious, unfounded rumors to (**acquit, generate**) discord and conflict in our school!

12. It was upsetting to see that his best friend was trying to (**discredit, scan**) his record as the best receiver on the team.

You may wish to provide students with an explanation and example of a related form.

Completing the Sentence

Choose the word from the word bank that best completes each of the following sentences. Write the correct word or form of the word in the space provided.

acquit	generate	ovation	reverie	strife
discredit	ingratitude	plight	scan	topple

1. The TV program made us keenly aware of the _____**plight**_____ of retired people trying to live solely on Social Security payments.

2. She richly deserved the audience's _____**ovation**_____ for her brilliant performance of Lady Macbeth.

3. We learned that even unfavorable reviews of a new book may help to _____**generate**_____ a certain amount of public interest in it.

4. The evidence against the accused man proved to be so weak that the jury had no choice but to _____**acquit**_____ him.

5. As I sincerely appreciate all my parents have done for me, how can you accuse me of _____**ingratitude**_____?

6. The famous Leaning Tower of Pisa looks as though it might _____**topple**_____ over any minute.

7. The sudden racket produced by a noisy car radio jolted me out of my deep and peaceful _____**reverie**_____.

8. As it is clear that his only interest is to make money for himself, his plan for building a new highway has been completely _____**discredited**_____.

9. Because the members of my family disagree on so many matters, the dinner table is often the scene of much verbal _____**strife**_____.

10. I don't have the time to read every word of that long newspaper article, but I'll_____**scan**_____ it quickly to get the main idea.

Encourage students to look for context clues. See page 7.

Definitions

Note the spelling, pronunciation, part(s) of speech, and definition(s) of each of the following words. Then write the appropriate form of the word in the blank space in the illustrative sentence(s) following.

1. deem
(dēm)

(*v.*) to think, believe; to consider, have an opinion

Most people _____**deem**_____ it a wise plan to set aside savings for the future.

2. devastate
(dev' ə stāt)

(*v.*) to destroy, lay waste, leave in ruins

Failure or harsh criticism can _____**devastate**_____ a person who has shaky self-esteem.

3. elusive
(ē lü' siv)

(*adj.*) difficult to catch or to hold; hard to explain or understand

According to legend, Zorro, the heroic Mexican character, was too _____**elusive**_____ for local police to capture.

4. idolize
(ī' dəl īz)

(*v.*) to worship as an idol, make an idol of; to love very much

Teens who _____**idolize**_____ a movie star may repeatedly see the same movie featuring that actor or actress.

5. keepsake
(kēp' sāk)

(*n.*) something kept in memory of the giver; a souvenir

Before my grandmother died, she made me a special quilt as a _____**keepsake**_____ of her love.

6. mortal
(môr' təl)

(*n.*) a being that must eventually die; (*adj.*) of or relating to such a being; causing death, fatal; possible, conceivable

In the mythology of many cultures, a heavenly god can come down to Earth and act as a _____**mortal**_____.

The soldier was the only one in her battalion to suffer a _____**mortal**_____ injury.

7. petty
(pet' ē)

(*adj.*) unimportant, trivial; narrow-minded; secondary in rank, minor

You say my complaint is _____**petty**_____, but to me it is an issue of great importance.

8. repent
(ri pent')

(*v.*) to feel sorry for what one has done or has failed to do

As people grow older and gain more maturity, some of them come to _____**repent**_____ their youthful mistakes.

Practice with synonyms and antonyms is on page 66.

9. revocation
(rev ə kā′ shən)

(*n.*) an act or instance of calling back, an annulment, cancellation

His failure to complete the job according to schedule led to a _____ revocation _____ of his contract.

10. strand
(strand)

(*n.*) a beach or shore; a string of wire, hair, etc.; (*v.*) to drive or run aground; to leave in a hopeless position

We asked the waiter to take back the soup when we discovered a _____ strand _____ of hair in it.

I don't want to be the third out in the inning and _____ strand _____ the two base runners.

Using Context

*For each item, determine whether the **boldface** word from pages 62–63 makes sense in the context of the sentence. Circle the item numbers next to the six sentences in which the words are used correctly.*

1. Critics praised the historical novelist for giving such a clear, **elusive** account of the Louisiana Purchase within a work of fiction.

2. The star athlete commented that children who dream of playing sports should work hard on the field rather than **idolize** the current players.

3. This small jar filled with sand from the beach is a **keepsake** to remind me of the amazing week I had during my vacation.

4. The clever detective was able to piece together the mystery based on a single **strand** of the perpetrator's hair he found at the scene of the crime.

5. She offered a **revocation** to all involved by saying she was proud to have us as volunteers.

6. An earthquake of that magnitude has the potential to **devastate** entire regions.

7. I fear it makes no difference to my unforgiving friend how I **repent** for hurting his feelings.

8. When the main characters in the movie found a note warning them that they were in "**mortal** danger," I couldn't help but yell at the screen and tell them to turn back.

9. We don't have the time for you to **deem** for hours about what decision to should make.

10. The **petty** car is said to be more energy-efficient, but I don't think I'd feel safe in such a small vehicle.

Choosing the Right Word

*Select the **boldface** word that better completes each sentence. You might refer to the passage on pages 56–57 to see how most of these words are used in context. Note that the choices might be related forms of the Unit words.*

1. In Shakespeare's *A Midsummer Night's Dream*, which character speaks the line, "Lord, what fools these (**mortals, keepsakes**) be"?

2. We should respect our national leaders, but we should not (**idolize, deem**) them and assume that they can do no wrong.

3. The children stood on the southern (**revocation, strand**) and waved at the boats sailing into the harbor.

4. A special edition of poems by the noted writer was presented as a (**revocation, keepsake**) to all who attended her eightieth birthday party.

5. Since you are the only one of us who has had experience with this kind of problem, we shall do whatever you (**deem, idolize**) necessary.

6. Our father often says that he has never stopped (**repenting, devastating**) the decision he made many years ago to give up the study of medicine.

7. Are we going to allow (**elusive, petty**) quarrels to destroy a friendship that has endured for so many years?

8. Katie purchased a (**revocation, keepsake**) box to store letters and photographs.

9. While the actors were busy rehearsing, the manager ran away with all the money and left them (**stranded, repented**) in a strange town.

10. Many diseases that have disappeared in the United States continue to (**devastate, idolize**) countries in other parts of the world.

11. Once order had been restored, the leaders of the opposition called for the (**revocation, keepsake**) of martial law.

12. In my composition, I tried to give a definition of "humor," but I found the idea too (**petty, elusive**) to pin down.

You may wish to provide students with an explanation and example of a related form.

Completing
the Sentence

Choose the word from the word bank that best completes each of the following sentences. Write the correct word or form of the word in the space provided.

| deem | elusive | keepsake | petty | revocation |
| devastate | idolize | mortal | repent | strand |

1. Regardless of what you might think proper, I do not __**deem**__ it necessary for someone of your age to wear an evening gown to the dance.

2. Though that actress's name and face are all but forgotten today, she used to be __**idolized**__ by adoring fans all over the world.

3. The wound at first did not appear to be too serious, but to our great grief it proved to be __**mortal**__.

4. I plan to save this old notebook as a(n) __**keepsake**__ of one of the best and most enjoyable classes I have ever had.

5. The hurricane so __**devastated**__ a large section of the coast that the president declared it a disaster area.

6. Why argue about such __**petty**__ matters when there are so many important problems to deal with?

7. Instead of telling us how much you __**repent**__ your outrageous conduct, why don't you sincerely try to reform?

8. The defendant was warned that another speeding ticket would result in the __**revocation**__ of her driver's license.

9. Tom is not a very fast runner, but he is so __**elusive**__ that he is extremely hard to tackle on the football field.

10. The rope is made of many __**strands**__ of fiber woven together.

Encourage students to look for context clues. See page 7.

Synonyms

*Choose the word or form of the word from this Unit that is the same or most nearly the same in meaning as the **boldface** word or expression in the phrase. Write that word on the line. Use a dictionary if necessary.*

1. to **desert** them on a dangerous island — strand
2. **exonerate** him of all charges — acquit
3. a reputation **defamed** by false reports — discredited
4. **search** the night sky for shooting stars — scan
5. not concerned by **insignificant** matters — petty
6. saved a **memento** of her trip — keepsake
7. suffered a **deadly** wound — mortal
8. **judge** her worthy to take over the company — deem
9. **unseat** the corrupt dictator — topple
10. unable to **produce** enough heat — generate
11. could not identify that **puzzling** scent — elusive
12. **revere** and respect our ancestors — idolize
13. power to **demolish** an entire community — devastate
14. immersed in **contemplation** — reverie
15. pitied her for the **difficult situation** she was in — plight

Antonyms

*Choose the word or form of the word from this Unit that is most nearly opposite in meaning to the **boldface** word or expression in the phrase. Write that word on the line. Use a dictionary if necessary.*

1. **rejoice over** their role in the demonstration — repent
2. a ruling that produced **harmony** — strife
3. resulted in a **ratification** of the agreement — revocation
4. deserved the **heckling** that he received — ovation
5. a surprising display of **gratefulness** — ingratitude

Writing: Words in Action

Answers to the prompt will vary.

How is the traditional approach to disease and healing similar to or different from contemporary approaches? Write a brief essay comparing traditional healing to modern-day healing. Support your comparison using at least two details from the passage (pages 56–57) and three or more words from this Unit.

Vocabulary in Context

*Some of the words you have studied in this Unit appear in **boldface** type. Read the passage below, and then circle the letter of the correct answer for each word as it is used in context.*

In his novel *Three Men in a Boat*, Jerome K. Jerome (1859–1927) asserts his belief that our lives are dominated by our stomachs. It is just not possible to think clearly or work effectively, he says, unless our stomachs are agreeable. The source of our deepest emotions is not the heart, but the digestive tract. He advises us to think before we eat, and to be mindful of the stomach's reactions to particular kinds of food and drink. The stomach's **ingratitude** can be a terrible thing, and disagreement between the processes of digestion and thought can quickly turn into **mortal strife**. If you upset your stomach, you can **repent** your error, but there can be no **revocation** of the offending food.

After eggs and bacon in the morning, Jerome tells us, the stomach says, "Work!" After a heavy steak dinner, the stomach says, "Sleep!" The way to win your stomach's friendship, Jerome explains, is tea. Jerome's words deserve a heartfelt **ovation** from tea drinkers everywhere.

"After a cup of tea," he claims, "the stomach says to the brain, 'Now rise, and show your strength. Be eloquent, and deep, and tender. See, with a clear eye, into Nature and into life; spread your white wings of quivering thought, and soar over the whirling world, up through the blazing stars to the gates of eternity!'"

Over 100 years after Jerome wrote these words about how good tea makes a person feel, a team of university researchers found that tea does contain elements with health benefits and may help lower a tea drinker's risk for certain diseases.

---

1. What is the meaning of **ingratitude** as it is used in paragraph 1?
   a. resentment
   b. rudeness
   c. thanklessness
   d. disloyalty

2. **Mortal** comes from the Latin word **mors**. **Mors** most likely means
   a. death
   b. agony
   c. heart
   d. bitterness

3. The word **strife** means about the same as
   a. anguish
   b. fear
   c. enmity
   d. conflict

4. Which word means the same as **repent** as it is used in paragraph 1?
   a. berate
   b. betray
   c. regret
   d. ignore

5. In paragraph 1, what does the use of the word **revocation** suggest about the food?
   a. It should be savored.
   b. It can't be removed.
   c. It is limitless.
   d. It is enjoyable.

6. What does the word **ovation** most likely mean as it is used in paragraph 2?
   a. vote of thanks
   b. smile of approval
   c. gift of love
   d. round of applause

See pages T29–T31 for assessment options.

UNIT 5

Note that not all of the Unit words are used in this passage. *Bungle, remorse, smug,* and *tarry* are used in the passage on page 79.

*Read the following passage, taking note of the **boldface** words and their contexts. These words are among those you will be studying in Unit 5. It may help you to complete the exercises in this Unit if you refer to the way the words are used below.*

Continue Space Exploration, Now!
<Persuasive Speech>

The United States should continue to support an active program of space exploration. Opponents of such a policy have **blustered** that space exploration is a waste of resources. Why spend money on rockets, they argue, when desperate needs here on Earth are so **acute**? Billions of the planet's **inhabitants** struggle from day to day. The **numbing** curses of war, famine, and poverty cry out for attention and relief.

For all but the most stubborn and **headstrong**, however, this argument can be convincingly **refuted**. For the entire **duration** of the space program's existence—a little more than half a century—the budget of the National Aeronautics and Space Administration (NASA) has averaged under one percent of total federal annual expenditures. One must keep these numbers in perspective. In a country where appetites are often **ravenous**, Americans spend nearly twenty times more money at restaurants every year than the government spends on NASA! Even a brief **synopsis** of costs and budgets shows that space exploration does not account for major outlays.

But how about astronaut safety? Opponents in the **fray** over space policy point to the risks

Apollo 15 astronaut on the moon, 1971

of human spaceflight. They argue that these risks justify an end to space exploration. It is true that the space shuttle disasters of 1986 and 2003 marked major **setbacks** for NASA. In over 50 years, however, only 18 people worldwide have died in spaceflights. This one **facet** of the debate over future policy certainly elicits strong emotions. Yet the vast majority of astronauts undergo rigorous training. To **pacify** the critics, some have suggested that spaceflights should depend on robotics, which are less costly and risky than manned flights. It may well be cheaper and safer to organize unmanned missions into space. Human intelligence and flexibility, though, will still be invaluable for many purposes. Astronauts, moreover, have served as powerful role models for generations of young people.

Fidelity to balance and fairness demands an evaluation of the numerous benefits derived from the space program so far. These include many advances in technology. What are some of these breakthroughs? Among them are satellites, microchips, and fuel cells. Take just one example. Satellites have vastly improved global communications. Better weather forecasts from satellites save lives. More accurate data make research on climate change possible. The demands and challenges of space exploration have meant that scientists and inventors can't risk being complacent. Ever bolder objectives in space require ever more ingenious responses.

Finally, the most important reason to press on in space is psychological, not material. The writer and inventor Arthur C. Clarke won fame

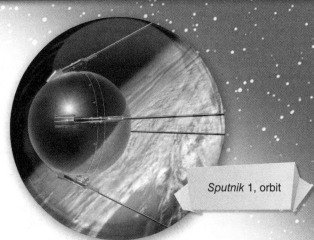

Sputnik 1, orbit

for his achievements in science and science fiction. In one essay, Clarke offered this insightful **commentary** on human nature. He said that civilization cannot exist without new frontiers and that people have a physical and spiritual need for them. Clarke was right. The fascination with the *Apollo 11* moon landing of July 1969 swept the world. Humanity should continue to press forward in space. This effort is not so much to explore space's **eerie** depths but rather to explore the soul and timeless aspirations of humans themselves.

Audio

For iWords and audio passages, go to **SadlierConnect.com**.

Space Shuttle *Discovery* launch, Kennedy Space Center, September 9, 1994

Definitions

Note the spelling, pronunciation, part(s) of speech, and definition(s) of each of the following words. Then write the appropriate form of the word in the blank space in the illustrative sentence(s) following.

1. bluster
(bləs' tər)

(*v.*) to talk or act in a noisy and threatening way; to blow in stormy gusts; (*n.*) speech that is loud and threatening

When we saw harsh winds _____**bluster**_____ around our tent, we decided to change our plans for the weekend.

Dad's manner is all _____**bluster**_____, but beneath it all, he's really a kind-hearted man.

2. commentary
(käm' ən ter ē)

(*n.*) a series of notes clarifying or explaining something; an expression of opinion

Our spiritual leader gave us a _____**commentary**_____ on the true meaning of charity.

3. eerie
(ē' rē)

(*adj.*) causing fear because of strangeness; weird, mysterious

It is a lot of fun to tell _____**eerie**_____ ghost stories around a campfire.

4. fidelity
(fi del' ə tē)

(*n.*) the state of being faithful; accuracy in details, exactness

The knight made an oath of _____**fidelity**_____ to the king.

5. headstrong
(hed' strôŋ)

(*adj.*) willful, stubborn

Even the most patient caregiver may feel challenged when faced with a _____**headstrong**_____ child.

6. pacify
(pas' ə fī)

(*v.*) to make peaceful or calm; to soothe

The factory owners hope to _____**pacify**_____ the angry protesters with promises of higher wages.

7. ravenous
(rav' ə nəs)

(*adj.*) greedy; very hungry; eager for satisfaction

Exercising vigorously for several hours gives me a _____**ravenous**_____ appetite.

8. refute
(ri fyüt')

(*v.*) to prove incorrect

After analyzing the situation, I now know a foolproof way to _____**refute**_____ the original claim.

Synonyms and antonyms are provided at SadlierConnect.com.

9. **remorse**
(ri mors')

(*n.*) deep and painful regret for one's past misdeeds; pangs of conscience

When the driver realized what a terrible accident he had caused, he was overcome with _____**remorse**_____.

10. **synopsis**
(si nap' sis)

(*n.*) a brief statement giving a general view of some subject, book, etc.; a summary

The teacher's guide gives a _____**synopsis**_____ of the plot of each story in the collection.

Using Context

*For each item, determine whether the **boldface** word from pages 70–71 makes sense in the context of the sentence. Circle the item numbers next to the six sentences in which the words are used correctly.*

1. The general praised the troops for their brave and **headstrong** actions.

2. When writing a persuasive essay, you must clearly state a particular idea and then offer reasons or examples to **pacify** it.

(3.) The **commentary** in the introduction to *The Hobbit* was very enlightening, and it definitely helped me to understand and appreciate the story.

4. With no moon above, the campsite would have been completely **ravenous** had it not been for the light of the campfire and our lanterns.

(5.) The player apologized from his **bluster** against the umpire and promised to show more self-control in the future.

(6.) The **eerie** story was about a scarecrow that seemed to look in one direction on one day and in another direction the next.

7. In just under an hour, the challenger was able to **refute** the chess game and claim the title of world champion.

(8.) German shepherds are often used as police dogs and military dogs because they show great **fidelity** to their owners as well as above-average intelligence.

(9.) Villains in modern superhero stories generally do not show any **remorse** for their crimes and misdeeds.

(10.) As soon as I saw the **synopsis** online, I was eager to read the book and reserved a copy at the library.

Choosing the Right Word

*Select the **boldface** word that better completes each sentence. You might refer to the passage on pages 68–69 to see how most of these words are used in context. Note that the choices might be related forms of the Unit words.*

1. The character Scrooge in Charles Dickens's *A Christmas Carol* starts out as a (**headstrong, ravenous**) miser, but he undergoes a great change of heart.

2. "It's your job to help (**pacify, bluster**) the conquered area," the general said, "not to add fuel to an already explosive situation."

3. On the camping trip out West, some of the children were frightened when they first heard the (**headstrong, eerie**) howls of coyotes at night.

4. My lawyer prepared to (**bluster, refute**) the outrageous accusations against me.

5. The idea that most people usually behave in a calm and reasonable way is (**refuted, pacified**) by all the facts of history.

6. The lost hikers, having endured several days in the blistering sun, became discouraged after sighting (**headstrong, ravenous**) vultures circling overhead.

7. The fact that so many people are still living in poverty is indeed a sad (**fidelity, commentary**) on our civilization.

8. With a winter storm (**blustering, refuting**) outside, what could be more welcome than a warm room, a good meal, and my favorite TV program?

9. When I realized how deeply I had hurt my dear friend with my careless insult, I suffered a terrible pang of (**remorse, fidelity**).

10. If you read no more than a (**remorse, synopsis**) of the plot of any one of Shakespeare's plays, you will get very little idea of what it is all about.

11. Although I don't agree with all her ideas, I must admire her unshakable (**fidelity, synopsis**) to them.

12. I keep telling you things for your own good, but you're just too (**eerie, headstrong**) to listen.

You may wish to provide students with an explanation and example of a related form.

Completing the Sentence

Choose the word from the word bank that best completes each of the following sentences. Write the correct word or form of the word in the space provided.

bluster	eerie	headstrong	ravenous	remorse
commentary	fidelity	pacify	refute	synopsis

1. Do you think it is a good idea to try to _____**pacify**_____ the weeping child by giving her a lollipop?

2. The program contained a(n) _____**synopsis**_____ of the opera, so we were able to follow the action even though the singing was in Italian.

3. Some children are as docile as sheep; others are as _____**headstrong**_____ as mules.

4. Since the convicted felon had shown no _____**remorse**_____ for his crimes, the judge sentenced him to the maximum prison term allowed.

5. I had a(n) _____**eerie**_____ feeling that we were being followed and that something bad might happen.

6. The accused person must be given every chance to _____**refute**_____ the charges against him or her.

7. By _____**blustering**_____ in a loud, confident voice, he tried to convince us that he had nothing to do with the accident.

8. The newscaster on my favorite TV program not only tells the facts of the news but also offers a(n) _____**commentary**_____ that helps us to understand it.

9. No one can question her complete _____**fidelity**_____ to basic American ideas and ideals.

10. We had eaten only a light breakfast before hiking for hours in the crisp mountain air, so you can imagine how _____**ravenous**_____ we were by lunchtime.

Encourage students to look for context clues. See page 7.

Definitions

Note the spelling, pronunciation, part(s) of speech, and definition(s) of each of the following words. Then write the appropriate form of the word in the blank space in the illustrative sentence(s) following.

1. acute
(ə kyüt′)

(*adj.*) with a sharp point; keen and alert; sharp and severe; rising quickly to a high point and lasting for a short time
One who is an _____**acute**_____ observer of human nature may notice subtle changes in people's behavior.

2. bungle
(bəŋ′ gəl)

(*v.*) to act or work clumsily and awkwardly; to ruin something through clumsiness
If we _____**bungle**_____ this project, we may never get another chance to prove ourselves as a worthy team.

3. duration
(dù rā′ shən)

(*n.*) the length of time that something continues or lasts
Even though the story was hard to follow, my friends decided to stay for the _____**duration**_____ of the opera.

4. facet
(fas′ ət)

(*n.*) one aspect or side of a subject or problem; one of the cut surfaces of a gem
One important _____**facet**_____ of problem solving is to recognize when a solution makes no sense.

5. fray
(frā)

(*n.*) a brawl, a noisy quarrel; (*v.*) to wear away by rubbing; make ragged or worn; to strain, irritate
After the two loudest students began arguing, the whole class jumped into the _____**fray**_____.
A faucet that drips continuously can _____**fray**_____ anyone's nerves.

6. inhabitant
(in hab′ ə tənt)

(*n.*) one living permanently in a given place
Although she enjoys traveling to exotic places, she's a lifelong _____**inhabitant**_____ of this small town.

7. numb
(nəm)

(*adj.*) having lost the power of feeling or movement; (*v.*) to dull the feelings of; to cause to lose feeling
Bitter cold may leave your toes _____**numb**_____.
This injection will _____**numb**_____ the area so that the doctor can stitch the cut painlessly.

8. setback
(set′ bak)

(*n.*) something that interferes with progress; a disappointment, unexpected loss or defeat; a step-like recession in a wall
A broken toe can be a major _____**setback**_____ for a skater who hopes to qualify for the Olympics.

Practice with synonyms and antonyms is on page 78.

9. **smug**
   (sməg)

(*adj.*) overly self-satisfied, self-righteous
Just because he got the lead in the school play doesn't justify his irritating air of _____**smug**_____ superiority.

10. **tarry**
    (tar′ ē)

(*v.*) to delay leaving; to linger, wait; to remain or stay for a while
He will be tempted to _____**tarry**_____ longer if he thinks that this might be their last visit together.

Using Context

*For each item, determine whether the **boldface** word from pages 74–75 makes sense in the context of the sentence. Circle the item numbers next to the six sentences in which the words are used correctly.*

(**1.**) The parents were worried that their children didn't have the patience to remain seated for the **duration** of such a long car ride.

(**2.**) Having **acute** attention to detail is an excellent skill for a future editor such as yourself.

3. When he refused to **tarry** any of the work for the group project, I decided to ask the teacher for a different partner.

(**4.**) For the social studies assignment, each of us will draw a section of the relief map that shows one **facet** of the landscape of the school grounds.

(**5.**) My hands are **numb** from shoveling snow without wearing gloves, but I'm regaining some feeling now.

6. Her **smug** expression when she saw the grade on her paper was a sure sign that she had not done well.

7. When I finally got a moment to myself, the **fray** of silence helped to settle my thoughts and gave me a few minutes of peace.

(**8.**) The last-minute withdrawal of a runner from our relay team was a major **setback** that kept us from advancing to the finals.

9. Cheers of amazement erupted from the crowds when the star hitter went on to **bungle** two home runs in the eighth inning.

(**10.**) Someone stopped me on the street to ask directions, mistaking me for an **inhabitant** of this magnificent city.

Choosing the Right Word

*Select the **boldface** word that better completes each sentence. You might refer to the passage on pages 68–69 to see how most of these words are used in context. Note that the choices might be related forms of the Unit words.*

1. The bloodhound's (**numb, acute**) sense of smell led the trackers to the bank robber's hideout in record time.

2. Maria's illness, after she had been chosen for the leading role in the class show, was a serious (**setback, inhabitant**) to our plans.

3. Since it had seemed that winter would (**tarry, bungle**) forever, we were all heartily glad when it finally quit dragging its heels and departed.

4. When the plane encountered turbulence, we had to remain seated with our seat belts fastened for the (**duration, setback**) of the flight.

5. Each time she answered a question correctly, she rewarded herself with a (**smug, numb**) little smile of self-congratulation.

6. We cannot assume that all the people one sees on the streets of a large city are actually (**facets, inhabitants**) of the place.

7. The victims of the disaster were so (**numbed, tarried**) by the scope of the tragedy that they scarcely showed any emotion at all.

8. After the way you (**bungled, numbed**) the job of arranging the class trip, I can never again trust you with anything important.

9. There is so much wear and tear on the ropes in this pulley system that they become (**frayed, tarried**) in only a few days.

10. The strength of this book lies in the author's ability to describe and explain different (**setbacks, facets**) of human experience.

11. His (**numb, acute**) analysis of the housing problem in our town gave us a clear idea of what we would have to overcome.

12. Have you ever wondered if there is life on other planets and, if so, what the (**frays, inhabitants**) might look like?

You may wish to provide students with an explanation and example of a related form.

Completing the Sentence

Choose the word from the word bank that best completes each of the following sentences. Write the correct word or form of the word in the space provided.

| acute | duration | fray | numb | smug |
| bungle | facet | inhabitant | setback | tarry |

1. His _____**smug**_____ expression showed how highly he valued his own opinions and scorned the views of others.

2. Our team suffered a tough _____**setback**_____ when our best player was hurt in the first few minutes of play.

3. Is it true that the _____**inhabitants**_____ of Maine are often called "Mainiacs"?

4. When my two sisters began their bitter quarrel, only Mother had enough nerve to enter the _____**fray**_____ and tell them to stop.

5. Warmth and understanding are two outstanding _____**facets**_____ of her memorable personality.

6. After the dentist gave me an injection of novocaine, the whole side of my jaw and face turned _____**numb**_____.

7. Although the rain was heavy, it was of such short _____**duration**_____ that it didn't interfere with our plans.

8. Because of our inexperience and haste, we _____**bungled**_____ the little repair job so badly that it became necessary to replace the entire motor.

9. Because I _____**tarried**_____ at the book fair, I was ten minutes late for my piano lesson.

10. Anyone who has never had a sprained ankle will find it hard to imagine how _____**acute**_____ the pain is.

Encourage students to look for context clues. See page 7.

End Set B

Unit 5 ■ *77*

Synonyms

*Choose the word or form of the word from this Unit that is the same or most nearly the same in meaning as the **boldface** word or expression in the phrase. Write that word on the line. Use a dictionary if necessary.*

1. tried to **disprove** her argument — refute
2. bored by the pundit's detailed **analysis** — commentary
3. had **penetrating** pain in the right shoulder — acute
4. reflected off the **cut surfaces** of the diamond — facets
5. offer a brief **summation** of the movie — synopsis
6. the **span** of a thousand years — duration
7. lip-smacking sounds of the **famished** hikers — ravenous
8. swore **loyalty** to their leader — fidelity
9. broke up the parking lot **scuffle** — fray
10. was a **resident** in the apartment building — inhabitant
11. a shock that left them **dazed** and speechless — numb
12. to **mess up** his chances of winning — bungle
13. scared of the **spooky** shadow outside — eerie
14. intimidated by the speaker's **rant** — bluster
15. no sense of **guilt** for what happened — remorse

Antonyms

*Choose the word or form of the word from this Unit that is most nearly opposite in meaning to the **boldface** word or expression in the phrase. Write that word on the line. Use a dictionary if necessary.*

1. with a **discontented** look — smug
2. should not **rush** in the corridor — tarry
3. **anger** the demonstrators — pacify
4. able to control the **docile** horse — headstrong
5. expect yet another **triumph** — setback

Writing: Words in Action

Answers to the prompt will vary.

What is your position on funding space exploration? Should the United States continue to spend federal money to support NASA? Write an editorial persuading your audience to support or oppose funding space travel. Use at least two details from the passage (pages 68–69) and three or more words from this Unit.

Vocabulary in Context

*Some of the words you have studied in this Unit appear in **boldface** type. Read the passage below, and then circle the letter of the correct answer for each word as it is used in context.*

Sally Ride was born in Encino, California, in 1951. She received a bachelor's degree in physics and English from Stanford University. She continued her graduate studies in physics at Stanford as well, earning her master's degree and Ph.D. While studying at Stanford, an article in the student newspaper caught her **acute** eye. NASA was seeking astronaut candidates, and women could apply for the first time. Ride wanted to be free of **remorse** and not **bungle** this unique opportunity, so she did not **tarry** in submitting her application. Ride competed against 1,000 other applicants and received a coveted spot in the NASA astronaut program in 1978. She could not afford to be **smug** about her accomplishments; there was still a lot of work to do.

Ride completed NASA's training program and was eligible to go into space. On June 18, 1983, she stepped aboard the space shuttle *Challenger* and became the first American woman, and the youngest American ever, to go to space. This mission cemented Ride's status as a woman who broke barriers. After her first mission, she went back into space in October. She was assigned to a third shuttle mission, but her crew received a **setback** when their training was canceled due to the *Challenger* disaster in 1986.

After NASA, Ride became a physics professor at the University of California, San Diego. She cofounded Sally Ride Science to help young women pursue fields in science and math. Although Ride passed away in 2012, she lived an upstanding life and defied all expectations.

---

1. **Acute** comes from the Latin word **acutus. Acutus** most likely means
   a. untrained
   b. sharpened
   c. selective
   d. neutral

2. What is the meaning of **remorse** as it is used in paragraph 1?
   a. anger
   b. jealousy
   c. guilt
   d. frustration

3. What is the meaning of **bungle** as it is used in paragraph 1?
   a. to mess up
   b. to lose
   c. to attempt
   d. to discover

4. What does the word **tarry** most likely mean as it is used in paragraph 1?
   a. to decide
   b. to reschedule
   c. to linger
   d. to continue

5. The word **smug** means about the same as
   a. cautious
   b. timid
   c. persuasive
   d. self-satisfied

6. Which word means the same as **setback** as it is used in paragraph 2?
   a. disappointment
   b. announcement
   c. advantage
   d. recognition

See pages T29–T31 for assessment options.

UNIT 6

Note that not all of the Unit words are used in this passage. *Amiable, blight, limber, oracle,* and *vagabond* are used in the passage on page 91.

*Read the following passage, taking note of the **boldface** words and their contexts. These words are among those you will be studying in Unit 6. It may help you to complete the exercises in this Unit if you refer to the way the words are used below.*

The Fine Art of War: WWI Propaganda Images
<Textbook Entry>

The Great War Begins

Austrian Archduke Franz Ferdinand was assassinated in Sarajevo, Bosnia, in 1914 by a Serbian **partisan**. This event was the spark that ignited the tinderbox. Long-simmering international resentments and a complex and **befuddling maze** of military alliances erupted into the world's first global conflict: World War I (1914–1918).

The United States was neutral for the first three years. President Woodrow Wilson tried to play peacemaker. But by 1917, events like the torpedoing of passenger ships by German U-boats (submarines), which took a **gross** toll of civilian lives, convinced Wilson to declare war.

Now the United States was one of the Allies (along with France, Great Britain, Russia, Italy, and Japan).

The War at Home

When World War I began, propaganda campaigns were waged on all sides. Propaganda aimed to win the hearts and minds of citizens and discourage the enemy. The United States entered the war in 1917. Its publicity machine went into overdrive to **induce** public support. In a speech to the nation, President Wilson said, "The world must be made safe for democracy." With that **clarity** of vision, Wilson **debuted** the new Committee on Public Information (CPI), which, along with other government agencies such as the U.S. Food Administration, mobilized support for the war effort. Journalist George Creel, a **boisterous** supporter of America's entry into the war, led the CPI.

Creel hired 150,000 writers, actors, artists, and others to help drum up American support for the war. CPI planned a clear **agenda**. It had plenty of freedom and **leeway** in its efforts. It presented pro-war speeches, articles, pamphlets, books, and films.

Division of Pictorial Publicity

The CPI writers, directors, actors, and speechmakers were successful in getting the message out. But there were still Americans out of reach. So Creel created the Division of Pictorial Publicity within the CPI. It is said that a bad cause requires many words. Creel needed few words for his mission. He hired well-known

U-boat attacks spurred the U.S. into WWI. The public was urged to help defeat the U-boat.

Flagg's iconic 1917 poster of Uncle Sam is still familiar.

patriotic messages worked. Soon, war fever swept the country.

The War to End All Wars Ends

In 1918, the **gory** war came to an end. It left 8.5 million dead and 20 million wounded. Germany signed a peace treaty that required it to **vacate** occupied countries and **reimburse** money to war victims. The harsh penalties forced the defeated nation to be **compliant**. With the end of the war came the end of the Committee on Public Information. CPI's U.S.-based work ended on November 11, 1918. Its overseas operations ended eight months later. Its images are still used and still powerful today.

artists, illustrators, and cartoonists to create posters, banners, and advertisements for the war effort.

Newspapers and magazines were full of powerful images that packed a punch. Roadside billboards urged citizens to join the army or navy, buy bonds, knit socks for soldiers, **conserve** scarce food, and guard against the danger of spies.

Images as a Recruiting Tool

James Montgomery Flagg created some of the most memorable posters. His famous "I Want You" image of Uncle Sam compelled young men to enlist. (Uncle Sam was a fictional grey-haired man used to represent the U.S. government.) Another famous example is a poster for the Treasury Department's Liberty Bonds. It shows an image of a German soldier with a bloody sword. Below him were the words "Beat Back the Hun with Liberty Bonds." ("Hun" was an insulting term for the Germans used by the Allies.) These

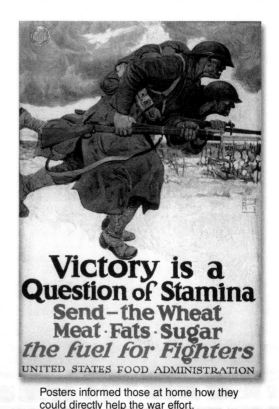

Posters informed those at home how they could directly help the war effort.

Audio

For iWords and audio passages, go to SadlierConnect.com.

Definitions

Note the spelling, pronunciation, part(s) of speech, and definition(s) of each of the following words. Then write the appropriate form of the word in the blank space in the illustrative sentence(s) following.

1. **amiable**
   (ā′ mē ə bəl)

   (*adj.*) friendly, good-natured
   Marty, whose sense of humor and good spirits never fail, is an _____**amiable**_____ companion.

2. **befuddle**
   (bi fəd′ əl)

   (*v.*) to confuse, make stupid
   A difficult scientific experiment with many steps is likely to _____**befuddle**_____ most beginners.

3. **clarity**
   (klar′ ə tē)

   (*n.*) clearness, accuracy
   The vet explained with great _____**clarity**_____ how best to housebreak our new puppy.

4. **conserve**
   (kən sərv′)

   (*v.*) to preserve; to keep from being damaged, lost, or wasted; to save
   Responsible citizens try to _____**conserve**_____ our precious natural resources.

5. **gory**
   (gôr′ ē)

   (*adj.*) marked by bloodshed, slaughter, or violence
   The Civil War battle of Antietam is, to this day, the most _____**gory**_____ one-day fight in our history.

6. **induce**
   (in düs′)

   (*v.*) to cause, bring about; to persuade
   Can drinking warm milk _____**induce**_____ sleep?

7. **leeway**
   (lē′ wā)

   (*n.*) extra space for moving along a certain route; allowance for mistakes or inaccuracies; margin of error
   Experienced planners allow _____**leeway**_____ of a week or so in case a project runs into snags or delays.

8. **limber**
   (lim′ bər)

   (*adj.*) flexible; (*v.*) to cause to become flexible
   Serious dancers develop _____**limber**_____ bodies.
   Runners _____**limber**_____ up before a race.

Synonyms and antonyms are provided at SadlierConnect.com.

9. **oracle**
(ôr' ə kəl)

(*n.*) someone or something that can predict the future; someone who gives astute answers or advice that seems authoritative

According to Greek legend, people sought prophecy from the great _____oracle_____ at Delphi.

10. **vagabond**
(vag' ə bänd)

(*n.*) an idle wanderer; a tramp; (*adj.*) wandering; irresponsible

The _____vagabond_____ carried his few belongings in a shabby cardboard suitcase.

The _____vagabond_____ life interests some people, but it doesn't appeal to me.

Using Context

*For each item, determine whether the **boldface** word from pages 82–83 makes sense in the context of the sentence. Circle the item numbers next to the six sentences in which the words are used correctly.*

(**1.**) I did not let my younger brother and sister watch the horror movie because I knew that they would be upset by several of its **gory** scenes.

(**2.**) The real murderer in the mystery novel planted a series of false clues in order to **befuddle** the police.

(**3.**) Please don't waste your time; nothing you have to say could **induce** me to change my mind at this point.

4. To find the shortest **leeway** up the mountain, the explorers studied the map that had been left behind by the previous expedition.

(**5.**) The **clarity** of the images coming from the exploration of Mars is amazing, especially when you consider the distance between that planet and Earth.

(**6.**) In 1960, accompanied by his dog Charley, writer John Steinbeck set off on a **vagabond** journey to find out what the America of his day was really like.

7. While one side fought fiercely to capture the **amiable** fort, the other side fought just as fiercely to defend it.

(**8.**) During a drought, people need to pitch in and find ways to **conserve** water on a daily basis.

9. The small, **limber** village lies in the shadow of the mighty volcano.

10. The diagram shows that each planet's path around the sun is shaped like an **oracle**.

Choosing the Right Word

*Select the **boldface** word that better completes each sentence. You might refer to the passage on pages 80–81 to see how most of these words are used in context. Note that the choices might be related forms of the Unit words.*

1. To become an all-around athlete, you not only need a strong and (**induced, limber**) body, but also a quick, disciplined mind.

2. If you want to get a clear picture of just what went wrong, you must not (**befuddle, induce**) your mind with all kinds of wild rumors.

3. What I thought was going to be a(n) (**amiable, vagabond**) little chat with my boss soon turned into a real argument.

4. Many a student dreams about spending a (**vagabond, limber**) year idly hiking through Europe.

5. Students must take many required courses, but they also have a little (**oracle, leeway**) to choose courses that they find especially interesting.

6. Don't let the (**clarity, leeway**) of the water fool you into supposing that it's safe for drinking.

7. This video game is not appropriate for children or minors due to its violent and (**amiable, gory**) content.

8. Over the years, so many of the columnist's predictions have come true that he is now looked on as something of a(n) (**vagabond, oracle**).

9. In her graphic description of the most gruesome scenes in the horror film, Maria left out none of the (**amiable, gory**) details.

10. Because he is an expert gymnast and works out every day, his body has remained as (**limber, gory**) as that of a boy.

11. As we moved higher up the mountain, I was overcome by dizziness and fatigue (**induced, befuddled**) by the thin air.

12. An experienced backpacker can give you many useful suggestions for (**befuddling, conserving**) energy on a long, tough hike.

Completing the Sentence

Choose the word from the word bank that best completes each of the following sentences. Write the correct word or form of the word in the space provided.

amiable	clarity	gory	leeway	oracle
befuddle	conserve	induce	limber	vagabond

1. The high standard of excellence that the woman had set for herself left her no _____**leeway**_____ for mistakes.

2. Why do you always ask me what's going to happen? I'm no _____**oracle**_____!

3. For years, his restless spirit led him to wander the highways and byways of this great land like any other footloose _____**vagabond**_____.

4. No matter what you may say, you cannot _____**induce**_____ me to do something that I know is wrong.

5. How can a _____**befuddled**_____ mind make decisions needed to drive safely in heavy traffic?

6. Because our energy resources are limited, we must try to do find ways to _____**conserve**_____ fuel.

7. I was not prepared for the _____**gory**_____ sight that met my eyes at the scene of that horrible massacre.

8. Before the game starts, the players _____**limber**_____ up by doing a few deep knee bends, sit-ups, and other exercises.

9. Because of her outgoing and _____**amiable**_____ personality, she is liked by nearly everyone at school.

10. Ms. Fillmer explained with such _____**clarity**_____ how to go about changing a tire that I felt that even someone as clumsy as I could do it.

Encourage students to look for context clues. See page 7.

Definitions

Note the spelling, pronunciation, part(s) of speech, and definition(s) of each of the following words. Then write the appropriate form of the word in the blank space in the illustrative sentence(s) following.

1. agenda
(ə jen′ də)

(*n.*) the program for a meeting; a list, outline, or plan of things to be considered or done

Our recycling plan is on today's _____ **agenda** _____.

2. blight
(blīt)

(*n.*) a disease that causes plants to wither and die; a condition of disease or ruin; (*v.*) to destroy, ruin

Dutch elm disease was a _____ **blight** _____ that forever changed the look of my neighborhood.

She was determined not to let low test scores _____ **blight** _____ her hopes of going to college.

3. boisterous
(boi′ strəs)

(*adj.*) rough and noisy in a cheerful way; high-spirited

The bus was filled with _____ **boisterous** _____ children.

4. compliant
(kəm plī′ ənt)

(*adj.*) willing to do what someone else wants; obedient

A _____ **compliant** _____ dog is easy to discipline.

5. debut
(dā′ byü)

(*n.*) a first public appearance; a formal entrance into society; (*v.*) to make a first appearance

She made her _____ **debut** _____ as lead in the play.

Many theaters will _____ **debut** _____ the film tonight.

6. gross
(grōs)

(*adj.*) coarse, vulgar; very noticeable; total; overweight; (*n.*) an overall total (without deductions); twelve dozen; (*v.*) to earn

They responded to the _____ **gross** _____ injustice in an unsatisfactory manner.

A _____ **gross** _____ of pencils lasts all year.

She expects to _____ **gross** _____ $3,000 in tips.

7. maze
(māz)

(*n.*) a network of paths through which it is hard to find one's way; something very mixed-up and confusing

It was a challenge to navigate the _____ **maze** _____.

8. partisan
(pärt′ ə zən)

(*n.*) a strong supporter of a person, party, or cause; one whose support is unreasoning; a resistance fighter, guerrilla; (*adj.*) strongly supporting one side only

That candidate is a _____ **partisan** _____ of term limits.

_____ **Partisan** _____ hometown fans can be hostile to those from out of town.

Practice with synonyms and antonyms is on page 90.

9. **reimburse**
(rē im bərs')

(v.) to pay back; to give payment for
When you go on business trips, the company will
_____ **reimburse** _____ all of your traveling expenses.

10. **vacate**
(vā' kāt)

(v.) to go away from, leave empty; to make empty; to void, annul
We have a lot of cleaning up to do before we
_____ **vacate** _____ the apartment for good.

Using Context

*For each item, determine whether the **boldface** word from pages 86–87 makes sense in the context of the sentence. Circle the item numbers next to the six sentences in which the words are used correctly.*

1. I don't feel strongly about these political issues either way, so I guess you might say I'm truly a **partisan**.

2. I tried to **reimburse** the kind stranger who paid for my coffee, but he insisted it was his treat.

3. We hurried to **vacate** our home before the exterminators started fumigating it.

4. The weather forecast indicates that conditions will be cool and **boisterous** with high winds, so be sure to wear a jacket.

5. Next month, the art museum will **debut** an exhibition of newly discovered photography from the postwar period.

6. The film director made a **gross** oversight when she failed to thank any of her family members or mentors in her award acceptance speech.

7. During the holiday season, the city comes alive with spectacular window displays, dazzling lights, and a **blight** of festive attractions.

8. I felt overwhelmed just looking at all of the events and activities listed on the packed **agenda** of the conference's first day.

9. One of the children's favorite things to do at the farm's autumn carnival is to find their way out of the cornfield **maze**.

10. Students who do not submit their essays on time will have five points deducted from their grade for being **compliant**.

Choosing the Right Word

*Select the **boldface** word that better completes each sentence. You might refer to the passage on pages 80–81 to see how most of these words are used in context. Note that the choices might be related forms of the Unit words.*

VICTOR· ·HVGO·
·1859·

1. My sister made her (**agenda, debut**) in the Broadway production of *Les Misérables*, a musical based on Victor Hugo's novel.

2. The disc jockey promised to (**vacate, debut**) the band's long-awaited new song as soon as it was released by the recording company.

3. After all the deductions had been made from my (**gross, boisterous**) salary, the sum that remained seemed pitifully small.

4. The landlord ordered all tenants to (**vacate, reimburse**) the premises by noon.

5. Mr. Roth, our school librarian, may seem mild and easygoing, but he cracks down hard on (**compliant, boisterous**) students.

6. Because she is usually so (**compliant, partisan**), we were all surprised when she said that she didn't like our plans and wouldn't accept them.

7. One of the biggest problems facing the United States today is how to stop the (**blight, agenda**) that is creeping over large parts of our great cities.

8. This matter is so important to all the people of the community that we must forget (**boisterous, partisan**) politics and work together.

9. Poland was at the top of Adolf Hitler's (**maze, agenda**) of military conquests in the fall of 1939.

10. Until we were in (**compliance, debut**) with the neighborhood regulations, we could not build a tree house.

11. I will feel fully (**reimbursed, vacated**) for all that I have done for her if I can see her in good health again.

12. At the end of the long series of discussions and arguments, we felt that we were trapped in a (**maze, blight**) of conflicting ideas and plans.

You may wish to provide students with an explanation and example of a related form.

Completing the Sentence

Choose the word from the word bank that best completes each of the following sentences. Write the correct word or form of the word in the space provided.

agenda	boisterous	debut	maze	reimburse
blight	compliant	gross	partisan	vacate

1. Trying to untangle a badly snarled fishing line is like trying to find one's way through a(n) _____**maze**_____.

2. The crowd is so _____**partisan**_____ that the umpire is booed every time he makes a decision against the home team.

3. Each of the items on the _____**agenda**_____ for our meeting today will probably require a good deal of discussion.

4. None of us could possibly overlook the _____**gross**_____ error that the waiter had made in adding up our check.

5. The high point of the social season was the formal _____**debut**_____ of young ladies at the annual Society Ball.

6. You certainly have a right to cheer for your team, but try not to become too _____**boisterous**_____ and unruly.

7. If you would be kind enough to buy a loose-leaf notebook for me while you are in the stationery store, I'll _____**reimburse**_____ you immediately.

8. Because you are working with older and more experienced people, you should be _____**compliant**_____ with their requests and advice.

9. If the Superintendent of Schools should _____**vacate**_____ his position by resigning, the Mayor has the right to name someone else to the job.

10. We cannot allow the lives of millions of people to be _____**blighted**_____ by poverty.

Encourage students to look for context clues. See page 7.

Synonyms

Choose the word or form of the word from this Unit that is the same or most nearly the same in meaning as the **boldface** word or expression in the phrase. Write that word on the line. Use a dictionary if necessary.

1. a **hobo** who hopped freight trains _____ vagabond
2. cannot rely on their **one-sided** viewpoint _____ partisan
3. enough **latitude** for a beginner to succeed _____ leeway
4. the **schedule** for today's meeting _____ agenda
5. **repay** the worker for the money he spent _____ reimburse
6. became **submissive** when threatened with punishment _____ compliant
7. **bewildered** by the product's instructions _____ befuddled
8. lost in the **labyrinth** of tunnels _____ maze
9. made her **first appearance** in the play _____ debut
10. a **flagrant** misstatement of the situation _____ gross
11. a **horrific** spectacle on the battlefield _____ gory
12. regarded as an **authority** on Central America _____ oracle
13. an **affliction** certain to lead to disaster _____ blight
14. no choice but to **desert** the cabin _____ vacate
15. a speech to **bring about** calm _____ induce

Antonyms

Choose the word or form of the word from this Unit that is most nearly opposite in meaning to the **boldface** word or expression in the phrase. Write that word on the line. Use a dictionary if necessary.

1. the guitar player's **stiff** fingers _____ limber
2. socializing with our **gruff** neighbors _____ amiable
3. the **ambiguity** of his explanation _____ clarity
4. a **quiet** discussion about the election results _____ boisterous
5. to **waste** energy _____ conserve

Answers to the prompt will vary.

From the passage (pages 80–81), study the posters that became popular during World War I. Write a short essay that explains why these images were so effective in persuading Americans to support the war effort. Use at least two details from the passage and three or more words from this Unit.

Vocabulary in Context

*Some of the words you have studied in this Unit appear in **boldface** type. Read the passage below, and then circle the letter of the correct answer for each word as it is used in context.*

World War II was the first war ever fought to a musical soundtrack. The BBC Forces Programme was established in 1940, and U.S. Armed Forces Radio started broadcasting in 1942. Radio gave the troops abroad a vital sense of connection with the nation, the values, and the people they were fighting for, and song was uniquely effective in expressing the conflicting emotions of the time.

Wartime songs tend to be patriotic, sentimental, or comic—some, such as Guy Lombardo's "Ma! I Miss Your Apple Pie" and Irving Berlin's "Oh, How I Hate to Get Up in the Morning," were all three. Stars such as Frank Sinatra and Bing Crosby played an important part in boosting morale. In Britain, two **amiable vagabond** comedians (and surprisingly **limber** dancers), Bud Flanagan and Chesney Allen, mixed laughter and tears with a repertoire that included "We're Going to Hang out the Washing on the Siegfried Line" and the tearjerker "Underneath the Arches."

The definitive voices of the period were female, however. Jo Stafford, Vera Lynn, Dinah Shore, the Andrews Sisters, and Marlene Dietrich gave voice to all the sweethearts, wives, and mothers who were waiting and hoping for the safe return of their loved ones, husbands and sons. Their voices brought comfort, hope, encouragement, and inspiration. They saw into the future like benign **oracles**, and set the **agenda** for peace and happiness. They were a remedy for the **blight** of war. They made promises that would be kept—and the title of the greatest song of the war was the greatest promise of all: "We'll Meet Again."

---

1. What is the meaning of **amiable** as it is used in paragraph 2?
   a. humorous
   c. friendly
   b. roguish
   d. hearty

2. The word **vagabond** means about the same as
   a. wandering
   c. untrustworthy
   b. destitute
   d. crooning

3. What is the meaning of **limber** as it is used in paragraph 2?
   a. adaptable
   c. talented
   b. clumsy
   d. lithe

4. Which word means the same as **oracles** as it is used in paragraph 3?
   a. well-wishers
   c. fortune-tellers
   b. witches
   d. clairvoyants

5. **Agenda** comes from the Latin word **agere. Agere** most likely means
   a. to arrange
   c. to imagine
   b. to do
   d. to plan

6. What does the word **blight** most likely mean as it is used in paragraph 3?
   a. uncertainty
   c. disease
   b. weakness
   d. scandal

See pages T29–T31 for assessment options.

Vocabulary for Comprehension
Part 1

*Read "Oseola McCarty: 1908–1999," which contains words in **boldface** that appear in Units 4–6. Then answer the questions.*

Oseola McCarty: 1908–1999

Oseola McCarty left school after sixth grade to help care for an ailing relative. She was sorry not to be able to continue her education, but her family needed her.

(5) Pursuing an education was an **elusive** dream to this lifelong **inhabitant** of Mississippi. She eked out a living washing and ironing other people's clothing and lived most of her life in a small house her

(10) uncle had once owned.

For seventy-five years, Oseola McCarty served her customers. McCarty believed in hard work, and she was 86 years old before she finally retired. She boiled,

(15) hand-scrubbed, and hang-dried her customers' laundry instead of using a washing machine or a dryer. She would iron clothes until 11 o'clock at night. "Hard work gives your life meaning," she once

(20) said. McCarty also lived a frugal lifestyle and walked wherever she had to go.

McCarty earned little money yet managed to put aside a small amount almost every week. She knew it was wise

(25) to plan for the future, and she never felt right about taking money out of her bank account. The money she put into the bank was earning interest. What must have seemed like **petty** deposits of nickels and

(30) dimes eventually grew into a fortune. By the time McCarty was 87, she had nearly $300,000.

McCarty's dreams of education had never faded. She thought she was too old

(35) to attend college but felt no **remorse** about her life. Instead she thought of an **agenda** to help others attend college. She gave $150,000 of her life's savings to the University of Southern Mississippi. All she

(40) asked of the university was that it use the money for scholarships for deserving students from southern Mississippi who could not afford college. Suddenly this elderly laundry woman became a local

(45) hero.

Oseola McCarty's generosity touched people, and many were moved to make their own contributions to increase the Oseola McCarty Endowed Scholarship

(50) Fund. Since the fund was first established, the university has been able to award many scholarships in McCarty's name.

Although McCarty became a rich woman through her dutiful saving, she

(55) remained a straightforward, honest, and humble person. Her **commentaries** on life were right to the point. "If you want to feel proud of yourself," she once said, "you've got to do things you can be proud of."

(60) McCarty also had a simple explanation for her ability to live so modestly and save so much of what she earned: "My secret was contentment. I was happy with what I had," she said. When Oseola McCarty

(65) died at the age of 91, people throughout the United States remembered her with pride and admiration.

1. Which sentence **best** states the author's purpose in "Oseola McCarty: 1908–1999"?
   A) The author persuades the reader about the benefits of saving money.
   B) The author tells an inspirational true story.
   C) The author explains ways to help others.
   D) The author tells an inspirational fictional story.

2. As used in line 5, what does the word **elusive** suggest about Oseola McCarty's dream of pursuing an education?
   A) It was temporary.
   B) It was difficult to achieve.
   C) It was cherished.
   D) It was easily fulfilled.

3. What does the word **inhabitant** most likely mean as it is used in line 6?
   A) fan
   B) resident
   C) visitor
   D) student

4. **Part A**
   Which word **best** describes the author's tone in paragraphs 2 and 3 (lines 11–32)?
   A) pitying
   B) critical
   C) respectful
   D) disbelieving

   Part B
   Which statement from the passage **best** supports your answer to Part A?
   A) "For seventy-five years, Oseola McCarty served her customers." (lines 11–12)
   B) "She would iron clothes until 11 o'clock at night." (lines 17–18)
   C) "The money she put into the bank was earning interest." (lines 27–28)
   D) "What must have seemed like petty deposits of nickels and dimes eventually grew into a fortune." (lines 28–29)

5. According to the passage, what are **petty** deposits (line 29)?
   A) major
   B) insignificant
   C) narrow-minded
   D) sensible

6. Based on the evidence in lines 28–32, which statement **best** describes how McCarty amassed her wealth?
   A) Out of sight, out of mind.
   B) Live only in the here and now.
   C) Here today, gone tomorrow.
   D) Slow and steady wins the race.

7. Which word means the opposite of **remorse** in line 35?
   A) regret
   B) sympathy
   C) guiltlessness
   D) confusion

8. What does the word **agenda** mean as it is used in line 37?
   A) plan
   B) dream
   C) way
   D) contest

9. What does the word **commentaries** most likely mean as it is used in line 56?
   A) keepsakes
   B) remarks
   C) ideas
   D) writings

10. Which statement **best** provides an inference that is supported by "Oseola McCarty: 1908–1999"?
    A) Live as if today were your last day on earth.
    B) The most important thing in life is a college education.
    C) One person can make a big difference in the lives of others.
    D) Without an education, a person is permanently disadvantaged.

Vocabulary for Comprehension
Part 2

*Read these passages, which contain words in **boldface** that appear in Units 4–6. Then choose the best answer to each question based on what is stated or implied in the passage(s). You may refer to the passages as often as necessary.*

Questions 1–10 are based on the following passages.

Passage 1

A puppet is a figure of a person or animal moved by human aid. Throughout recorded history puppets and puppet theater have been popular all over the
(5)　world. Some historians claim that puppets date back into Cro-Magnon times, around 30,000 BCE. Puppets have enjoyed enduring popularity, and some puppets have become famous through movies.
(10)　Over time, many types of puppet and styles of puppet entertainment have developed. There are hand or glove puppets, rod puppets, marionettes or string puppets, and shadow figures, in
(15)　which an audience views the puppet's shadows through a translucent screen.
Puppetry is diverse, and any **synopsis** of its origins will necessarily leave out some of the cultures that contributed to its
(20)　development. It is fair to say, however, that two distinct traditions developed in the **maze** of this art's history. One tradition was centered in Europe, the other in Asia. The western tradition, found chiefly in Europe,
(25)　performed folk plays for popular audiences. An outstanding example is the Punch and Judy show, which featured two main characters: the **headstrong** Pulcinella (Mr. Punch) and his wife Judy.
(30)　Often **boisterous** and violent, this entertainment showcased farce and slapstick comedy. This type of puppet theater reached its height in England in the early 1700s.

Passage 2

(35)　The eastern tradition in puppetry is remarkably diverse. Puppet performances are popular in numerous Asian countries. One widespread type of performance is shadow puppet theater, common in India,
(40)　Indonesia, Malaysia, Thailand, and Cambodia. In these performances, puppets are two-dimensional and made of buffalo hide. The puppeteer, known as the *dalang* in Indonesia, manipulates all
(45)　the figures on one side of an illuminated screen. The audience watches the action from the other side. Performances include a musical ensemble of percussion instruments known as the *gamelan*.
(50)　Called *wayang kulit* in Indonesia, shadow puppetry is **deemed** one of the country's most distinctive cultural traditions.
Two ancient Indian epics **generated** the storylines and most of the characters of
(55)　*wayang kulit*. These epics, the *Ramayana* and the *Mahabharata*, were probably composed sometime between 400 BCE and 400 CE. In the *Ramayana*, the hero rescues his kidnaped wife. In the
(60)　*Mahabharata*, five brothers must wage a **devastating** war against their cousins. Although many shadow plays exhibit great **fidelity** to the epic stories, there is **leeway** for the addition of new characters.
(65)　As a night-long performance unfolds, the eerie shadows and hypnotic musical accompaniment may **induce** a state of **reverie** in the audience. Such is the magic of *wayang kulit*

You may wish to ask students to write a few paragraphs that cite evidence from both passages in answer to the following prompt: What are some of the similarities and differences between the western and eastern traditions of puppetry?

1. According to Passage 1, historians believe that puppets may
   A) be a product of medieval cultures.
   B) be a very ancient form of art.
   C) have become less popular over time.
   D) have originated in China.

2. As it is used in line 17, "synopsis" most nearly means
   A) essay.
   B) interpretation.
   C) outline.
   D) judgement.

3. From details in Passage 2, it can reasonably be inferred that the effect of shadow puppet theater is often
   A) explosive.
   B) satirical.
   C) hypnotic.
   D) subversive.

4. As it is used in line 51, "deemed" most nearly means
   A) judged.
   B) confirmed.
   C) investigated.
   D) nominated.

5. As it is used in line 63, "fidelity" most nearly means
   A) duplication.
   B) transformation.
   C) loyalty.
   D) recognition.

6. Passage 1 differs from Passage 2 primarily because it
   A) claims that puppetry has a narrow, specialized appeal.
   B) acknowledges that puppets have an ancient history.
   C) presents a broader discussion, including a definition and historical summary.
   D) argues that the western tradition is more significant than the eastern tradition.

7. Which choice provides the best evidence for the answer to the previous question?
   A) Lines 1–2 ("A puppet . . . aid")
   B) Lines 12–16 ("There are . . . screen")
   C) Lines 17–20 ("Puppetry . . . development)
   D) Lines 36–37 ("Puppet . . . countries")

8. Passage 1 and Passage 2 are similar in that both passages stress
   A) the ingenious features of puppetry.
   B) the widespread popularity of puppetry.
   C) the epic tales underlying puppet traditions.
   D) the contributions of slapstick comedy to puppetry.

9. Passage 1 describes the use of puppetry to tell European folk plays, while Passage 2
   A) describes the use of puppets to tell epic Indian storylines.
   B) explains how to make a puppet out of buffalo hide.
   C) claims that puppet shows were first performed in Italy.
   D) describes a popular puppet show called Punch and Judy.

10. As it is used in line 68, "reverie" most nearly means
    A) blackout.
    B) distraction.
    C) boredom.
    D) trance.

Synonyms

*From the word bank below, choose the word that has the same or nearly the same meaning as the **boldface** word in each sentence and write it on the line. You will not use all of the words.*

acute	eerie	headstrong	ovation
amiable	fray	limber	petty
compliant	gory	mortal	ravenous
debut	gross	numb	smug

1. The **spooky** story sent chills down my spine.   _____eerie_____

2. It is extremely important for everyone to behave in a **submissive** manner during the fire drill.   _____compliant_____

3. We must not let **insignificant** matters get in the way; instead, we should stay focused on our main goal.   _____petty_____

4. All sports require a certain level of physical fitness, but for gymnastics, athletes need to be particularly **supple**.   _____limber_____

5. If you need to have a cavity filled, the dentist might give you a shot that will temporarily **deaden** the feeling in your mouth.   _____numb_____

6. Both critics and audiences are looking forward to the film's **coming-out** at the upcoming festival in Toronto.   _____debut_____

7. According to legend, the werewolf is a **voracious** creature that is half human and half beast.   _____ravenous_____

8. I can't bear the thought of giving up my favorite pair of jeans, even though they have begun to **unravel** at the knee.   _____fray_____

9. The reviewer's **clever** analysis helped me gain a better understanding of the book.   _____acute_____

10. Is the main character in this myth a **human** or a god?   _____mortal_____

11. It would be a **flagrant** exaggeration to call the mild cold that you are experiencing a "dreadful illness."   _____gross_____

12. When the **hurrahs** ended, the band treated the audience to one more song.   _____ovation_____

Two-Word Completions

Select the pair of words that best completes the meaning of each of the following sentences.

1. In the third century, bands of savage barbarians repeatedly broke through the frontier defenses of the Roman province of Gaul, _____ the countryside with fire and sword, and either slew or carried off the _____.
a. pacified … vagabonds
b. scanned … partisans
c. blighted … oracles
d. devastated … inhabitants

2. The defense was able to _____ the prosecution's case so convincingly that the members of the jury _____ the defendant after only five minutes of deliberation.
a. topple … discredited
b. bungle … reimbursed
c. refute … acquitted
d. devastate … befuddled

3. The TV special not only brought in huge sums of money to help relieve the _____ of millions of Africans suffering from the effects of a severe famine but also _____ a great deal of sympathy for them.
a. plight … generated
b. setback … induced
c. strife … conserved
d. duration … deemed

4. After the speech in which Thomas Paine _____ against unfair taxes, it became obvious to all colonists that his _____ was to promote freedom.
a. blustered … agenda
b. idolized … ingratitude
c. vacated … keepsake
d. repented … revocation

5. When the new government came to power, its first order of business was to _____ a country that had been torn by _____ and revolution for over ten years.
a. topple … ingratitude
b. pacify … strife
c. conserve … remorse
d. strand … fidelity

6. "The Scholar Gypsy" tells the tale of a poor student who left school to join a band of _____. He and his companions roamed the countryside endlessly, never _____ in one place for long.
a. bunglers … vacating
b. inhabitants … deeming
c. vagabonds … tarrying
d. partisans … generating

7. "I want to maintain _____ to the book in bringing this story to the screen," the director instructed the scriptwriter. "However, I recognize that one has to have a little _____ when translating print into film."
a. fidelity … leeway
b. clarity … synopsis
c. partisan … commentary
d. strife … facet

Denotation and Connotation

When you look up a word in a dictionary, you find its definition, or its **denotation**. A word's denotation is its literal meaning, and it conveys a neutral tone.

Many words have additional shades of meaning called connotations. **Connotations** are the emotional associations we have with words. A word might have several synonyms, or words that have related meanings, but each synonym will have a particular connotation that sets it apart from the others. Connotations can be positive, negative, or neutral.

Consider these synonyms for the neutral word *remembrance*.

> *memento   souvenir   keepsake   relic*

Memento, souvenir, and *keepsake* have positive connotations, whereas *relic* has a more negative one, suggesting something old and outdated.

Look at these examples of words that have similar denotations but very different connotations.

NEUTRAL	POSITIVE	NEGATIVE
pacify	soothe	placate
pleased	proud	smug
agenda	proposal	conspiracy

Expressing the Connotation

Read each sentence. Select the word in parentheses that better expresses the connotation (positive, negative, or neutral) given at the beginning of the sentence.

negative **1.** The shop owner does not want people to (**loiter**, **tarry**) in front of her store.

neutral **2.** Some people (**idolize**, **admire**) the idea of physical beauty, but I think personality is more important.

negative **3.** One member banged his shoe on the desk, prompting a (**fray**, **disagreement**) among the politicians.

positive **4.** Ruby is a (**determined**, **headstrong**) child, and she prefers getting dressed on her own.

neutral **5.** Our cat is quite (**elusive**, **mystifying**) and seldom makes an appearance when we have company.

positive **6.** When they heard that their troop had sold the most cookies, the scouts responded with (**unruly**, **boisterous**) shouts and applause.

negative **7.** The criticism he made was (**minor**, **petty**), but nobody in class took offense.

neutral **8.** You should be (**compliant**, **submissive**) when addressing a police officer if he stops your car.

Classical Roots

re—back; again

The Latin root *re* appears in **repent** (page 62), **revocation** (page 63), **refute** (page 70), **remorse** (page 71), and **reimburse** (page 87). Some other words based on the same root are listed below.

rebuke	refrain	renege	retract
redeem	relic	restraint	revive

From the list of words above, choose the one that corresponds to each of the brief definitions below. Write the word in the blank space in the illustrative sentence below the definition. Use a dictionary if necessary.

1. to go back on a promise

They were surprised when the buyer suddenly decided to _____**renege**_____ on the deal.

2. to take back something that has been said, offered, or published

The angry candidate demanded that the newspaper _____**retract**_____ the scandalous story.

3. to hold oneself back; a repeated verse, chorus

On Thanksgiving, it is always hard for me to _____**refrain**_____ from eating too much delicious food.

4. a device that restricts or confines; control over the expression of one's feelings or behavior

The police officers placed _____**restraints**_____ on the violent prisoner.

5. something that has survived the passage of time

We marveled at the delicate artistry in the Indian _____**relics**_____ we saw at the museum.

6. to scold, express sharp disapproval; a scolding

The babysitter had to _____**rebuke**_____ the children for misbehaving after dinner.

7. to give new life to; to restore

Lively cheers from a hopeful crowd may _____**revive**_____ a team's dampened spirits.

8. to buy back; to make up for; to fulfill a pledge

Consumers who _____**redeem**_____ discount coupons they clip from magazines and newspapers can lower their weekly grocery bills.

UNIT 7

Note that not all of the Unit words are used in this passage. *Fatality, illicit, inflammatory, memorandum,* and *writhe* are used in the passage on page 111.

*Read the following passage, taking note of the **boldface** words and their contexts. These words are among those you will be studying in Unit 7. It may help you to complete the exercises in this Unit if you refer to the way the words are used below.*

Made for the Shade
<Informational Essay>

Most people who wear sunglasses might say they wear shades to protect their eyes from the sun's harmful ultraviolet rays or to ward off glare. They aren't **prevaricating**. Those *are* the most popular reasons people wear sunglasses. But the "coolness factor" is another reason. With so many shapes, sizes, and colors to choose from, just about everyone can pick shades that look stylish. But modern sunglasses are a far cry from earlier models.

People today might not **relish** wearing the "sunglasses" of the ancient Inuit. The Inuit wore sun goggles made from bone, ivory, and wood. These were fashioned into eye coverings with slits so the wearer could see. These goggles were functional, but not exactly a fashion statement.

Roman emperors used a more glamorous way of protecting their eyes. Supposedly, the emperor Nero shielded his eyes with pieces of emerald. But lowly citizens were not **authorized** to do the same, even if they could afford the gems.

In the twelfth century, Chinese judges hid their eyes behind planes of smoky quartz crystals to appear detached or impartial. The judges could **immerse** themselves in the trial without betraying their thoughts about the alleged **culprit** or witnesses. This gesture **quashed** any suspicion that they were taking sides.

Centuries later, sunglasses similar to modern shades were developed. Around 1750, British optician, designer, and inventor James Ayscough experimented with tinted lenses. He **dissected** and remade existing spectacles to create shaded ones. He was trying to correct specific eye ailments. While he might have felt his early efforts **pathetic**, he **persevered**. Although Ayscough was not designing the glasses for sun protection, he is still known as the father of modern sunglasses.

Snow goggles helped protect the Inuit from snow blindness.

Advancements in the manufacture of sunglasses followed over the years. In 1929, entrepreneur Sam Foster started selling his own inexpensive shades in Atlantic City, New Jersey. That is when sunglasses really became both fashionable and functional. Foster founded Foster Grant—still a successful company today.

Foster could not have picked a better time to start his company. As the film industry took off in the twentieth century, sunglasses became popular among movie stars. Silent-film stars wore shades to disguise red eyes caused by lamps used while shooting films. Even after this problem was fixed, stars continued to wear shades—probably for the glamour factor. Or perhaps celebrities who want to remain incognito believe that the public is **gullible** enough not to recognize a star wearing shades.

Although celebrities and the general public alike wear them to be fashionable, sunglasses have become a staple in various professions. In 1936, photography pioneer Edwin H. Land developed polarized sunglasses using his patented Polaroid filter. These fast became popular with fishermen. The polarized lenses reduced glare and allowed fishermen to see into the water. There are also special shades for athletes, airline pilots, and astronauts. Astronauts need sunglasses for inside the spacecraft as well as out. Sunlight is much stronger in space.

Nowadays, sunglasses are more popular than ever. It is a **testimonial** to their staying power. Some people **expend** time carefully

Audrey Hepburn
in *Breakfast at Tiffany's*

scouring websites for the odd or unusual pair of shades. A person might look at vintage shades and **reminisce** about the past. But **dawdling** fondly over old memories and the "good old days" might be a case of looking at the world through rose-colored glasses. If only those who yearn for vintage shades could see the primitive methods of blocking the sun's rays, they might not see sunglasses in such a romantic light.

Astronauts require eye protection from
the sun outside and inside their spacecraft.

Audio

For iWords and
audio passages, go to
SadlierConnect.com.

Definitions

Note the spelling, pronunciation, part(s) of speech, and definition(s) of each of the following words. Then write the appropriate form of the word in the blank space in the illustrative sentence(s) following.

1. culprit
(kəl′ prit)

(*n.*) a person who has committed a crime or is guilty of some misconduct; an offender

Thanks to their efficient tracking methods, the police were able to catch the _____ **culprit** _____ red-handed.

2. dawdle
(dôd′ əl)

(*v.*) to waste time; to be idle; to spend more time in doing something than is necessary

It's relaxing to _____ **dawdle** _____ in the shower, but it wastes water.

3. expend
(ek spend′)

(*v.*) to pay out, spend; to use up

The most experienced long-distance runners learn not to _____ **expend** _____ their energy too soon.

4. gullible
(gəl′ ə bəl)

(*adj.*) easily fooled, tricked, or cheated

Are you _____ **gullible** _____ enough to believe everything you hear on the radio?

5. immerse
(i mərs′)

(*v.*) to plunge or dip into a fluid; to involve deeply

I find it's easier to _____ **immerse** _____ my entire body in a swimming pool than try to get used to the water slowly.

6. inflammatory
(in flam′ ə tôr ē)

(*adj.*) causing excitement or anger; leading to unrest, violence, or disorder

The candidate made an _____ **inflammatory** _____ speech that incensed all those who heard it.

7. persevere
(pər sə vēr′)

(*v.*) to keep doing something in spite of difficulties; to refuse to quit even when the going is tough

The patient needs to _____ **persevere** _____ with the painful exercises in order to be able to walk normally again.

8. quash
(kwäsh)

(*v.*) to crush, put down completely

Swift military action was required to _____ **quash** _____ the revolt before anyone was injured.

Synonyms and antonyms are provided at SadlierConnect.com.

9. **testimonial**
(tes' tə mō' nē əl)

(*n.*) a statement that speaks to a person's character or to the benefits of a product; expressing the value and worth of someone or something

The famous athlete's _____testimonial_____ about the thirst-quenching drink made an impression on TV viewers.

10. **writhe**
(rīth)

(*v.*) to make twisting or turning movements in a way that suggests pain or struggle

It's so sad to see an injured bird _____writhe_____ in pain.

Using Context

*For each item, determine whether the **boldface** word from pages 102–103 makes sense in the context of the sentence. Circle the item numbers next to the six sentences in which the words are used correctly.*

(1.) After participating in the special music program, each student wrote a **testimonial** to explain what he or she had gotten out of it.

(2.) When you are on vacation, you can just **dawdle** or relax in other ways that you can't during the rest of the year.

3. It is **inflammatory** that we catch the 9:15 a.m. bus to the city if we want to get to the show on time.

4. Because I don't have any time to read it, I decided to **expend** my subscription to the weekly newsletter.

(5.) My little brother dislikes pea soup so much that just the mention of it makes him **writhe** with disgust.

6. When a windstorm is predicted, homeowners should move trash cans, outdoor tables and chairs, and other **gullible** objects to a safe, sheltered location.

(7.) The owners of the store downtown breathed a sigh of relief once the **culprit** behind the thefts was behind bars.

8. The scientists will **persevere** the treetops in an attempt to locate nests of the endangered species of eagle.

(9.) We will not allow this loss to **quash** our hopes for a winning season and perhaps even the state championship.

(10.) If you **immerse** those wilted lettuce leaves in cold water for a minute or two, they will regain some of their crispness.

Choosing the Right Word

*Select the **boldface** word that better completes each sentence. You might refer to the passage on pages 100–101 to see how most of these words are used in context. Note that the choices might be related forms of the Unit words.*

1. Though he was losing his hearing, Beethoven (**expended, immersed**) himself in his music.

2. She is so worried about appearing (**inflammatory, gullible**) that she sometimes refuses to believe things that are well supported by facts.

3. The charges against the suspected mugger will probably not hold up in court, so the district attorney has decided to (**writhe, quash**) them.

4. She was so deeply (**immersed, expended**) in the book she was reading that she did not even hear us enter the room.

5. His sticky fingers and the crumbs around his mouth convinced us that he was the (**culprit, testimonial**) in the Case of the Empty Cookie Jar.

6. Because my sister is so (**gullible, inflammatory**), I have to avoid reading scary stories to her before her bedtime.

7. We were impressed with Ella's (**testimonial, culprit**), as she described how a new shampoo made her hair grow faster.

8. When the class comedian imitated my way of speaking, it was all I could do not to (**writhe, immerse**) with embarrassment.

9. It was plain from the way that he (**dawdled, persevered**) over breakfast that he was in no hurry to visit the dentist.

10. Dictators like Hitler and Mussolini used (**gullible, inflammatory**) language to stir up the emotions of the crowds they addressed.

11. In spite of all your talk about how hard it is to get into medical school, I intend to (**persevere, dawdle**) in my plans to become a doctor.

12. She (**expends, dawdles**) so much time and energy on small matters that she can't prepare properly for the things that are really important.

You may wish to provide students with an explanation and example of a related form.

Completing the Sentence

Choose the word from the word bank that best completes each of the following sentences. Write the correct word or form of the word in the space provided.

culprit	expend	immerse	persevere	testimonial
dawdle	gullible	inflammatory	quash	writhe

1. The children won't _____**dawdle**_____ over their homework if they know they'll be getting cheese and crackers as soon as they finish.

2. The dictator ordered his secret police to _____**quash**_____ any attempt to organize a protest rally.

3. We tried to hold Tom steady, but he _____**writhed**_____ with pain as the doctor put splints on his broken leg.

4. Do you really think that I am _____**gullible**_____ enough to believe his foolish story about being a member of the Olympic team?

5. "Only a bigot would dare to make such a rude and _____**inflammatory**_____ remark, even in jest," I replied.

6. No matter how talented you may be, you will never be successful unless you learn to _____**persevere**_____ in what you undertake.

7. Because he was seen near the scene of the crime at the time the deed was committed, he was suspected of being the _____**culprit**_____.

8. Before you _____**immerse**_____ yourself in the bath, be sure to test the temperature of the water.

9. Is it wise to _____**expend**_____ so much of your hard-earned money on things that you don't really want or need?

10. The new library that will bear Ann Parker's name is a(n) _____**testimonial**_____ to her commitment to teaching children how to read.

Encourage students to look for context clues. See page 7.

End Set A

Definitions

Note the spelling, pronunciation, part(s) of speech, and definition(s) of each of the following words. Then write the appropriate form of the word in the blank space in the illustrative sentence(s) following.

1. authorize
(ô′ thə rīz)

(*v.*) to approve or permit; to give power or authority to
I wonder if Congress will someday _____**authorize**_____ U.S. citizens to cast official votes over the Internet.

2. dissect
(di sekt′)

(*v.*) to cut apart in preparation for scientific study; to analyze with great care
I can't wait to _____**dissect**_____ a frog in biology class next week.

3. fatality
(fā tal′ ə tē)

(*n.*) an event resulting in death; an accidental death
The driver slammed on the brakes, but it was too late to prevent the traffic _____**fatality**_____.

4. illicit
(i lis′ it)

(*adj.*) not permitted, unlawful, improper
Students will be suspended for one week if they bring any _____**illicit**_____ materials to school.

5. memorandum
(mem ə ran′ dəm)

(*n.*) a note to aid one's memory; an informal note or report (*pl.,* memorandums *or* memoranda)
The principal's weekly _____**memorandum**_____ reminds teachers of programs, deadlines, and special events.

6. pathetic
(pə thet′ ik)

(*adj.*) marked by strong emotion, especially pity and sorrow; able to move people emotionally; worthy of pity; woefully inadequate or lacking
It was a _____**pathetic**_____ sight to see so many starving people desperately begging for food.

7. prevaricate
(pri var′ ə kāt)

(*v.*) to lie, tell an untruth; to mislead on purpose
His reputation has suffered because of his unfortunate tendency to _____**prevaricate**_____.

8. relish
(rel′ ish)

(*n.*) enjoyment or satisfaction; something that adds a pleasing flavor; (*v.*) to enjoy greatly
She opened the tiny box with _____**relish**_____, knowing that it contained a piece of jewelry.
Now that I've learned about Japan in class, I _____**relish**_____ the chance to travel there.

Practice with synonyms and antonyms is on page 110.

9. **reminisce**
(rem ə nis')

(*v.*) to recall one's past thoughts, feelings, or experiences
At the family reunion, we got to hear 94-year-old Tía
Luzia _____reminisce_____ about life in old Havana.

10. **scour**
(skaůr)

(*v.*) to clean or polish by hard rubbing; to examine with
great care; to move about quickly in search of
The pot roast was delicious, but it won't be any fun
to _____scour_____ the burned roasting pan.

Using Context

*For each item, determine whether the **boldface** word from pages 106–107 makes sense in the context of the sentence. Circle the item numbers next to the six sentences in which the words are used correctly.*

1. The movie star was known best for her **illicit** laughter, which had the power to bring a smile to anyone's face.

(2.) Before the manager left for vacation, he decided to **authorize** his assistant to sign for any packages that arrived.

3. The student began to **scour** and pout when scolded by the teacher for disrupting the class.

(4.) When the store owner realized how many employees were arriving late to work, she issued a **memorandum** reminding them of the importance of punctuality.

(5.) In the original fairy tale "The Little Mermaid" by Hans Christian Andersen, the mermaid loses not only the prince, but also her life—a **pathetic** ending compared to what happens in the movie.

6. Instead of carefully examining the car for signs of damage, the driver decided to simply **dissect** what happened and casually drove away.

(7.) As I sat down to read the newest book by my favorite author, I shut out all distractions and began to **relish** every page I was reading.

(8.) If our proposal to lower the local speed limit does not get the required number of votes to pass, it could mean the **fatality** of our plan to make our town a safer place.

(9.) Whenever I smell cinnamon, I can't help but **reminisce** about the treats my grandmother used to bake for me.

10. I continue to **prevaricate** over whether I should try out for the basketball team or audition for the chorus.

Choosing the Right Word

*Select the **boldface** word that better completes each sentence. You might refer to the passage on pages 100–101 to see how most of these words are used in context. Note that the choices might be related forms of the Unit words.*

1. With the skill of a trained debater, she (**prevaricated, dissected**) her opponent's arguments one by one to reveal their basic weaknesses.

2. No one (**relishes, prevaricates**) being reminded of his or her mistakes, but if you are wise you will try to learn from such criticism.

3. What good does it do for the president of the Student Council to issue (**fatalities, memorandums**) if no one takes the trouble to read them?

4. Whenever my Aunt Joan hears a hit from the 1990s on the radio, she starts to (**reminisce, relish**) about her days in high school.

5. We learned in our social studies class that the Constitution (**dissects, authorizes**) the president to arrange treaties with foreign countries.

6. His scheme to make money by preparing term papers for other students is not only completely (**pathetic, illicit**) but immoral as well.

7. I am afraid that our ambitious plan to modernize the gym has become a (**fatality, memorandum**) of the School Board's economy drive.

8. When it became known that four explorers were lost in the jungle, special search parties were sent out to (**prevaricate, scour**) the area for them.

9. I spent three hours (**authorizing, scouring**) my room, looking for my homework.

10. Is there any sight more (**pathetic, illicit**) than a kitten stranded in a tree?

11. The more he tried to protect himself by (**scouring, prevaricating**), the more he became entrapped in his own web of lies.

12. Although our coach can spend hours (**scouring, reminiscing**) about his victories, he doesn't have an equally good memory for his defeats.

You may wish to provide students with an explanation and example of a related form.

Completing the Sentence

Choose the word from the word bank that best completes each of the following sentences. Write the correct word or form of the word in the space provided.

authorize	fatality	memorandum	prevaricate	reminisce
dissect	illicit	pathetic	relish	scour

1. This pass _____**authorizes**_____ you to visit certain rooms in this museum that are not open to the general public.

2. After we had _____**dissected**_____ the animal, we had to point to each of its important organs and explain its main function.

3. Our supervisor prepared a(n) _____**memorandum**_____ that reminded the salespeople of the procedures to be followed during the holiday season.

4. Cracking down on _____**illicit**_____ drug traffic is one of the biggest problems facing law-enforcement agencies.

5. The story of the homeless child was so _____**pathetic**_____ that it moved us all to tears.

6. You may be tempted to _____**prevaricate**_____, but in the long run it will be to your advantage to own up to the truth about your unfortunate error.

7. You may not _____**relish**_____ being told that your carelessness was responsible for the accident, even though it happens to be true.

8. I love to listen to my grandfather _____**reminisce**_____ about his boyhood adventures in Coney Island.

9. We had to _____**scour**_____ the walls for hours to get rid of the dirt and grease with which they were encrusted.

10. Many people were injured in the explosion, but luckily there was not a single _____**fatality**_____.

Encourage students to look for context clues. See page 7.

End Set B

Synonyms

*Choose the word or form of the word from this Unit that is the same or most nearly the same in meaning as the **boldface** word or expression in the phrase. Write that word on the line. Use a dictionary if necessary.*

1. **carry on** despite many setbacks _____ persevere
2. is certainly no time to **fib** _____ prevaricate
3. caught the **wrongdoer** in the act _____ culprit
4. a **tribute** to his good deeds _____ testimonial
5. not **permitted** to use her parent's car _____ authorized
6. **scrub** the kitchen floor _____ scour
7. **take pleasure in** eating good food _____ relish
8. **examine** the facts point by point _____ dissect
9. **recall thoughts** about their wedding day _____ reminisce
10. **utilize** all the money in the savings account _____ expend
11. upsetting to learn the **heartbreaking** details _____ pathetic
12. **submerge** the vegetables in cold water _____ immerse
13. **suppressed** the children's excitement with more homework _____ quashed
14. sent a **reminder** to the club members _____ memorandum
15. so **trusting** that he gave away too much personal information _____ gullible

Antonyms

*Choose the word or form of the word from this Unit that is most nearly opposite in meaning to the **boldface** word or expression in the phrase. Write that word on the line. Use a dictionary if necessary.*

1. an accident that resulted in a **minor injury** _____ fatality
2. **hurry** while walking home from school _____ dawdle
3. participating in **legal** activities _____ illicit
4. a snake that **lies still** _____ writhes
5. made **calming** remarks to the group _____ inflammatory

Writing: Words in Action

Answers to the prompt will vary.

Suppose you are in charge of an advertising campaign for a company that manufactures sunglasses. Your job is to write a television commercial that introduces a new line of shades and persuades viewers to purchase them. Use at least two details from the passage (pages 100–101) and three or more words from this Unit.

Vocabulary in Context

*Some of the words you have studied in this Unit appear in **boldface** type. Read the passage below, and then circle the letter of the correct answer for each word as it is used in context.*

Colorblindness happens when cells in the retina that allow the brain to perceive color are abnormal. The most common type of color vision deficiency is red-green colorblindness. This color vision deficiency makes it difficult to distinguish between red and green.

A glass scientist invented lenses that were originally intended to protect surgeons' eyes from lasers. These lenses were also designed to help surgeons distinguish between different human tissue in an effort to prevent a **fatality** during a surgical procedure. In 2002, while **writhing** and jumping during a game of flying disk, this scientist lent these glasses to a colorblind friend. While wearing the glasses, his friend could finally see the orange cones on the field. Years after this accidental discovery, glasses for the colorblind were officially born.

It would seem like these glasses would be beneficial for everyone. One vision scientist, however, has strong concerns about these colorblind glasses. He released a **memorandum** intended to **quash** interest in these glasses by arguing that they were not based in "solid science." This vision scientist also argued that this new company is taking advantage of people by making **illicit** claims that the glasses can cure colorblindness. The company behind the colorblind glasses responded to this **inflammatory** claim by stating that these glasses do not "cure" colorblindness in the same way that reading glasses don't cure farsightedness. They simply help 80 percent of colorblind people see colors that they couldn't see previously. Regardless of the debate, some colorblind people have experienced a sensation that others have taken for granted since birth: seeing the world in color.

---

1. What is the meaning of **fatality** as it is used in paragraph 2?
   a. casualty   c. injury
   b. accident   d. judgment

2. In paragraph 2, what does **writhing** suggest about the way the scientist moved?
   a. He was spinning.   c. He was kicking.
   b. He was posing.   d. He was twisting.

3. Which word means the same as **memorandum** as it is used in paragraph 3?
   a. invitation   c. speech
   b. article   d. note

4. **Quash** comes from the Latin word **quassare**. **Quassare** most likely means
   a. to leave   c. to crush
   b. to disagree   d. to lament

5. Which word means the same as **illicit** as it is used in paragraph 3?
   a. improper   c. undisputed
   b. exclusive   d. factual

6. The word **inflammatory** means about the same as
   a. causing fear   c. causing worry
   b. causing anger   d. causing sadness

UNIT 8

Note that not all of the Unit words are used in this passage. *Cascade, immobile, impassable, martial,* and *perishable* are used in the passage on page 123.

*Read the following passage, taking note of the **boldface** words and their contexts. These words are among those you will be studying in Unit 8. It may help you to complete the exercises in this Unit if you refer to the way the words are used below.*

From Big Dream to Big Top
<Interview>

This month, Teen Talk Magazine *interviews Mike Quintus Bessy, an aerialist with the Empire Circus. Mike tells TT about the history of the circus, his job, and circus life.*

Editor's Note: Englishman Philip Astley (1742–1814) is one of the most important figures in circus history. He was a skilled equestrian who opened a popular riding school and performing arena, and then became a circus impresario when he built Astley's Amphitheatre in London in 1770. Astley worked hard, took risks, gained money and **affluence**, and was living proof that there is no luck except when there is discipline.

TT: Mike, many circus performers are born into a family of performers, but your parents are dentists. What made you want to join the circus?

Mike Q. Bessy: When I was quite young, I read a book about Philip Astley. I was fascinated and started taking tumbling classes. Astley is known as the father of the modern circus because his circus is the **template** for the circuses we see today.

TT: How did Astley go about founding a circus?

MQB: From the **onset**, Astley had a passion for horses. He enlisted in a cavalry regiment and then took up performing. One of his specialties was to **retrieve** a handkerchief from the ground while his horse cantered. He could maintain his balance better if his horse traveled in circles, so that's why he had a ring for his circus. Back then, animals and trick riders were the stars, and Astley's circus supposedly featured a horse that could perform card tricks and a pig that could solve math problems. I would pay to see that!

TT: What was a typical show like back in Astley's time?

MQB: Astley staged massive spectacles featuring a **minimum** of 100 horses and riders.

Philip Astley was one of the great showmen of his time.

There would also be fireworks, music, magicians, tightrope walkers, clowns, performing dogs… you name it! Well, except for wild-animal acts—that **innovation** came later. There was a stage, a circular pit, and audience galleries. There was no **partition** between the stage and the arena, so the shows were held simultaneously. The amphitheatre was rebuilt a number of times after fires, and it was eventually demolished in the 1890s because bad decisions and bad luck left the owner in **arrears**. Meanwhile, Astley retired from performing when he was still in his 30s, but he was often the ringmaster, dressed in his customary military costume.

Astley's Amphitheatre was home to the first true modern circus.

TT: The story goes that although Astley was charming, he also had a quick temper. I guess even circus folk aren't always happy-go-lucky.

MQB: It's a mistake to assume that circus performers are happy and **jovial** 100 percent of the time. We're all **crotchety** sometimes—even clowns!

TT: Besides a taste for adventure, what makes a good aerialist?

MQB: You have to have a strong, **taut** body, and you must be alert, quick, and **nimble** to fly through the air and catch your partners.

TT: Do you feel as if the circus is your home?

MQB: I do, although I know some people don't care for circuses. They think the atmosphere is a little creepy and **sinister**, or they're uncomfortable with crowds, or they harbor an image of elephants in **manacles** and chains. It makes me **cringe** to hear that animals are abused. I believe most circuses treat their animals with kindness and respect, the same way Philip Astley cared for his beloved horses.

Audio

For iWords and audio passages, go to SadlierConnect.com.

Definitions

Note the spelling, pronunciation, part(s) of speech, and definition(s) of each of the following words. Then write the appropriate form of the word in the blank space in the illustrative sentence(s) following.

1. arrears
(ə rērz')

(*n., pl.*) unpaid or overdue debts; an unfinished duty
Bad spending habits and unexpected expenses left my aunt in _____**arrears**_____.

2. cascade
(kas kād')

(*n.*) a steep, narrow waterfall; something falling or rushing forth in quantity; (*v.*) to flow downward (like a waterfall)
We were thrilled when we hit the jackpot, which produced a _____**cascade**_____ of loudly jangling coins.
I watched the clear, sparkling water _____**cascade**_____ down the mountainside.

3. crotchety
(kräch' ə tē)

(*adj.*) cranky, ill-tempered; full of odd whims
It is unfortunate that the teacher asked me to work with the most _____**crotchety**_____ partner in the class.

4. impassable
(im pas' ə bəl)

(*adj.*) blocked so that nothing can go through
Fallen trees formed an _____**impassable**_____ barrier across the highway after the storm.

5. manacle
(man' ə kəl)

(*n., usually pl.*) a handcuff, anything that chains or confines; (*v.*) to chain or restrain (as with handcuffs)
The kidnappers clamped _____**manacles**_____ on their frightened hostages.
The guards _____**manacled**_____ the uncooperative prisoner to the chair.

6. martial
(mär' shəl)

(*adj.*) warlike, fond of fighting; relating to war, the army, or military life
The army band plays _____**martial**_____ music as the troops formally march past the visiting general.

7. partition
(pär tish' ən)

(*n.*) something that divides (such as a wall); the act of dividing something into parts or sections; (*v.*) to divide or subdivide into parts or shares
A cloth _____**partition**_____ in the study gave each of us some privacy.
If you like, we can easily _____**partition**_____ the backyard into four separate play areas.

Synonyms and antonyms are provided at SadlierConnect.com.

8. **perishable**
(per' ə shə bəl)

(*adj.*) likely to spoil or decay
You must keep _____**perishable**_____ foods chilled, or they will spoil.

9. **sinister**
(sin' ə stər)

(*adj.*) appearing evil or dangerous; threatening evil or harm
A _____**sinister**_____ message left on our voicemail made us suspect the caller had the wrong number.

10. **taut**
(tôt)

(*adj.*) tightly drawn, tense; neat, in good order
The _____**taut**_____ chain kept the dog in the yard.

Using Context

*For each item, determine whether the **boldface** word from pages 114–115 makes sense in the context of the sentence. Circle the item numbers next to the six sentences in which the words are used correctly.*

1. Many **martial** animals can be found in the desert; they rest during the day to escape the heat and become active at night when the temperature drops.

2. In many comedy shows, a **crotchety** boss causes difficulties in the main character's life.

3. You will find that this apple has an interesting taste; it is sweet and **taut** at the same time.

4. The king ordered the guards to remove the prisoner's **manacles** and release him.

5. Does a diamond **cascade** more brightly than any other kind of gem?

6. The new owner will **partition** the large piece of land into twelve different lots and build a house on each one.

7. Farming can be an unpredictable business; one year you might find yourself in **arrears**, while the next year you might make a good profit.

8. Mozart's **perishable** talent became evident when he began composing music at age five.

9. If you want to play the villain in this skit, you will have to develop and practice a **sinister** laugh.

10. Two hours after the blizzard had ended, some of the city's streets had been plowed, but most were completely **impassable**.

Choosing the Right Word

*Select the **boldface** word that better completes each sentence. You might refer to the passage on pages 112–113 to see how most of these words are used in context. Note that the choices might be related forms of the Unit words.*

1. We learned in our history class that the ancient Romans were very fine soldiers and excelled in all the (**martial, perishable**) arts.

2. This facial cream claims that it will help keep your skin (**taut, impassable**) and youthful.

3. The first thing the bankrupt firm must do with its funds is pay the (**arrears, manacles**) due on the employees' wages.

4. Normally, I'm very even tempered, but I can become a little (**martial, crotchety**) when I'm tired or hungry.

5. I felt that there was something thoroughly (**sinister, taut**) about the way he kept trying to duck questions on that subject.

6. More than once, our skillful running backs managed to find a way through our opponents' supposedly (**impassable, sinister**) line.

7. In the eighteenth century, Russia, Prussia, and Austria made a series of deals to (**partition, manacle**) and annex Poland right out of existence.

8. In the moment of danger, my nerves were so (**taut, sinister**) that I would have screamed if someone had touched me.

9. Of all the different types of writing, humor may be the most (**perishable, martial**), since each generation has its own idea of what is funny.

10. Instead of acting as though you were permanently (**manacled, cascaded**) to your small circle of friends, you should try to meet new people.

11. Her blond hair fell upon her shoulders like a shimmering (**partition, cascade**) of gold.

12. In Charles Dickens's well-loved novel, Mr. Scrooge is introduced as a (**martial, crotchety**) character, but he becomes happy and merry by the end of the story.

You may wish to provide students with an explanation and example of a related form.

Completing the Sentence

Choose the word from the word bank that best completes each of the following sentences. Write the correct word or form of the word in the space provided.

arrears	crotchety	manacle	partition	sinister
cascade	impassable	martial	perishable	taut

1. I know that my payments on the car are in _____**arrears**_____, but I will catch up as soon as I get my next paycheck.

2. During the war years, the government tried all kinds of propaganda to arouse the _____**martial**_____ spirit of the people.

3. Today _____**perishable**_____ foods are transported in refrigerated trucks to prevent spoilage.

4. We made use of a(n) _____**partition**_____ to break up the floor space into a large number of small offices.

5. Unless you pull the ropes _____**taut**_____, the tennis net will sag.

6. All roads throughout the area became _____**impassable**_____ as a result of the record-breaking snowstorm.

7. The sunlight caught the waters of the stream as they _____**cascaded**_____ over the steep cliff and formed a brilliant rainbow.

8. Sherlock Holmes detected in the wicked scheme the _____**sinister**_____ hand of the evil Professor Moriarty.

9. Although we are sure that the prisoners will make no attempt to escape, the law requires us to place _____**manacles**_____ on them.

10. The more we tried to humor the _____**crotchety**_____ crossing guard, the more irritable and demanding he seemed to become.

Encourage students to look for context clues. See page 7.

Definitions

Note the spelling, pronunciation, part(s) of speech, and definition(s) of each of the following words. Then write the appropriate form of the word in the blank space in the illustrative sentence(s) following.

1. **affluence**
   (af′ lü əns)

   (*n.*) wealth, riches, prosperity; great abundance, plenty
   Education, hard work, and a very strong desire to succeed can raise a person from poverty to _____**affluence**_____.

2. **cringe**
   (krinj)

   (*v.*) to shrink back or hide in fear or submissiveness
   My father told me to be brave and not to _____**cringe**_____ when the doctor vaccinated me.

3. **immobile**
   (i mō′ bəl)

   (*adj.*) not movable; not moving
   Models must remain _____**immobile**_____ for a long time in order for an artist to draw or paint them accurately.

4. **innovation**
   (i nō vā′ shən)

   (*n.*) something new, a change; the act of introducing a new method, idea, device, etc.
   Our furnace has an energy-saving _____**innovation**_____ that turns the heat on and off at certain intervals.

5. **jovial**
   (jō′ vē əl)

   (*adj.*) good-humored, in high spirits; merry
   My _____**jovial**_____ friend is very entertaining and is always the life of the party.

6. **minimum**
   (min′ ə məm)

   (*n.*) the smallest possible amount; (*adj.*) the lowest permissible or possible
   I need to sleep a _____**minimum**_____ of seven hours every night.
   The _____**minimum**_____ age to get a driver's license in this state is sixteen.

7. **nimble**
   (nim′ bəl)

   (*adj.*) quick and skillful in movement, agile; clever
   As the _____**nimble**_____ climber scaled Mount Everest, it looked as if she was barely exerting any energy at all.

8. **onset**
   (än′ set)

   (*n.*) the beginning, start (especially of something violent and destructive); an attack, assault
   At the _____**onset**_____ of the heavy storm, frightened people ran to find shelter.

Practice with synonyms and antonyms is on page 122.

9. retrieve
(ri trēv')

(v.) to find and bring back, get back; to put right, make good
I don't relish having to _____retrieve_____ the tennis balls every time you hit them over the fence!

10. template
(tem' plit)

(n.) a pattern, typically in the form of metal, wood, or plastic; something that is used as a model to imitate
The carpenter created a wooden _____template_____ for a stair step so that he could easily construct the staircase.

Using Context

*For each item, determine whether the **boldface** word from pages 118–119 makes sense in the context of the sentence. Circle the item numbers next to the six sentences in which the words are used correctly.*

(1.) Even though my grandfather is in his late 80s, he welcomes every new **innovation** in technology and actively tries to learn how to use it.

2. When meeting new people, I try to project a sense of **affluence** and comfort with myself, but on the inside I'm extremely nervous.

3. The **jovial** music coming from the orchestra suggested that something bad was about to happen in the play.

(4.) When I tried to pay for my $7 purchase with a credit card, the cashier directed me to a sign that said the **minimum** credit card purchase was $20.

(5.) The career counselor helped the job candidate to fill in the résumé **template** with her specific employment information.

(6.) I tried to **retrieve** the tiny gem that had fallen between the seats of the car, but unfortunately, I was unable to locate it.

(7.) The doctor advised the athlete that his injury would heal more quickly if he kept his leg mostly **immobile**—only moving it when absolutely necessary.

8. After a day walking around in ill-fitting shoes, I was so **nimble** that I could barely set one foot in front of the other.

(9.) You should really prepare for a snowstorm before it hits, rather than at its **onset**.

10. I saw her **cringe** as she checked her messages and figured she must have received a funny message from someone.

Choosing the Right Word

*Select the **boldface** word that better completes each sentence. You might refer to the passage on pages 112–113 to see how most of these words are used in context. Note that the choices might be related forms of the Unit words.*

1. Robin Hood's faithful merry men were not only (**immobile, jovial**) companions, but brave and clever fighters as well.

2. The self-styled "tough guy" (**cringed, retrieved**) in terror and begged the police not to shoot.

3. The speed with which the boxer darted about the ring made his lumbering opponent seem utterly (**nimble, immobile**) by comparison.

4. To keep a (**nimble, jovial**) mind, doctors advise working on crossword puzzles or learning a foreign language.

5. Everyone in the auditorium (**retrieved, cringed**) when the singer hit a sour note while performing his most famous song.

6. Thanks to my brother's (**templates, innovations**) to a classic recipe, we won first prize at the fair for best hot sauce.

7. Some hikers are surprised when they get a poison ivy rash, as its (**cringe, onset**) can sometimes be several days after the encounter with the vine.

8. Despite all his efforts, he was never able to (**retrieve, cringe**) the fine reputation he had lost by that crooked deal.

9. Did you know that most computer software provides several different (**templates, onsets**) for letter writing?

10. Although we all recognize that there must be changes, it is a mistake to think that every (**template, innovation**) is necessarily an improvement.

11. A high school student looking for a vacation job usually can't expect to earn more than the (**immobile, minimum**) wage.

12. Although we are proud of our high standard of living, we should not forget that there are those who do not share in this (**affluence, minimum**).

You may wish to provide students with an explanation and example of a related form.

Completing the Sentence

Choose the word from the word bank that best completes each of the following sentences. Write the correct word or form of the word in the space provided.

affluence	immobile	jovial	nimble	retrieve
cringe	innovation	minimum	onset	template

1. I was able to _____**retrieve**_____ my baggage promptly after leaving the plane.

2. I don't expect you to be a hero, but do you have to _____**cringe**_____ in that cowardly fashion whenever anyone so much as disagrees with you?

3. We plan to update the _____**template**_____ of our school brochure to make it more attractive and readable.

4. The patients will have a much better chance to recover quickly if they receive treatment at the _____**onset**_____ of the fever.

5. His back injury was so severe that he has been placed in a cast and will have to remain _____**immobile**_____ for months.

6. The feeling of _____**affluence**_____ I had when I was paid lasted only until I had finished taking care of my bills.

7. The _____**jovial**_____ mood of our cheerful little gathering changed abruptly to sorrow when news of the tragedy came over the radio.

8. Frank Lloyd Wright was a great American architect who was responsible for many _____**innovations**_____ in the design of buildings.

9. It's a pleasure to watch the expert typist's _____**nimble**_____ fingers move swiftly over the keyboard.

10. Can you explain why there is not only a maximum speed limit but also a(n) _____**minimum**_____ speed limit on many modern highways?

Encourage students to look for context clues. See page 7.

End Set B

Synonyms

*Choose the word or form of the word from this Unit that is the same or most nearly the same in meaning as the **boldface** word or expression in the phrase. Write that word on the line. Use a dictionary if necessary.*

1. a **menacing** look in his eyes — sinister
2. begged not to be **shackled** — manacled
3. worked overtime to pay off loans **in default** — (in) arrears
4. fruit and vegetables that are **likely to spoil** — perishable
5. resisting the latest **modernization** — innovation
6. huge mansions that are a sign of **wealth** — affluence
7. in a **grouchy** mood — crotchety
8. **divide** the pie into 8 pieces — partition
9. packed up before the **outset** of the long hike — onset
10. under strict **military** law — martial
11. made a cabinet based on the **mock-up** — template
12. **cowered** when the storm approached — cringed
13. as confetti **spilled** onto the stage — cascaded
14. **recover** data from my computer — retrieve
15. installed to make it remain **stationary** — immobile

Antonyms

*Choose the word or form of the word from this Unit that is most nearly opposite in meaning to the **boldface** word or expression in the phrase. Write that word on the line. Use a dictionary if necessary.*

1. happen to be in an **unblocked** lane — impassable
2. the **maximum** height for a desk — minimum
3. a **morose** expression on her face — jovial
4. pulled at the **loose** rope — taut
5. had **clumsy** hand movements — nimble

Writing: Words in Action

Answers to the prompt will vary.

Some people believe that animals should not be trained to perform in circuses. Others believe that circus animals' amazing feats show how intelligent they are. Write a brief essay stating your position on this topic. Use examples from your reading (pages 112–113) and personal experience. Use three or more words from this Unit.

Vocabulary in Context

*Some of the words you have studied in this Unit appear in **boldface** type. Read the passage below, and then circle the letter of the correct answer for each word as it is used in context*

On October 12, 1779, James Boswell suggested to his friend Samuel Johnson that the pair of them should travel to Ireland. Johnson declined, remarking that he saw no sense in going to all the trouble of traveling from one country to another, where they would lack the comforts and conveniences of home.

Johnson's obstinacy could be an **impassable** obstacle. Boswell, however, was determined. He tried to interest his **crotchety** friend in the natural beauties of the country. Boswell remembered how impressed he had been himself by the spectacular volcanic landscapes of the northeast coast. In particular, he regarded the Giant's Causeway as a source of endless wonder rather than a **perishable** thrill. This unique rock formation was formed fifty or sixty million years ago, in the aftermath of an enormous volcanic eruption. A large area of the coast was buried under a deep layer of molten lava that extended far out to sea. Rapid cooling caused the lava to contract as it solidified into 173 acres of interlocking hexagonal columns, some as high as forty feet. They have a **martial** air as they stand, proud and **immobile**, before they **cascade** into the Irish Sea.

"Is not the Giant's Causeway worth seeing?" Boswell asked.

"Worth seeing?" Johnson replied. "Yes. But not worth going to see."

To bring sights to those who, like Johnson, were reluctant or unable to travel was the goal of all early circuses. Circus trains traveled the country so that ordinary citizens could see lions, elephants, and international entertainment, all without leaving the comfort of their hometown.

---

1. What is the meaning of **impassable** as it is used in paragraph 2?
   a. weighty
   b. colossal
   c. unmanageable
   d. unpleasant

2. In paragraph 2, what does the use of the word **crotchety** suggest about Johnson?
   a. He was irrational.
   b. He was selfish.
   c. He was stubborn.
   d. He was cranky.

3. The word **perishable** means about the same as
   a. worthless
   b. short-lived
   c. immortal
   d. cheap

4. **Martial** comes from the Latin proper noun **Mars. Mars** is most likely
   a. the Roman god of war
   b. the red planet
   c. a sacred mountain
   d. the Roman god of thought

5. Which word means the same as **immobile** as it is used in paragraph 2?
   a. fearless
   b. commanding
   c. still
   d. distinct

6. What does the word **cascade** most likely mean as it is used in paragraph 2?
   a. dive
   b. march
   c. parade
   d. plunge

Note that not all of the Unit words are used in this passage. *Discretion, misrepresent, optional, rendezvous,* and *rotund* are used in the passage on page 135.

*Read the following passage, taking note of the **boldface** words and their contexts. These words are among those you will be studying in Unit 9. It may help you to complete the exercises in this Unit if you refer to the way the words are used below.*

From Fire Arrows to Space Flight: A History of Rockets
<Informational Essay>

As early as 400 BCE, **logical** and observant inventors in Greece used steam to propel simple devices. A man named Archytas used steam to send a wooden pigeon gliding along high wires. These early steam-propelled devices were of little practical use. They were mainly used for entertainment. Over a thousand years later and thousands of miles away from Greece, Chinese alchemists learned to make gunpowder. By around 1100 CE, the Chinese were using gunpowder to make fireworks, which were used for celebrations. Simple grenade-like bombs were used in war. Before long, the Chinese learned to use gunpowder to propel "fire arrows" through the air. The same basic principle of propulsion was at work in Archytas's **giddy** pigeon and in Chinese fire arrows. But the special properties of gunpowder made the fire arrows useful tools of war.

In 1232, Chinese soldiers used fire arrows to defeat Mongol invaders at the Battle of Kai-Keng. This is the first known use of rockets in the history of warfare. To make these simple rockets, the Chinese filled a short bamboo tube with gunpowder. They capped one end of the tube. Then they attached it to an arrow. Then the gunpowder was ignited. It produced fire, smoke, and gas that escaped through the open end of the tube. This force propelled the rocket through the air. The arrow helped to keep the rocket steady during flight, though its course remained quite **variable**. These earliest rockets may not always have done much damage on **impact**. But a **deluge** of many fire arrows could cause **outright** fear in the enemy. Gaining something in defeat, the Mongols learned to make similar rockets. The new technology spread rapidly across Asia and Europe. But improvements in the basic design proceeded slowly at a **sluggish** pace until more modern days.

By the **verge** of the industrial age, military rockets were becoming more effective weapons. In 1780, Hyder Ali of Mysore, a kingdom in India, used heavy, iron-cased rockets to defeat British forces. His son, Tipu Sultan, used the same rockets against the British with similar success. Mysorean rockets were not used merely to scare and **intimidate** the enemy. They were deadly weapons that cut down troops in their path.

Early Chinese fire arrow rockets, c. 1000

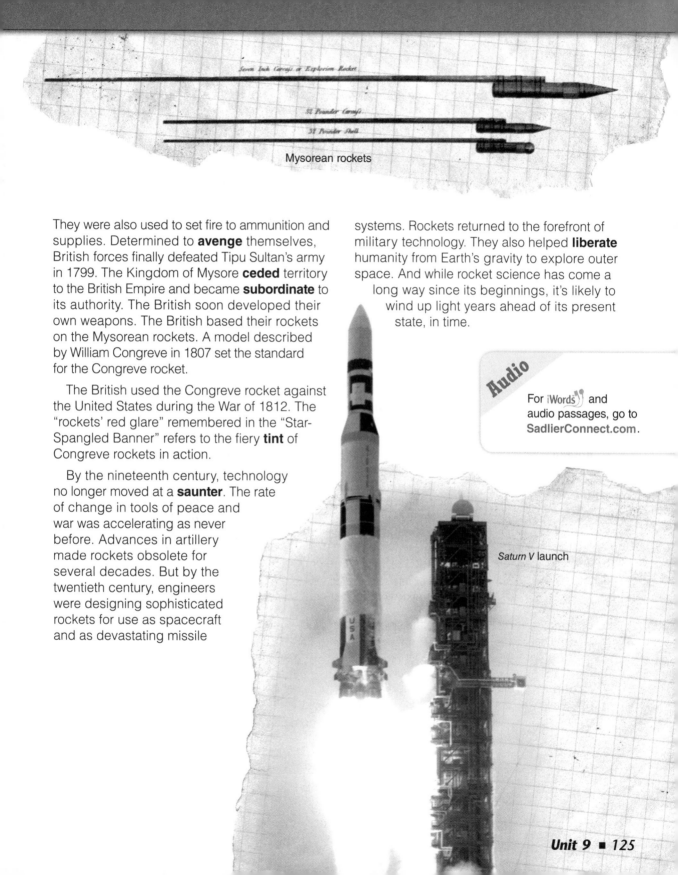

Mysorean rockets

They were also used to set fire to ammunition and supplies. Determined to **avenge** themselves, British forces finally defeated Tipu Sultan's army in 1799. The Kingdom of Mysore **ceded** territory to the British Empire and became **subordinate** to its authority. The British soon developed their own weapons. The British based their rockets on the Mysorean rockets. A model described by William Congreve in 1807 set the standard for the Congreve rocket.

The British used the Congreve rocket against the United States during the War of 1812. The "rockets' red glare" remembered in the "Star-Spangled Banner" refers to the fiery **tint** of Congreve rockets in action.

By the nineteenth century, technology no longer moved at a **saunter**. The rate of change in tools of peace and war was accelerating as never before. Advances in artillery made rockets obsolete for several decades. But by the twentieth century, engineers were designing sophisticated rockets for use as spacecraft and as devastating missile

systems. Rockets returned to the forefront of military technology. They also helped **liberate** humanity from Earth's gravity to explore outer space. And while rocket science has come a long way since its beginnings, it's likely to wind up light years ahead of its present state, in time.

Audio

For iWords and audio passages, go to SadlierConnect.com.

Saturn V launch

Definitions

Note the spelling, pronunciation, part(s) of speech, and definition(s) of each of the following words. Then write the appropriate form of the word in the blank space in the illustrative sentence(s) following.

1. avenge
(ə venj′)

(*v.*) to get revenge for, get even for, settle a score; to punish someone or get satisfaction for a wrong or injury

In Shakespeare's *Hamlet*, the title character vows to _____**avenge**_____ his father's death.

2. deluge
(del′ yüj)

(*n.*) a great flood; a heavy fall of rain; anything that comes in a vast quantity (like a flood); (*v.*) to flood

Owners are hoping this summer will bring a _____**deluge**_____ of visitors to their new theme park in Minneapolis.

A torrential downpour _____**deluged**_____ the entire town.

3. giddy
(gid′ ē)

(*adj.*) dizzy; light-headed; lacking seriousness

After the long and grueling race, the marathoner felt _____**giddy**_____ and exhausted.

4. impact
(*n.*, im′ pakt;
v., im pakt′)

(*n.*) the striking of one object against another; the shock caused by a collision; (*v.*) to affect, especially forcefully

The _____**impact**_____ of the car crash destroyed both vehicles, but miraculously no one was hurt.

Budget cuts will _____**impact**_____ the number of hours the public library can stay open.

5. liberate
(lib′ ə rāt)

(*v.*) to free from bondage or domination; to release

The police _____**liberated**_____ the anxious hostages after sixteen hours of confinement.

6. optional
(äp′ shə nəl)

(*adj.*) left to one's own choice; not required

The hotel will charge us for breakfast and dinner, but lunch is _____**optional**_____.

7. rotund
(rō tənd′)

(*adj.*) rounded and plump; full or rich in sound

My friends like to display the largest and most _____**rotund**_____ pumpkin outside their front door.

8. saunter
(sôn′ tər)

(*v.*) to stroll; walk in an easy, leisurely way; (*n.*) a stroll

The star _____**sauntered**_____ past his adoring fans.

It's such a beautiful day to take a _____**saunter**_____.

Synonyms and antonyms are provided at SadlierConnect.com.

9. subordinate
(adj., n.,
sə bôr′ də nət;
v., sə bôr′ də nāt)

(adj.) lower in rank or position, secondary; (n.) one who is in a lower position or under the orders of someone else; (v.) to put in a lower or secondary position

A corporal is ____subordinate____ to a sergeant.

Let's ask a ____subordinate____ to help us file.

Parents often ____subordinate____ their own wishes for the sake of their children's needs.

10. verge
(vərj)

(n.) the point at which something begins or happens; a border; (v.) to incline, tend toward, approach; to be in the process of becoming something else

I was on the ____verge____ of tears today.

That chatter ____verges____ on baby talk.

Using Context

*For each item, determine whether the **boldface** word from pages 126–127 makes sense in the context of the sentence. Circle the item numbers next to the six sentences in which the words are used correctly.*

1. During their yearly migration, giant herds of zebra and wildebeest **verge** across the grasslands.

(2.) The children were in such a **giddy** mood that they refused to take anything that the babysitter said seriously.

(3.) The frustrated colonists increasingly felt the need to **liberate** themselves from English rule.

(4.) Is our attendance at the annual association meeting in New York City required, or is it **optional**?

(5.) Most residents feel that the construction of the high-rise apartment building will have a positive **impact** on the neighborhood.

6. No light reaches the most **rotund** part of the ocean; it is completely dark there.

(7.) The new supervisor was not pleased to witness the casual way in which some employees would **saunter** into the office nearly twenty minutes late for work.

8. Winning a gold medal is the **subordinate** goal of every Olympic athlete.

9. When you write an essay or a report, you must be sure to **avenge** any details that are not directly related to your topic.

(10.) As soon as the hugely popular singer announced her new concert schedule, a **deluge** of fans tried to buy tickets online.

Choosing the Right Word

*Select the **boldface** word that better completes each sentence. You might refer to the passage on pages 124–125 to see how most of these words are used in context. Note that the choices might be related forms of the Unit words.*

1. In times of crisis, we may be called on to (**deluge, subordinate**) our personal interests to the needs of the nation as a whole.

2. The invitation to the party said that formal wear was (**optional, giddy**).

3. If you know that you are late for school, why do you (**saunter, liberate**) along as though you had all the time in the world?

4. It is shocking to see how, in just a few years, the lean young athlete has allowed himself to become flabby and (**giddy, rotund**).

5. It is good for you to "stand up for your rights," but you should not do so in a way that (**verges, subordinates**) on discourtesy.

6. We had regarded her as a rather (**subordinate, giddy**) young girl, but in this tough situation she showed that she had courage and good sense.

7. Wasn't it annoying to see Michael (**verge, saunter**) into the party as though he were the coolest person ever to walk the face of the earth?

8. Modern household appliances have done much to (**liberate, deluge**) homemakers from tedious and time-consuming chores.

9. I plan to write a term paper that will discuss the different ways in which commercial television has had a major (**impact, verge**) on American life for more than sixty years.

10. Though once her peer, I became Caitlin's (**impact, subordinate**) when she was promoted to company president.

11. Many Western films include a character who is out to (**saunter, avenge**) a wrong done to a close friend or relative.

12. Letters of protest (**deluged, verged**) the Mayor's office when he proposed an increase in the sales tax.

You may wish to provide students with an explanation and example of a related form.

Completing the Sentence

Choose the word from the word bank that best completes each of the following sentences. Write the correct word or form of the word in the space provided.

avenge	giddy	liberate	rotund	subordinate
deluge	impact	optional	saunter	verge

1. We believe that the world is now on the _____ **verge** _____ of new and exciting developments that may dramatically change the way we live.

2. As a young and inexperienced employee, you cannot expect to hold more than a(n) _____ **subordinate** _____ job in that big company.

3. Every eye was on us as we _____ **sauntered** _____ down Main Street in our new outfits.

4. Many people say that they become quite _____ **giddy** _____ when they look down from the top of a tall building.

5. According to the eyewitness, the great _____ **deluge** _____ that arrived after the hurricane caused more damage than the winds.

6. By not ordering _____ **optional** _____ features, we can hold down the cost of the new car we want to buy.

7. Many older residents of Paris can still recall the day in 1944 when Allied troops _____ **liberated** _____ the city from German occupation.

8. Uncle Eddie, with his _____ **rotund** _____ figure, is often called on to play Santa Claus.

9. Even fans sitting high in the stands could hear the _____ **impact** _____ when the big fullback crashed into the line.

10. Next year, when we have a stronger, more experienced team, we hope to _____ **avenge** _____ the crushing defeat we have just suffered.

Encourage students to look for context clues. See page 7.

End Set A

Definitions

Note the spelling, pronunciation, part(s) of speech, and definition(s) of each of the following words. Then write the appropriate form of the word in the blank space in the illustrative sentence(s) following.

1. cede
(sēd)

(*v.*) to give up, surrender; to hand over to another
Spain _____ceded_____ territory to France.

2. discretion
(dis kresh' ən)

(*n.*) good judgment; care in speech and action; freedom to judge or choose
My teacher suggested I use _____discretion_____ in dealing with my difficult classmate.

3. intimidate
(in tim' ə dāt)

(*v.*) to make timid or frighten by threats; to use fear to get someone to do (or not to do) something
Bullies may try to _____intimidate_____ us, but if we act brave and stand tall, we can diminish their threats.

4. logical
(läj' ə kəl)

(*adj.*) reasonable; making use of reason and good sense
Our parents are constantly encouraging us to look for _____logical_____ solutions to our problems.

5. misrepresent
(mis rep ri zent')

(*v.*) to give a false or untrue idea
If witnesses _____misrepresent_____ the facts, the defense attorney has proof to support our story.

6. outright
(aùt'rīt)

(*adj.*) complete; instantaneous; without reservation, thoroughgoing; (*adv.*) completely, instantaneously
When the teacher asked her why she didn't do her homework, she told an _____outright_____ lie.
Even though they had already heard it several times, the hilarious joke made them laugh _____outright_____.

7. rendezvous
(rän' dā vü)

(*v.*) to meet in accordance with a plan; (*n.*) a meeting by agreement; a meeting place
Let's all agree to _____rendezvous_____ by the fountain on Saturday afternoon.
They kept their _____rendezvous_____ a secret.

8. sluggish
(sləg' ish)

(*adj.*) lazy; slow-moving; not active, dull
After a big lunch, I feel _____sluggish_____.

Practice with synonyms and antonyms is on page 134.

9. **tint**
   (tint)

(n.) a delicate color or hue; a slight trace of something;
(v.) to give color to something; to dye

He's painting his room a _____tint_____ of blue.

I want to _____tint_____ my sunglass lenses pink.

10. **variable**
    (vâr' ē ə bəl)

(adj.) likely to undergo change; changeable; (n.) a
value or quantity that varies; a symbol for such

Spring weather can be extremely _____variable_____.

In math, the letter x can stand for a _____variable_____.

Using Context

*For each item, determine whether the **boldface** word from pages 130–131 makes sense in the context of the sentence. Circle the item numbers next to the six sentences in which the words are used correctly.*

(1.) The size of the government building alone was enough to **intimidate** me, not to mention the high rank of the officials working inside of it.

(2.) Is your decision based on a **logical** assessment of the situation, or on your gut feelings about it?

(3.) The **tint** of pink in your cheeks suggests that the wind has picked up a bit.

(4.) The celebrity refused to give private interviews to reporters for fear that they would twist her words and **misrepresent** her character.

5. I plan to **cede** my favorite dress back from my sister before she gets a stain on it.

6. The rainfall was not particularly heavy, but the **sluggish** way in which the drops hit the roof was enough to remind me of its presence.

(7.) One of the guests at the event showed **outright** disrespect for the queen when he did not stand up as she entered the room.

8. The safest way to descend the steep hill into the valley is to maintain a slow and **variable** driving speed.

(9.) We agreed that we would individually research the subject and then **rendezvous** in the library later this afternoon to discuss what we find.

10. In the novel, the main character is hiding a **discretion**, and the reader must figure out what it is.

Choosing the Right Word

*Select the **boldface** word that better completes each sentence. You might refer to the passage on pages 124–125 to see how most of these words are used in context. Note that the choices might be related forms of the Unit words.*

1. I knew my dog was not feeling well when he suddenly became (**logical, sluggish**) and refused to get up.

2. At the State Fair, we separated to visit different exhibits, but we agreed to (**tint, rendezvous**) at the refreshment stand at five o'clock.

3. The aged millionaire, wishing to spend his last years in peace and quiet, (**ceded, intimidated**) all his business interests to his sons.

4. A fastball pitcher will often try to (**misrepresent, intimidate**) an opposing batter by "shaving" him with an inside pitch.

5. There are times in life when you should be guided more by your feelings, without trying to be strictly (**outright, logical**) about everything.

6. I look forward to the time when my parents will agree that I have reached the "age of (**discretion, misrepresentation**)."

7. Only the (**sluggish, outright**) repeal of this unfair nuisance tax will satisfy the voters.

8. This biased editorial has deliberately (**misrepresented, ceded**) the stand of our candidate on the important issues of the election.

9. Many people, unhappy with what nature has given them, seek to improve their appearance by (**tinting, ceding**) their hair.

10. We held a meeting to discuss why the sale of tickets to the class dance has been so (**sluggish, variable**) and what we can do about it.

11. It is up to the teacher's (**discretion, variable**) what topics can be chosen for our research papers.

12. He soon learned that the moods of a youngster—happy one moment, miserable the next—can be as (**variable, sluggish**) as the winds.

You may wish to provide students with an explanation and example of a related form.

Completing the Sentence

Choose the word from the word bank that best completes each of the following sentences. Write the correct word or form of the word in the space provided.

cede	intimidate	misrepresent	rendezvous	tint
discretion	logical	outright	sluggish	variable

1. Her argument was so _____**logical**_____ that she convinced us that her solution to the math problem was the correct one.

2. You may like to live where the sun shines all the time, but I prefer a more _____**variable**_____ climate.

3. By late September, the leaves on the trees in the woods have begun to take on their normal autumn _____**tint**_____.

4. Our "truth in advertising" laws are designed to discourage manufacturers from _____**misrepresenting**_____ the virtues of their products.

5. When they realized that sweet talk and flattery were getting them nowhere, they tried to _____**intimidate**_____ me into doing what they wanted.

6. The two groups of hikers, setting out from different points, have planned a(n) _____**rendezvous**_____ at four o'clock at Eagle Rock.

7. Because of the lawyer's long experience in legal matters, we left it to his _____**discretion**_____ how to proceed with the case.

8. After the heavy meal, we felt so _____**sluggish**_____ that we just sat in the living room and watched whatever was on television.

9. After being defeated in a war that lasted from 1846 to 1848, Mexico was forced to _____**cede**_____ vast territories to the United States.

10. The force of the head-on collision was so severe that the drivers of both vehicles were killed _____**outright**_____.

Encourage students to look for context clues. See page 7.

Synonyms

*Choose the word or form of the word from this Unit that is the same or most nearly the same in meaning as the **boldface** word or expression in the phrase. Write that word on the line. Use a dictionary if necessary.*

1. as if they had an **appointment** with danger _____ rendezvous
2. felt **woozy** from spinning in a circle _____ giddy
3. the **round** cauldron over the fire _____ rotund
4. the **effect** of the ruling on the community _____ impact
5. felt weak and **lethargic** _____ sluggish
6. need a **rational** explanation _____ logical
7. **stroll** through the lovely village _____ saunter
8. rejected her idea **utterly** _____ outright
9. the yellowish **hue** of the water _____ tint
10. on the **brink** of a new beginning _____ verge
11. **exaggerate** the truth _____ misrepresent
12. had to **yield** that point in the debate _____ cede
13. **retaliate for** the attack on the innocent _____ avenge
14. could **bully** us into giving in _____ intimidate
15. thankful for their **good judgment** _____ discretion

Antonyms

*Choose the word or form of the word from this Unit that is most nearly opposite in meaning to the **boldface** word or expression in the phrase. Write that word on the line. Use a dictionary if necessary.*

1. a reminder that attendance is **mandatory** _____ optional
2. **imprisoned** the rebels _____ liberated
3. **superior** to the others on the team _____ subordinate
4. a **steady** position on education policy _____ variable
5. information that came in a **trickle** _____ deluge

Writing: Words in Action

Answers to the prompt will vary.

Think about how Archytas's wooden pigeon in the passage (pages 124–125) led to the invention of rockets. Write a letter to Archytas in which you tell him some of the effects, or consequences, of his invention over the centuries. Use at least two details from the passage and three or more words from this Unit.

Vocabulary in Context

*Some of the words you have studied in this Unit appear in **boldface** type. Read the passage below, and then circle the letter of the correct answer for each word as it is used in context.*

Now that missions to Mars have become almost routine, it would be easy to **misrepresent** the challenges confronting Project Gemini in the 1960s. NASA designed Gemini as a response to President John F. Kennedy's goal of sending a man to the moon and back. Kennedy did not want the United States to **cede** leadership in space exploration to the Soviet Union. With Gemini's accomplishments, an American **rendezvous** with the moon was indeed achieved by the Apollo project in July 1969.

Gemini means "twins" in Latin. True to this name, each manned Gemini flight had a crew of two astronauts. There were ten manned missions in all. Each flight was launched by a Titan II rocket. The distinctive Gemini space capsule had a **rotund** base and tapered to a pointed tip. The project had three major objectives. First, NASA wanted to verify the endurance of the astronauts and their equipment for lengthy periods of spaceflight. A minimum of eight days would be needed for a flight to the moon and back. Secondly, the astronauts needed practice docking maneuvers with another vehicle. This operation was an essential component of a mission to the moon. Finally, the astronauts had to practice Extra-Vehicular Activity (EVA). With extreme **discretion,** they performed various tasks outside the protection of the spacecraft. The first astronaut to demonstrate this capability was Edwin "Buzz" Aldrin on Gemini 12.

The total cost of Project Gemini has been estimated to be $1.3 billion (in 1967 dollars). Some critics regarded the program as **optional,** but it fired up the public imagination.

---

1. What is the meaning of **misrepresent** as it is used in paragraph 1?
   a. exaggerate   **c.** conceal
   b. minimize   **d.** falsify

2. Cede comes from the Latin word **cedere. Cedere** most likely means
   a. to yield   **c.** to steal
   b. to praise   **d.** to inform

3. What is the meaning of **rendezvous** as it is used in paragraph 1?
   a. meeting   **c.** skirmish
   b. confrontation   **d.** salute

4. The word **rotund** means about the same as
   a. bloated   **c.** plump
   b. awkward   **d.** agile

5. Which word means the same as **discretion** as it is used in paragraph 2?
   a. negligence   **c.** bravado
   b. courage   **d.** prudence

6. What does the word **optional** most likely mean as it is used in paragraph 3?
   a. mandatory   **c.** not required
   b. temporary   **d.** elaborate

See pages T29–T31 for assessment options.

Vocabulary for Comprehension
Part 1

*Read "Two Friends," which contains words in **boldface** that appear in Units 7–9. Then answer the questions.*

Two Friends
by Guy de Maupassant

Besieged Paris was in the throes of famine. Its days of **affluence** had passed, and everyone had to subsist with the **minimum** amount possible. Even the

(5) sparrows on the roofs and the rats in the sewers were growing scarce. People were eating anything they could get.

Monsieur Morissot, watchmaker by profession with a tendency to **dawdle**, was

(10) sauntering along the boulevard one bright January morning. Hands in his trousers pockets and stomach empty, he suddenly came face-to-face with an acquaintance— Monsieur Sauvage, a fishing chum.

(15) Before the war it was Morissot's habit, every Sunday morning, of setting forth with a bamboo rod in his hand and a tin box on his back. He took the Argenteuil train, got out at Colombes, and walked

(20) thence to the Ile Marante. The moment he arrived he began fishing.

Every Sunday he met in this very spot Monsieur Sauvage, a stout, **jovial** man, a draper in the Rue Notre Dame de Lorette,

(25) and an ardent fisherman. They often spent half the day side by side, rod in hand and feet dangling over the water, and a warm friendship had sprung up between them.

Some days they did not speak. At other

(30) times they were immersed in conversation. Never an inflammatory word passed between them. They understood each other perfectly without the aid of words, having similar tastes and feelings.

(35) In the spring, when the early sun caused a light mist to float on the water

and gently warmed the backs of the two anglers, Morissot would remark:
"My, but it's pleasant here."

(40) To which the other would reply:
"I can't imagine anything better!"
These few words sufficed to make them understand and appreciate each other.
In the **variable** autumn weather, toward

(45) day's end, the sunset shed a blood-red glow over the sky. The reflection of the crimson clouds **tinted** the river red, brought a glow to the faces of the two friends. As the sun gilded the trees,

(50) whose leaves were turning at the first touch of winter, Monsieur Sauvage would sometimes smile and say:
"What a glorious spectacle!"
And Morissot would answer, without

(55) taking his eyes from his float:
"Isn't this better than the boulevard?"
On this day, as soon as they recognized each other they shook hands cordially, affected at the thought of meeting

(60) under such changed circumstances.
Monsieur Sauvage murmured:
"These are sad times!"
Morissot shook his head mournfully.
"And such weather! This is the first

(65) fine day of the year."
The sky was of a bright, cloudless blue. They reminisced as they walked along, side by side, reflective and sad.
"And to think of the fishing!" said

(70) Morissot. "What good times we had!"

From "Two Friends" by Guy de Maupassant—Public Domain

1. What is the author's purpose in the first paragraph (lines 1–7)?
A) to describe Paris
B) to compare past and present Paris life
C) to reveal the awful economic situation
D) to show the residents' resourcefulness

2. What does the word **affluence** mean as it is used in line 2?
A) wealth
B) newness
C) history
D) dominance

3. Which word means the opposite of **minimum** as it is used in line 4?
A) melancholy
B) pessimism
C) realism
D) maximum

4. What does the word **dawdle** most likely mean as it is used in line 9?
A) delay
B) reflect
C) argue
D) rush

5. What does the word **jovial** in line 23 **most likely** suggest about Monsieur Sauvage?
A) He is competitive.
B) He is young.
C) He is merry.
D) He is formal.

6. According to the passage, what is **variable** (line 44) weather?
A) mild weather
B) changing weather
C) colorful weather
D) harsh weather

7. As it is used in line 47, what does the word **tinted** mean?
A) polluted
B) cooled
C) created
D) colored

8. Part A
How has the relationship between Monsieur Sauvage and Monsieur Morissot evolved over time?
A) The friends are unable to communicate with each other.
B) The war altered their friendship.
C) An argument destroyed their friendship.
D) The friends have become closer over the years.

Part B
Which choice provides the **best** evidence for the answer to the previous question?
A) "he met in this very spot Monsieur Sauvage" (lines 22–23)
B) "a warm friendship had sprung up between them" (lines 27–28)
C) "brought a glow to the faces of the two friends" (lines 47–48)
D) "meeting under such changed circumstances" (lines 59–60)

9. Why is the memory of the fishing experiences important to the two friends?
A) It calls to mind a happier time before the war.
B) They recall their financial struggles before they became wealthy.
C) They recall a time when they were rivals.
D) They remember the day they first met.

10. Which sentence **best** states what the passage is about?
A) A man reflects on a warm friendship that existed before the war began and then unexpectedly meets the old friend.
B) Difficult circumstances forge a stronger friendship between two men, who have much to discuss when they meet by their old fishing hole.
C) Two friends share an unbreakable bond of friendship after the war.
D) While on fishing trips, two men daydream about pre-war life in Paris.

Vocabulary for Comprehension
Part 2

*Read this passage, which contains words in **boldface** that appear in Units 7–9. Then choose the best answer to each question based on what is stated or implied in the passage. You may refer to the passage as often as necessary.*

Questions 1–10 are based on the following passage.

This passage is adapted from Alice Dunbar Nelson, "The Fisherman of Pass Christian." Published in 1899.

You've never been for a hay-ride and fish-fry on the shores of the Mississippi Sound, have you? When the summer boarders and the Northern visitors

(5) undertake to give one, it is a dull affair. During those times, due regard is had for one's clothes, and there are servants to **expend** energy on the hardest work. Then it isn't enjoyable at all. But sometimes

(10) the boys and girls who live there make up their minds to have fun. Then you may depend upon its being just the best kind.

This time there were twenty boys and girls, a mamma or so, several papas,

(15) and a grizzled fisherman to quash any **inflammatory** behavior. The cart was vast and solid, and two comfortable, sleepy-looking mules to pull it. There were also tin horns, some guitars, an accordion,

(20) and a quartet of much praised voices. The hay in the bottom of the wagon was freely mixed with pine needles, whose prickiness through your hose was compensated for by its delicious

(25) fragrance.

After a triumphantly noisy passage down the beach one comes to the almost **impassable** stretch of heavy sand that lies between Pass Christian proper and

(30) Henderson's Point. This is a hard pull for the mules, and the more ambitious riders

get out and walk. Then, after a final strain through the shifting sands, bravo! The shell road is reached, and one goes

(35) cheering through the pine-trees to Henderson's Point.

If ever you go to Pass Christian, you must have a fish-fry at Henderson's Point. To **dissect** the landscape is to notice the

(40) pine-thicketed, white-beached peninsula jutting out from the land. One side of the land is on the verge of the waters of the Sound and the other is purred over by the blue waves of the Bay of St. Louis. Here

(45) is the beginning of the great three-mile trestle bridge to the town of Bay St. Louis. Tonight from the beach could be seen the lights of the villas glittering across the Bay like masses of unsleeping eyes.

(50) Here upon a firm stretch of white sand camped the **giddy** merry-makers. At the **onset** of the event, a great fire of driftwood and pine cones tossed its flames at a radiant moon in the sky, and

(55) the fishers were casting their nets in the sea. The more daring of the girls waded in the water, holding pine-torches, spearing flounders with **nimble** hands and peering for soft-shell crabs.

(60) Annette had wandered farther in the shallow water than the rest. Suddenly she fell over a stone. The **impact** of the fall caused the torch to drop and splutter at her feet. With a little helpless cry she

(65) **scoured** the stretch of unfamiliar beach and water to find herself all alone.

1. Why does the author begin with a description of summer boarders and Northern visitors to the Mississippi Sound?
   A) to detail each part of their elaborate hay-rides and fish-fries
   B) to contrast their dull entertainment with the residents' joyful entertainment
   C) to show the variety within the landscape of the Mississippi Sound
   D) to narrate the servants' experiences while working on the Mississippi Sound

2. What is the main idea of the third paragraph (lines 26–36)?
   A) Getting from Pass Christian to Henderson's Point is difficult but worthwhile in the end.
   B) Some young people prefer to walk to Henderson's Point rather than ride the mules.
   C) It takes a long time to arrive at the shell road leading to Henderson's Point.
   D) Riders on mules are noisy as they move from Pass Christian to Henderson's Point.

3. As it is used in line 28, the word "impassable" means
   A) hilly.
   B) flat.
   C) vast.
   D) blocked.

4. It can reasonably be inferred that the author uses the word "you" in the first and fourth paragraphs of the passage to
   A) show that the reader has similarities with residents of the Mississippi Sound.
   B) make the reader sympathize with the main characters in the story.
   C) bring the reader directly into the events of the story.
   D) connect to the reader's prior knowledge about the Mississippi Sound.

5. Lines 39–49 serve to
   A) describe the villas that overlook Henderson's Point.
   B) present the specific landscape of Henderson's Point.
   C) compare Henderson's Point with other local beaches.
   D) illustrate a fish-fry at Henderson's Point.

6. As it is used in line 39, the word "dissect" means to
   A) discover a new idea.
   B) analyze in great detail.
   C) paint a landscape.
   D) find language for an emotion.

7. As it is used in line 51, the word "giddy" means
   A) lacking seriousness.
   B) lacking energy.
   C) lacking maturity.
   D) lacking personality.

8. As it is used in line 52, the word "onset" means
   A) decrease
   B) beginning
   C) closing
   D) peak

9. It can reasonably be inferred that Annette
   A) is a summer boarder at the Mississippi Sound.
   B) wants to separate herself from the merry-makers.
   C) is one of the more daring girls in the group.
   D) works as a servant for the boarders and visitors.

10. Which choice provides the best evidence for the answer to the previous question?
    A) Lines 3–5 ("When the … dull affair")
    B) Lines 6–8 ("During … hardest work")
    C) Lines 50–51 ("Here … merry-makers")
    D) Lines 56–59 ("The more … crabs")

Synonyms

*From the word bank below, choose the word that has the same or nearly the same meaning as the **boldface** word in each sentence and write it on the line. You will not use all of the words.*

affluence	impassable	outright	rendezvous
cascade	logical	perishable	sluggish
illicit	minimum	persevere	template
immobile	nimble	relish	tint

1. The intense heat, combined with the large breakfast I had consumed, made me feel **lethargic** all day long.

_____ sluggish _____

2. Before ticket-holders can enter the concert venue, they must have their bags checked for **unauthorized** materials.

_____ illicit _____

3. After a long run, I was able to eat my dinner with great **pleasure**, knowing I'd worked for the calories.

_____ relish _____

4. Because of her **keen** wit, she is always the first to make a quip that surprises and amuses everyone in the room.

_____ nimble _____

5. I had seen pictures of the magnificent waterfall, but watching the gleaming waters **rush** over the rocks was an entirely different sight in person.

_____ cascade _____

6. I thought I was looking at a statue until someone explained that it was actually an **unmoving** man covered in silver spray paint!

_____ immobile _____

7. Although he comes from a life of **opulence**, he knows the value of a hard day's work and never takes anything for granted.

_____ affluence _____

8. I know she claims to be able to speak Spanish fluently, but that is just an **out-and-out** lie.

_____ outright _____

9. These shelves I ordered appear to have green **tone** even though their description says they are white.

_____ tint _____

10. Doctors recommend that one cup of fruit is the **least** you should eat in a day, and they will never discourage you from eating more.

_____ minimum _____

11. The highway is **closed** because of an accident that is blocking all four lanes.

_____ impassable _____

12. I appreciate his wacky sense of humor most of the time, but when I want a **sensible** answer to a question, I wish he'd just be serious.

_____ logical _____

Two-Word Completions

Select the pair of words that best completes the meaning of each of the following sentences.

1. The bully down the block is so big and so _____ that I find myself unconsciously _____ in fear every time he looks in my direction.
a. sinister … dawdling
b. martial … sauntering
c. intimidating … cringing
d. rotund … prevaricating

2. The _____ of their sudden collision left one of the players _____ on the ice in agony, while the other was hurled five feet into the air.
a. impact … writhing
b. testimonial … cringing
c. onset … scouring
d. fatality … verging

3. During "Operation Dragnet," the police _____ the city in search of the two _____ who had pulled off the daring bank robbery.
a. quashed … innovators
b. immersed … fatalities
c. deluged … subordinates
d. scoured … culprits

4. After Grandpa _____ a large investment in an obviously crooked scheme and lost most of his savings as a result, I said that he could no longer be so _____ when it came to taking the advice of financial "wizards."
a. deluged … giddy
b. authorized … gullible
c. reminisced … jovial
d. intimidated … taut

5. The spy was a double agent, a person of great _____, who, though tormented by enemies and allies alike, proceeded to carry out secretive and sometimes _____ deeds.
a. discretion … sinister
b. arrears … crotchety
c. culprit … optional
d. innovation … pathetic

6. Joan of Arc spent most of her brief career as the "warrior maiden of France," attempting to _____ lands that the French had been forced to _____ to England as a result of English victories in the initial stages of the Hundred Years' War.
a. avenge … authorize
b. partition … expend
c. retrieve … cede
d. liberate … misrepresent

7. The Emancipation Proclamation _____ enslaved people in the South once and for all from the _____ that bound them to a life of servitude and humiliation.
a. liberated … manacles
b. immersed … arrears
c. retrieved … discretion
d. subordinated … memoranda

WORD STUDY

Idioms

In the passage, "Made for the Shade" (see pages 100–101), the author says that nostalgia for the past "might be a case of looking at the world through rose-colored glasses."

Looking at the world "through rose colored glasses" is having an overly positive or optimistic view. An **idiom** is an informal phrase or expression whose words should not be interpreted literally. We learn idioms from everyday usage, and they become so ingrained in our daily speech that we often forget we are using them.

Choosing the Right Idiom

*Read each sentence. Use context clues to figure out the meaning of each idiom in **boldface** print. Then write the letter of the definition for the idiom in the sentence.*

1. Greg, tired of doing all the work on the class project, asked his partner to **pull his own weight**. ___f___

2. Our class did not win first place at the tournament, but **that's the way the cookie crumbles**. ___g___

3. The mayor refused to **back down** on her position about the new hike and bike trail. ___h___

4. After a long day at school, Megan **lets off steam** by playing with her dog. ___c___

5. Jared was **up a creek** when he arrived at class without his books. ___i___

6. My brother tried to **butter me up**, hoping I would agree to wash the dishes. ___d___

7. It was difficult for the excited child to **sit tight** and wait his turn. ___e___

8. I really wish Jamie would quit **bugging** me about going to the football game. ___b___

9. How will Tonya react when she **gets wind of** the news that Leanne can run faster than she can? ___a___

10. If you're having a party, one of the best ways to **break the ice** is to play a name game. ___j___

a. hears about

b. annoying or pestering

c. releases energy or stress

d. flatter someone in order to gain something

e. be patient

f. take responsibility; do one's fair share

g. that's how things turn out differently than planned

h. retreat or give in

i. in a bad situation

j. start conversations; get people to relax

Classical Roots

log, logue—speech, word, discourse

The Greek root *log* appears in **logical** (page 130). The word means "capable of reasoning," and reasoning is expressed through speech and discourse. Some other words about speech or speaking are based on the same root. They are listed below.

apology	**dialogue**	**eulogy**	**neologism**
decalogue	**epilogue**	**monologue**	**prologue**

From the list of words above, choose the one that corresponds to each of the brief definitions below. Write the word in the blank space in the illustrative sentence below the definition. Use a dictionary if necessary.

1. a conversation between two or more people or characters; the lines in a script that are to be spoken; an airing of ideas or views
Abbott and Costello's wacky routine, "Who's on First?," is one of the funniest baseball ____**dialogues**____ in American comedy.

2. a long speech made by one person; a speech that monopolizes conversation; a series of jokes or comedic stories delivered by one comedian
The host's opening ____**monologue**____ is a staple of late-night television.

3. an introductory statement, act, or event; a preface; opening remarks
The novel's ____**prologue**____ offers background on the main character.

4. a set of ten authoritative rules or laws; (*usu. cap.*) the Ten Commandments (*in the Bible*)
The stained-glass window shows Moses holding the ____**Decalogue**____.

5. a concluding section at the end of a play or literary work, intended to provide further comment, interpretation, or information; an afterword
After the curtain fell, a narrator gave a brief ____**epilogue**____ to tie up loose ends.

6. words of regret to express remorse and ask pardon for an accident, fault, failure, or offense; an explanation, defense, or excuse
"I cannot accept your ____**apology**____," he explained, "I was at fault, not you."

7. a speech or written tribute composed to honor someone who has died
The Gettysburg Address is a ____**eulogy**____ to those who died in battle there.

8. a newly invented word, expression, or usage; new meaning for an old word
Evolving technology has led to many ____**neologisms**____, such as *smartphone* and *blog*, that have become part of our everyday language.

Note that not all of the Unit words are used in this passage. *Engulf, null and void, refurbish,* and *unerring* are used in the passage on page 155.

Read the following passage, taking note of the **boldface** words and their contexts. These words are among those you will be studying in Unit 10. It may help you to complete the exercises in this Unit if you refer to the way the words are used below.

Farewell, Blue Yodeler
<Obituary>

The Singing Brakeman.

June 1, 1933
Asheville Evening Post
by Floyd O. Merryll

With the passing last week of Jimmie Rodgers, the country lost a great performer. But it's a testament to the kind of man he was that many of his fans will take the loss personally, as if that Blue Yodeler, as we like to call him and will remember him, was a friend of ours. Thankfully, we've got his records to keep with us as **mementos**.

James Charles Rodgers was born in Meridian, Mississippi, in 1897. His mama died when he was just a kid, and Jimmie was raised by relatives in Mississippi and Alabama. When he was a little older, he returned to Meridian to live with his father, Aaron, who was a maintenance foreman on the Mobile and Ohio Railroad.

Jimmie had no **rigorous** musical training, but he learned to sing and play guitar. Still a boy, Jimmie proved to be a **nonconformist**. He secretly organized a traveling show. When Aaron Rodgers found out, he had the good sense to **foil** his son's plans—he tracked Jimmie down, and dragged him home. But the stunt was more than the **bumbling** behavior of an unruly kid. Jimmie showed the same **initiative** again, **formulating** a second plan to get out on the road and sing. He charged a pricey canvas tent in his father's name and hit the road to make music. His father might have understood Jimmie's love of music, but he probably didn't want the boy to **delude** himself about a musician's life. He set out again to **pry** his son from the road. Soon Aaron got Jimmie a job as a waterboy with the railroad. Within a few years, Jimmie was a brakeman on the New Orleans and Northeastern Railroad. Now Jimmie was a steady working man. But he never lost his love of music.

Jimmie came down with the deadly respiratory disease called tuberculosis in 1924, when he was 27 years old. As a **consequence** of that **abominable** disease, he had to quit his railroad job. Ever **resourceful**, Jimmie organized a traveling show and played across the Southeast. He worked as a brakeman again and later as a switchman but couldn't keep those jobs because of his tuberculosis. But his travels gave him a look at the whole **panorama** of Southern music. In 1927, Jimmie went to Asheville, North Carolina, where the city's first radio station had just hit the airwaves, and he played on the radio and earned himself a weekly slot. The exposure served him well in **subsequent** months. He recorded songs for a record company. One of them, "Blue Yodel," sold like hotcakes and made Jimmie Rodgers a star.

Propelled by fame, the Blue Yodeler traveled the country for the next few years. It was hard times for the nation. But while so many people were on the **dole** and looking for work, Jimmie was living his dream. He was making music, touring, and starring in a movie short called "The Singing Brakeman." Eventually, his illness caught up with him. During a recording session in New York City last week, he couldn't get through all of his songs. He took the day off to recover, but Jimmie was in a race against time. So before he'd sung his last song, Jimmie Rodgers was gone. But in a few years as a recording artist and a few more as a performer who rambled around the country, he made such a mark for **posterity** that we'll never forget him. Jimmie leaves behind his wife, Carrie, and daughter, Carrie Anita, and a legion of fans and recordings.

Farewell, Blue Yodeler.

Audio

For iWords and audio passages, go to **SadlierConnect.com.**

Left: Promotional photo for The Singing Brakeman

Inset: Jimmie posing with his sweet Model T Ford, in 1930

Definitions

Note the spelling, pronunciation, part(s) of speech, and definition(s) of each of the following words. Then write the appropriate form of the word in the blank space in the illustrative sentence(s) following.

1. **abominable**
(ə bäm′ ə nə bəl)

(*adj.*) arousing hatred; disgusting, detestable
Unfortunately, there are many _____**abominable**_____ ideas circulating on the Internet.

2. **consequence**
(kän′ sə kwens)

(*n.*) a result, effect; importance
Does he truly comprehend the _____**consequences**_____ of his actions?

3. **dole**
(dōl)

(*v.*) to give out in small amounts; (*n.*) money, food, or other necessities given as charity; a small portion
Let's _____**dole**_____ out scraps of food to the hungry dogs.
The people at the homeless shelter lined up to receive their weekly _____**dole**_____.

4. **formulate**
(fôr′ myə lāt)

(*v.*) to express definitely or systematically; to devise, invent; to state as a formula
The town board will _____**formulate**_____ a tax policy.

5. **memento**
(mə men′ tō)

(*n.*) something that serves as a reminder
This cap is a _____**memento**_____ of our recent trip.

6. **null and void**
(nəl and void)

(*adj.*) without legal force or effect; no longer binding
This contract becomes _____**null and void**_____ at noon.

7. **panorama**
(pan ə ram′ ə)

(*n.*) a wide, unobstructed view of an area; a complete survey of a subject; a continuously passing or changing scene; a range or spectrum
Displays of old picture postcards present an entertaining _____**panorama**_____ of twentieth-century life.

8. **pry**
(prī)

(*v.*) to pull loose by force; to look at closely or inquisitively; to be nosy about something
We can use this tool to _____**pry**_____ the lid off a can of paint.

Synonyms and antonyms are provided at SadlierConnect.com.

9. **resourceful**
(ri sôrs′ fəl)

(*adj.*) able to deal promptly and effectively with all sorts of problems; clever in finding ways and means of getting along

A _____**resourceful**_____ guide will know how to handle any questions or surprises that come up on the tour.

10. **subsequent**
(səb′ sə kwent)

(*adj.*) coming after; following in time, place, or order

The country enjoyed peace and prosperity in the years _____**subsequent**_____ to the war.

Using Context

*For each item, determine whether the **boldface** word from pages 146–147 makes sense in the context of the sentence. Circle the item numbers next to the six sentences in which the words are used correctly.*

(**1.**) I wouldn't say that the food at the picnic was **abominable**, but I wouldn't say that it was particularly good either.

(**2.**) After reaching the conclusion that the deed to the property was, in fact, a forgery, the judge declared it **null and void**.

3. The students shared their thoughts about the story's **memento** as well as its plot and characters.

(**4.**) Your good grades this semester are the direct **consequence** of your improved study habits.

5. In the workshop we learned how to **pry** baskets out of different materials, including vines, grass, and leaves.

(**6.**) The survivors of the shipwreck agreed to **dole** out the fresh water they had with them while waiting for rescuers to arrive.

7. The audience burst into applause as the star of the show began to sing the famous **panorama** that opens the second act.

(**8.**) You should make an effort to examine both sides of the issue before you **formulate** an opinion.

9. It will cost a **subsequent** amount of money to repair that old car—perhaps even more than the car is worth to begin with.

(**10.**) A **resourceful** cook can put together a great meal using ingredients that are already sitting in the refrigerator and the cupboard.

Choosing the Right Word

Select the **boldface** word that better completes each sentence. You might refer to the passage on pages 144–145 to see how most of these words are used in context. Note that the choices might be related forms of the Unit words.

1. When we reached the top of the volcano, the (**panoramic, resourceful**) view was well worth the five-hour hike.

2. The lawyer made the point that her client had been at the scene of the crime before the murder but not (**null and void, subsequent**) to it.

3. Sasha was pleasantly surprised with all the perks, such as free tickets, that the producers (**doled, formulated**) out to the actors.

4. Brad is the kind of (**abominable, resourceful**) quarterback who can always come up with something new when it is a matter of victory or defeat.

5. "We must (**formulate, pry**) a plan to deal with this new situation and carry it out as quickly as possible," the president said.

6. Our foreign policy embraces a vast (**consequence, panorama**) of aims and objectives, problems and concerns.

7. All these things in the attic may seem like a lot of junk to you, but to me they are priceless (**mementos, consequences**) of childhood.

8. By coaxing and questioning hour after hour, Tom finally managed to (**pry, dole**) the big secret from his sister.

9. Why is it that such hardworking, self-reliant people now have to depend on a (**panorama, dole**) of food and other necessities from charitable agencies?

10. Here I am on my first vacation in years, and I have to put up with this (**abominable, subsequent**) weather day after day!

11. He may look like an ordinary man, but he is in fact a figure of real (**panorama, consequence**) in the state government.

12. Since you have failed to carry out your promises, I must tell you that the agreement between us is now (**resourceful, null and void**).

You may wish to provide students with an explanation and example of a related form.

Completing the Sentence

Choose the word from the word bank that best completes each of the following sentences. Write the correct word or form of the word in the space provided.

abominable	dole	memento	panorama	resourceful
consequence	formulate	null and void	pry	subsequent

1. From the observation deck of the skyscraper one may enjoy a sweeping _____**panorama**_____ of the city.

2. At the time it occurred, that mistake didn't seem to be too important, but it had _____**consequences**_____ that still hurt me today.

3. These old photographs may not look like much, but I treasure them as a(n) _____**memento**_____ of the last summer my entire family spent together.

4. We must _____**formulate**_____ a detailed response that leaves no doubt about our position on this important issue.

5. The first meeting will be in the school auditorium, but all _____**subsequent**_____ meetings will be held in the homes of our members.

6. Anyone who _____**pries**_____ into someone else's business runs the risk of opening a can of worms.

7. Since I was able to prove in court that the salesperson had lied to me, the contract I had signed was declared _____**null and void**_____.

8. A truly _____**resourceful**_____ administrator always seems to be able to find an effective way of dealing with any problem that may come up.

9. You may think that the crude way he has behaved is slightly amusing, but I think it is _____**abominable**_____ and inexcusable.

10. During World War II, food became so scarce in Great Britain that the government _____**doled**_____ it out to consumers in very small amounts.

Encourage students to look for context clues. See page 7.

Definitions

Note the spelling, pronunciation, part(s) of speech, and definition(s) of each of the following words. Then write the appropriate form of the word in the blank space in the illustrative sentence(s) following.

1. **bumbling**
   (bəm′ bliŋ)

   (*adj.*) blundering and awkward; (*n.*) clumsiness
   The _____**bumbling**_____ burglars were so inept that they actually left some of their own money at the home they were planning to rob!
   The old cartoon character Mr. Magoo was well known for his _____**bumbling**_____.

2. **delude**
   (di lüd′)

   (*v.*) to fool, deceive; to mislead utterly
   Don't _____**delude**_____ yourself into thinking that you will become a famous concert pianist just because you played one song at the school's talent show.

3. **engulf**
   (en gəlf′)

   (*v.*) to swallow up, overwhelm, consume
   The truck was _____**engulfed**_____ in flames after its fuel tank exploded.

4. **foil**
   (foil)

   (*v.*) to defeat; to keep from gaining some end; (*n.*) a thin sheet of metal; a light fencing sword; a person or thing serving as a contrast to another
   The police will _____**foil**_____ the criminals' plot.
   Glum characters make a good _____**foil**_____ for the upbeat star of that new comedy.

5. **initiative**
   (i nish′ ə tiv)

   (*n.*) the taking of the first step or move; the ability to act without being directed or urged from the outside
   Dad is proud of my _____**initiative**_____ with chores.

6. **nonconformist**
   (nän kən fôr′ mist)

   (*n.*) a person who refuses to follow established ideas or ways of doing things; (*adj.*) of or relating to the unconventional
   Jake, a _____**nonconformist**_____, is not swayed by opinion.
   Her _____**nonconformist**_____ poetry appears in several small literary magazines.

7. **posterity**
   (pä ster′ ət ē)

   (*n.*) all of a person's offspring, descendants; all future generations
   Let's keep the photo album for _____**posterity**_____.

8. **refurbish**
   (ri fər′ bish)

   (*v.*) to brighten, freshen, or polish; to restore or improve
   The hotel _____**refurbished**_____ the décor of its lobby.

Practice with synonyms and antonyms is on page 154.

9. **rigorous**
   (rig' ər əs)

(*adj.*) severe, harsh, strict; thoroughly logical
"Boot camp" is the nickname for the place where new soldiers receive _____ **rigorous** _____ basic training.

10. **unerring**
    (ən er' iŋ)

(*adj.*) making no mistakes, faultless, completely accurate
Even a pilot with _____ **unerring** _____ judgment can be surprised by sudden changes in the weather.

Using Context

*For each item, determine whether the **boldface** word from pages 150–151 makes sense in the context of the sentence. Circle the item numbers next to the six sentences in which the words are used correctly.*

1. As much as I try to **engulf** the rules of certain sports, I always learn something new when I watch the actual games.

2. The employee-of-the-month award is given to someone who not only does the work assigned to him or her, but also takes **initiative** to accomplish other goals.

3. Your **unerring** ability to identify a given musical note demonstrates that you have perfect pitch.

4. She claims to be a **nonconformist**, but I usually see her doing what is expected of her.

5. I grimaced as I listened to my friend's **bumbling** speech, wishing I had encouraged him to practice more in front of me.

6. I set my alarm so that I can wake up to **rigorous** sounds, such as birds chirping or waves lapping the shore.

7. The **posterity** displayed by the ballerina showed how well she was trained and how often she had practiced.

8. The realtor assured the potential buyers that if they took some time to **refurbish** the old house, it would look as good as new.

9. Even though I know the superhero will always **foil** the plans of his nemesis, it's still fun to watch the bad guy get taken down.

10. From the crumbs leading to her room and the chocolate smudges across her face, I could **delude** that my sister ate the brownies I made for the bake sale.

Choosing the Right Word

*Select the **boldface** word that better completes each sentence. You might refer to the passage on pages 144–145 to see how most of these words are used in context. Note that the choices might be related forms of the Unit words.*

1. In devising the Constitution, the Founding Fathers sought to "secure the blessings of liberty to ourselves and our (**posterity**, **foils**)."

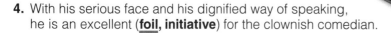

2. Perhaps he doesn't seem to be very bright, but he has a(n) (**bumbling**, **unerring**) instinct for anything that might make money for him.

3. We all know that it is a long time since the speeding laws in our community have been (**rigorously**, **unerringly**) enforced.

4. With his serious face and his dignified way of speaking, he is an excellent (**foil**, **initiative**) for the clownish comedian.

5. The war that began with Germany's invasion of Poland in 1939 spread until it had (**refurbished**, **engulfed**) almost the entire world.

6. One of the signs of a truly democratic nation is that it gives protection and freedom to (**initiatives**, **nonconformists**) who espouse unpopular views.

7. It is too late to attempt to (**delude**, **refurbish**) the old city charter; we must have a completely new plan for our city government.

8. Do you think the United States should take the (**initiative**, **foil**) in trying to bring about a compromise peace in the region?

9. Many comics get laughs for their (**unerring**, **bumbling**) antics on the stage.

10. If you think that you can get away with selling overpriced products to the people of this town, you are (**deluding**, **refurbishing**) yourself.

11. My father, an electrical engineer, is an expert at computing (**rigorous**, **unerring**) math problems.

12. She hopes to win the election by convincing voters that the city's troubles result from the (**unerring**, **bumbling**) policies of the present mayor.

You may wish to provide students with an explanation and example of a related form.

Completing the Sentence

Choose the word from the word bank that best completes each of the following sentences. Write the correct word or form of the word in the space provided.

bumbling	engulf	initiative	posterity	rigorous
delude	foil	nonconformist	refurbish	unerring

1. All that you will need to _____**refurbish**_____ that dilapidated old house is lots of time, lots of skill, lots of enthusiasm, and lots of money.

2. Rather than sit back and wait for the enemy to attack him, the general took the _____**initiative**_____ and delivered the first blow.

3. What a disappointment to hear that dull and _____**bumbling**_____ speech when we were expecting a clear, forceful, and interesting statement!

4. As a tennis player, Sue doesn't have much speed or power, but she hits the ball with _____**unerring**_____ accuracy.

5. Professional baseball players get themselves into shape for the upcoming season by undergoing a(n) _____**rigorous**_____ training period each spring.

6. Many an artist whose work has been overlooked in his or her own lifetime has had to trust to _____**posterity**_____ for appreciation.

7. The term "_____**nonconformist**_____" was first applied in the 1660s to English Protestants who dissented from the Church of England.

8. Like so many other young people, he has been _____**deluded**_____ into the false belief that there is an easy way to success.

9. Huge clouds of smoke and ash from the active volcano _____**engulfed**_____ the sleepy little villages that nestled on its flanks.

10. The alert employee _____**foiled**_____ an attempted robbery by setting off the alarm promptly.

Encourage students to look for context clues. See page 7.

End Set B

Synonyms

*Choose the word or form of the word from this Unit that is the same or most nearly the same in meaning as the **boldface** word or expression in the phrase. Write that word on the line. Use a dictionary if necessary.*

1. an **individualist** who defied all the rules — nonconformist
2. a dramatic **vista** of red rock formations — panorama
3. a comedian known for **clumsy** antics — bumbling
4. **meddled in** my personal affairs — pried (into)
5. showed **enterprise** when she started the project ahead of time — initiative
6. **tricked** by his claims of innocence — deluded
7. **obstructed** the burglar's escape plan — foiled
8. family traditions that are recorded for **future generations** — posterity
9. one day's **ration** of soup and bread — dole
10. **creative** in the way they used recycled materials — resourceful
11. the **outcome** of the war — consequence
12. huge waves that **envelop** the tiny beach — engulf
13. a precious **keepsake** of her childhood — memento
14. **prepare** a response for the defense — formulate
15. **restore** the old building — refurbish

Antonyms

*Choose the word or form of the word from this Unit that is most nearly opposite in meaning to the **boldface** word or expression in the phrase. Write that word on the line. Use a dictionary if necessary.*

1. discussed the issue at a **previous** meeting — subsequent
2. due to my **flawed** sense of direction — unerring
3. passed an **easy** exam — rigorous
4. declared **valid** by the courts — null and void
5. **lovely** behavior for a twelve-year-old — abominable

Writing: Words in Action

Answers to the prompt will vary.

Suppose that you are a musician who traveled with Jimmie Rodgers when he was a boy. Write a letter to persuade his father that Jimmie should travel with the show and hone his skills as a musician. Support your position with at least two details from the passage (pages 144–145) and three or more words from this Unit.

Vocabulary in Context

*Some of the words you have studied in this Unit appear in **boldface** type. Read the passage below, and then circle the letter of the correct answer for each word as it is used in context.*

Since the late 1940s, the unrivaled capital of country music has been Nashville, Tennessee. All other claims are **null and void.** Therefore, it is fitting that the Country Music Hall of Fame and Museum sits squarely in downtown Nashville. The Country Music Foundation took the **initiative** to establish the Hall of Fame in 1967. In 2001, this popular center moved into a larger, new facility. Finally, in 2014, money was raised to **refurbish** and expand the building, doubling its size to 350,000 square feet of exhibition space, archival storage, and educational classrooms.

Step into the museum and the exhibits **engulf** you in the experience of a truly American musical style. It is hard to express that experience in mere words. The museum offers a unique panorama. This spectacle extends from the early days of country music to the present. As though enveloped in **foil**, the artifacts, photographs, original recordings, text panels, posters, and interactive touchscreens all work together to reflect and preserve the development of country music. With an **unerring** eye and ear, the museum's curators have created a center rightly called "the Smithsonian of country music."

Attached to the museum is the Hall of Fame. Here, in a rotunda seventy feet high, are the bronze plaques honoring country music's finest artists. Back in 1961, one of the three original members was Jimmie Rodgers. The Hall of Fame now boasts more than 130 honorees, including Hank Williams, Johnny Cash, Dolly Parton, Taylor Swift, Gene Autry, and Loretta Lynn.

---

1. What is the meaning of **null and void** as it is used in paragraph 1?
a. canceled
b. valid
c. incomplete
d. private

2. In paragraph 1, what does the use of the word **initiative** suggest about the Country Music Foundation?
a. It had support.
b. It was stingy.
c. It had foresight.
d. It was tardy.

3. The word **refurbish** means about the same as
a. lengthen
b. broaden
c. heighten
d. improve

4. Which word means the same as **engulf** as it is used in paragraph 2?
a. immerse
b. blind
c. stretch
d. shove

5. **Foil** comes from the Latin word **folium. Folium** most likely means
a. a shiny tool
b. a thin sheet of metal
c. an iron shield
d. a cover for a record

6. What does the word **unerring** most likely mean as it is used in paragraph 2?
a. obvious
b. fashionable
c. faultless
d. unreliable

See pages T29–T31 for assessment options.

Note that not all of the Unit words are used in this passage. *Meteoric, parody, rend, replenish,* and *vandalism* are used in the passage on page 167.

Read the following passage, taking note of the **boldface** words and their contexts. These words are among those you will be studying in Unit 11. It may help you to complete the exercises in this Unit if you refer to the way the words are used below.

Here I Am: Galápagos Log
<Log>

Written by Samantha Z. Rosenstern, marine biologist with the Center for Island Research

Wed., *Apr. 12* After a delay at the airport, our research team arrived at the Galápagos. I often think that a good **alias** for these islands would be "reptile heaven." No land bridge ever linked the Galápagos with the coast of South America, over 600 miles away. As an unavoidable and **inevitable** consequence, reptiles **prevailed** over mammals in these spots of land straddling the equator. Only reptiles such as the giant tortoise and the land iguana possess the endurance to make long ocean crossings with no fresh water. The **dogged** persistence of these creatures made it possible for them to establish themselves here.

The name Galápagos refers to the islands' most prominent creatures. In old Spanish, *galápago* means "tortoise." Different giant tortoises have different shells. Some are dome-shaped, while others have an arched shell that looks like a saddle.

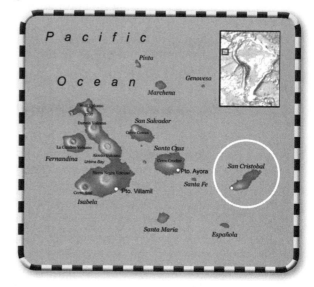

Sat., Apr. 15 My third day of field work on San Cristóbal Island at the eastern edge of the Galápagos archipelago. In mid afternoon, I **amble** down the beach. My leisurely pace would leave most of the Galápagos giant tortoises **dumbfounded**. I calculated that the **burly** giants move at about 0.2 miles per hour. That's barely ten percent of the rate of a human walker!

It really is true that human nature is the same the world over. This morning, I saw tour groups representing seven different nationalities. All were equally in awe of the animals of the Galápagos.

Thurs., Apr. 20 The population of saddlebacks on San Cristóbal has been estimated at 1,800. Long ago, there were tortoises at the southern

Conolophus subcristatus

Geochelone chathamensis

end of the island. That population is now **extinct**. The **relic** of a specimen of this race poses a new question: Were these tortoises the same as today's animals, named *Geochelone chathamensis*, or were they a different subspecies of giant tortoise?

One of my goals is to measure the impact of predators on tortoise hatchlings. The first newborns emerged this week after six months of incubation. I cannot help admiring their determination and **grit**. Feral dogs and goats, as well as hawks, are their chief enemies. If youngsters survive, however, they will enjoy a life on an epic scale. When fully grown, the males will weigh up to 800 pounds and measure over six feet from end to end. Amazingly, the tortoises have the longest life span of any creature on Earth—an estimated 150 years. No wonder there are so many gaps in the scientific literature about these animals. It is understandable that scientists' reports might be **distorted**. No one scientist could ever observe the tortoises' entire natural lifespan.

Wed., Apr. 26 Another goal of mine is to document dominance contests among adult saddlebacks. Last night I **rummaged** through my field notes from the last few weeks. Many of the dominance contests take place in plain view. As yet, I have witnessed only a few.

Fri., Apr. 28 Whatever the causes for their **ingrained** hostility, it is clear that superior height gives the winning tortoise its key advantage, as in the sparring contest I witnessed this morning. Saddlebacks can be especially aggressive toward one another. Is this because they have to **skimp** on sparse resources within their habitat, such as food, plants, water, and shade? Some more **sleuthing** during my next month here should answer these questions, as well as a few I haven't yet asked!

Audio

For iWords and audio passages, go to SadlierConnect.com.

Definitions

Note the spelling, pronunciation, part(s) of speech, and definition(s) of each of the following words. Then write the appropriate form of the word in the blank space in the illustrative sentence(s) following.

1. **alias**
   (ā′ lē əs)

   (*n.*) an assumed name, especially as used to hide one's identity; (*adv.*) otherwise called
   "Mr. Plante" was just one _____ **alias** _____ used by the elusive spy.
   Superman, _____ **alias** _____ Clark Kent, began as a comic book character created in 1938.

2. **distort**
   (dis tôrt′)

   (*v.*) to give a false or misleading account of; to twist out of shape
   A magazine known to _____ **distort** _____ the facts would be an unreliable source of information.

3. **dumbfounded**
   (dəm′ faùnd əd)

   (*adj.*) so amazed that one is unable to speak, bewildered
   When the shocking news finally reached us, we were completely _____ **dumbfounded** _____.

4. **extinct**
   (ek stiŋkt′)

   (*adj.*) no longer in existence; no longer active; gone out of use
   The _____ **extinct** _____ volcano is no longer a threat.

5. **inevitable**
   (in ev′ ə tə bəl)

   (*adj.*) sure to happen, unavoidable
   Is it _____ **inevitable** _____ that all comedies have happy endings?

6. **meteoric**
   (mē tē ôr′ ik)

   (*adj.*) resembling a meteor in speed; having sudden and temporary brilliance similar to a meteor's
   The young actor's _____ **meteoric** _____ rise to fame became legendary.

7. **parody**
   (par′ ə dē)

   (*n.*) a humorous or ridiculous imitation; (*v.*) to make fun of something by imitating it
   The audience roared with laughter at the comedy troupe's hilarious _____ **parody** _____.
   The new film successfully _____ **parodies** _____ political life in England.

8. **rend**
   (rend)

   (*v.*) to tear to pieces; split violently apart (*past tense*, rent)
   The abominable tactics of this trial could _____ **rend** _____ public confidence in the legal system.

Synonyms and antonyms are provided at SadlierConnect.com.

9. rummage
(rəm' əj)

(v.) to search through, investigate the contents of;
(n.) an active search; a collection of odd items

It can be an adventure to _____rummage_____
around our garage for remnants of our childhood.
She found an old saddle in the _____rummage_____.

10. vandalism
(van' dəl iz əm)

(n.) deliberate and pointless destruction of
public or private property

The city realizes that it needs to create tougher
laws to discourage _____vandalism_____.

Using Context

*For each item, determine whether the **boldface** word from pages 158–159 makes sense in the context of the sentence. Circle the item numbers next to the six sentences in which the words are used correctly.*

(1.) Some artists will **distort** familiar objects or human figures in their works to get viewers to see them in new ways.

(2.) Baby Face Nelson was the **alias** of an American gangster of the 1920s and 1930s whose real name was Lester Joseph Gillis.

(3.) In the performance of the Greek tragedy, the actors **rend** their clothes to express their grief.

4. You can tell that this message is written in secret code because the letters in every word are **dumbfounded**.

(5.) The scientists were amazed to find a salamander belonging to a species long believed to be **extinct**.

6. It would be **inevitable** for humans to survive in the thick, poisonous atmosphere that surrounds Venus.

(7.) Was the window broken during an act of **vandalism** or an attempted robbery?

8. Following a careful and **meteoric** examination of the crime scene, the investigators reported their findings to the police.

9. After watching a brief **parody**, students will be able to try out the 3D printer themselves.

(10.) The children liked to **rummage** through the pockets of every coat and jacket in the closet to look for loose change.

Choosing the Right Word

*Select the **boldface** word that better completes each sentence. You might refer to the passage on pages 156–157 to see how most of these words are used in context. Note that the choices might be related forms of the Unit words.*

1. There are several organizations whose goal is to protect endangered species, such as the giant panda, to keep them from becoming (**meteoric, extinct**).

2. With all of his absences and goofing off in class, it was (**inevitable, meteoric**) that he would not pass the test.

3. Suddenly, the stillness of the early morning hours was (**rent, rummaged**) by a single shot!

4. I hope to pick up some real bargains at the (**rummage, vandalism**) sale being held in our civic center.

5. His (**extinct, meteoric**) success at such an early age left him unprepared to handle the disappointments and failures that came to him later in life.

6. We scorn all those who would deliberately bend the truth and (**distort, rend**) history in order to suit the political needs of their day.

7. Don't you find those TV shows that (**parody, rummage**) famous people hilarious?

8. No, I wasn't (**inevitable, dumbfounded**) to be chosen the most popular member of the class, but maybe I was just a little surprised!

9. The aging actor trying to play the part of a young man seemed no more than a(n) (**alias, parody**) of the great performer he once was.

10. Nikki (**distorted, rummaged**) the truth about her whereabouts in order to conceal her alliance with the defendant.

11. To avoid a lot of unwanted attention, the famous rock star registered in the hotel under a(n) (**rummage, alias**).

12. Whether the window was broken accidentally or as an act of (**parody, vandalism**), the fact remains that it is broken and must be paid for.

You may wish to provide students with an explanation and example of a related form.

Completing the Sentence

Choose the word from the word bank that best completes each of the following sentences. Write the correct word or form of the word in the space provided.

alias	dumbfounded	inevitable	parody	rummage
distort	extinct	meteoric	rend	vandalism

1. Isn't it fun on a rainy day to _____**rummage**_____ about in the attic and look for interesting odds and ends?

2. The rock singer enjoyed a sudden _____**meteoric**_____ rise in popularity, but his career faded just as quickly as it had blossomed.

3. There is an old saying that nothing is really _____**inevitable**_____ except death and taxes.

4. We saw a bolt of lightning _____**rend**_____ a huge limb from the mighty oak tree.

5. As the buffalo began to decrease sharply in numbers, conservationists feared that the species might become totally _____**extinct**_____.

6. We were nothing less than _____**dumbfounded**_____ when we saw the immense damage that the hurricane had done in so brief a time.

7. Her face was so _____**distorted**_____ with pain and suffering that at first I did not recognize her.

8. The old con artist had used so many _____**aliases**_____ over the course of his criminal career that he sometimes forgot his real name!

9. Isn't it a shame that our school board must spend thousands of dollars every year just to repair the damage caused by _____**vandalism**_____?

10. Her ability to _____**parody**_____ the words and gestures of prominent Americans makes her an excellent comic impressionist.

Encourage students to look for context clues. See page 7.

End Set A

Definitions

Note the spelling, pronunciation, part(s) of speech, and definition(s) of each of the following words. Then write the appropriate form of the word in the blank space in the illustrative sentence(s) following.

1. **amble**
   (am' bəl)

   (v.) to walk slowly, stroll; (n.) an easy pace; a leisurely walk
   It's a lovely day to _____**amble**_____ to work and enjoy the many sights and sounds along the way.
   When we woke to see the sun shining, we planned a long _____**amble**_____ in the park.

2. **burly**
   (bər' lē)

   (adj.) big and strong; muscular
   That guy is as _____**burly**_____ as a lumberjack, so he would be the perfect one to help me move my furniture.

3. **dogged**
   (dôg' əd)

   (adj.) persistent, stubbornly determined, refusing to give up
   The troops fought with _____**dogged**_____ determination and courage.

4. **grit**
   (grit)

   (n.) very fine sand or gravel; courage in the face of hardship or danger; (v.) to grind; to make a grating sound
   Cars stall if _____**grit**_____ clogs a fuel line.
   It upsets me to see Dad get angry and _____**grit**_____ his teeth.

5. **ingrained**
   (in grānd')

   (adj.) fixed deeply and firmly; working into the grain or fiber; forming a part of the inmost being
   Biting my lower lip is an _____**ingrained**_____ habit.

6. **prevail**
   (pri vāl')

   (v.) to triumph over; to succeed; to exist widely, be in general use; to get someone to do something by urging
   We hope to _____**prevail**_____ over all obstacles we may encounter on this project.

7. **relic**
   (rel' ik)

   (n.) an object from the past with historical value or interest; a trace of an outdated custom; remaining fragments, ruins
   The old Model T in my grandfather's barn is a _____**relic**_____ of the first American touring cars.

8. **replenish**
   (ri plen' ish)

   (v.) to fill again, make good, replace
   Airport crews work quickly to _____**replenish**_____ a plane's supply of food, water, and safety supplies.

Practice with synonyms and antonyms is on page 166.

9. skimp
(skimp)

(v.) to save, be thrifty; to be extremely sparing with; to give little attention or effort to

If you _____**skimp**_____ on regular meals, you may be tempted to snack on too much junk food.

10. sleuth
(slüth)

(n.) a detective

A skilled _____**sleuth**_____ can find hidden clues in unusual places.

Using Context

*For each item, determine whether the **boldface** word from pages 162–163 makes sense in the context of the sentence. Circle the item numbers next to the six sentences in which the words are used correctly.*

1. The **grit** of my mother's hug was a welcome feeling after a summer away at camp.

2. The plot of the film seemed to **amble** quickly from one event to the next, and it was difficult to keep track of what was happening.

(3.) If you want to achieve your goals, you must be prepared to **prevail** over any opposition you face on your journey.

(4.) The main character of the comic book works as a **sleuth** by day and uses the clues she uncovers to fight crime as a superhero by night.

(5.) I admired every **relic** I saw in the history museum, wondering how each one could have remained intact over the centuries.

6. The speaker's message may have been well worth hearing, but his **ingrained** voice made it hard to make out any word he said.

(7.) It's amazing that she had no contacts in the technology industry yet became successful because of her **dogged** determination to create innovative products.

(8.) When I saw that our kitchen cupboards were empty, I rushed to the grocery store to **replenish** them before my guests arrived.

9. Even though I was short on cash, I decided to **skimp** myself by booking a day at the spa.

(10.) The character in the novel was described as being so **burly** that his nickname in town was "The Giant."

Choosing the Right Word

*Select the **boldface** word that better completes each sentence. You might refer to the passage on pages 156–157 to see how most of these words are used in context. Note that the choices might be related forms of the Unit words.*

1. The defenders of the Alamo put up a (**burly, dogged**) resistance against the enemy.

2. "I'll have two hot dogs with all the fixings," I said to the vendor, "and don't (**prevail, skimp**) on the mustard!"

3. The prejudices of a bigot are sometimes so (**ingrained, burly**) that it is very difficult to get rid of them.

4. When I discovered the abandoned cave that was used for an enemy hideout during WWII, I was amazed with how many war (**sleuths, relics**) still remained.

5. Is there anything more romantic than a nighttime (**amble, relic**) upon the moonlit decks of a mighty ocean liner?

6. Although it is sometimes hard, we must have faith that in the long run justice and decency will (**skimp, prevail**).

7. All I need is a meal, a hot shower, and a good night's sleep to (**replenish, prevail**) my energies.

8. After months of looking for employment, my sister, known for her (**skimpy, dogged**) persistence, finally obtained her dream job as a video game reviewer.

9. An art historian who is trying to verify the authenticity of a painting acts more like a (**sleuth, relic**) than a critic.

10. Isn't it foolish to think that just because of his (**dogged, burly**) physique he has no interest in art or music?

11. I know that you don't like the idea of painting the house, but you'll just have to (**replenish, grit**) your teeth and do it.

12. At one time, everyone wore hats, but now the custom is a (**relic, amble**) of a bygone age.

You may wish to provide students with an explanation and example of a related form.

Completing the Sentence

Choose the word from the word bank that best completes each of the following sentences. Write the correct word or form of the word in the space provided.

amble	dogged	ingrained	relic	skimp
burly	grit	prevail	replenish	sleuth

1. In the late nineteenth century, Sir Arthur Conan Doyle created one of the most famous _____**sleuths**_____ in literature, Sherlock Holmes.

2. Even though many people were criticizing and ridiculing him, he had the _____**grit**_____ to continue doing what he felt was right.

3. The cruise ship stopped at the port both to give the passengers a chance to go ashore and to _____**replenish**_____ the water supply.

4. We greatly admired the _____**dogged**_____ determination and patience that the disabled veteran showed in learning to master a wheelchair.

5. The old custom of celebrating the Fourth of July with a fireworks display still _____**prevails**_____ in many American towns.

6. Whenever our team needs a few yards to make a first down, we call on our big,_____**burly**_____ fullback to crash through the line.

7. There are archeological sites in Greece that contain sacred _____**relics**_____ that the ancients believed held supernatural powers.

8. After our furious gallop across the countryside, we allowed our tired horses to_____**amble**_____ back to the stable.

9. If you truly want to improve your math grades, you should not continue to _____**skimp**_____ so often on your homework.

10. The grime on the mechanic's hands was so deeply _____**ingrained**_____ even a thorough scrubbing couldn't entirely remove it.

Encourage students to look for context clues. See page 7.

End Set B

Synonyms

*Choose the word or form of the word from this Unit that is the same or most nearly the same in meaning as the **boldface** word or expression in the phrase. Write that word on the line. Use a dictionary if necessary.*

1. where science **reigns** over superstition   prevails
2. **refill** the empty bird feeder   replenish
3. showed **untiring** perseverance   dogged
4. amateur **investigator** Harriet the Spy   sleuth
5. admiring the **determination** of hardy pioneers   grit
6. discovered a **historical object**   relic
7. signed the document using an **assumed name**   alias
8. tried to **ridicule** the governor   parody
9. **willful destruction** of an historic statue   vandalism
10. **sift through** the attic for old clothes   rummage (around)
11. **stunned** by the price of the new shoes   dumbfounded
12. **deep-rooted** sense of right and wrong   ingrained
13. an action that would **tear apart** the political party   rend
14. protected by a **brawny** bodyguard   burly
15. ways to **misrepresent** the truth   distort

Antonyms

*Choose the word or form of the word from this Unit that is most nearly opposite in meaning to the **boldface** word or expression in the phrase. Write that word on the line. Use a dictionary if necessary.*

1. reviewing a **lackluster** career   meteoric
2. **raced** across the field together   ambled
3. usually **splurge** on the desserts   skimp
4. a **preventable** outcome   inevitable
5. photographs of the **surviving** species   extinct

Writing: Words in Action

Answers to the prompt will vary.

If you could choose a place anywhere in the world to visit for scientific research, where would it be? Why? What discovery would you hope to make? Write an essay supporting your choice, using specific examples, the reading (pages 156–157), and personal experience. Use three or more words from this Unit.

Vocabulary in Context

*Some of the words you have studied in this Unit appear in **boldface** type. Read the passage below, and then circle the letter of the correct answer for each word as it is used in context.*

The Humboldt Current, **alias** the Peru Current, is a cold-water current in the southeast Pacific Ocean. It runs parallel to southern Chile and Peru almost up to the equator, ranging nearly more than forty degrees of latitude. Experts have estimated that the current transports up to 700 million cubic feet of water per second. This rate may seem **meteoric**, but actually the current is relatively slow and shallow, with a width of 550 miles.

The regional ecosystem owes many of its major features to the Humboldt Current. It brings fog to the western coast of South America, for instance. But it also keeps this coastal region exceptionally arid. Without the current, there would be no Atacama Desert in northwestern Chile. Upwelling (ocean water rising up and flowing outward) in the Humboldt Current results in a remarkable abundance of nutrients. This, in turn, makes the waters off Chile, Peru, and Ecuador an outstanding fishing ground, especially for anchovies and sardines. Almost 20 percent of the world's fishing catch is said to come from the region.

Nature's bounty, however, is on the verge of collapse. Experts believe that overfishing is about to **rend** the balance of nature. There simply isn't sufficient time for species to **replenish** their numbers. In a kind of **parody,** commercial fleets are exploiting fish stocks with a greed that amounts to **vandalism.** The Peruvian anchovy, or anchoveta, is particularly threatened. This species accounts for a third of the global fishmeal industry, used to fatten farmed seafood. Because of the anchoveta's value, commercial fishing fleets ignore quotas and underreport catches.

---

1. **Alias** comes from the Latin word **alius.** **Alius** most likely means
   a. identical
   b. other
   c. alien
   d. legal

2. In paragraph 1, what does the use of the word **meteoric** suggest about the current?
   a. It is irregular.
   b. It is seasonal.
   c. It is rough.
   d. It is speedy.

3. What is the meaning of **rend** as it is used in paragraph 3?
   a. split
   b. unite
   c. restore
   d. emphasize

4. The word **replenish** means about the same as
   a. drain
   b. restock
   c. imitate
   d. magnify

5. Which word means the same as **parody** as it is used in paragraph 3?
   a. editorial
   b. transfer
   c. repetition
   d. travesty

6. What does the word **vandalism** most likely mean as it is used in paragraph 3?
   a. an act of selfish consumption
   b. an act of cautious preservation
   c. an act of willful destruction
   d. an act of prudent intervention

See pages T29–T31 for assessment options.

UNIT 12

Note that not all of the Unit words are used in this passage. *Abduct, compact, implement, strapping,* and *titanic* are used in the passage on page 179.

*Read the following passage, taking note of the **boldface** words and their contexts. These words are among those you will be studying in Unit 12. It may help you to complete the exercises in this Unit if you refer to the way the words are used below.*

Vampires We Have Known
<Humorous Essay>

To the extent that vampires make appearances in television dramas nowadays, and in movies and novels, too, we can say that we're all quite familiar with these creatures. That's an **indisputable** fact, is it not? And there's nothing **ambiguous** about the claim that there have been reports of vampires for hundreds of years already. The traditional legends of these ominous creatures seem to have **thrived** originally in eastern Europe. One early case stretches back to the year 1672 in old Croatia. There, a legend sprang up around a man named Jure Grando. He had died and been buried and some twenty years later was reportedly back on his feet. It is not precisely clear by what **incalculable** logic the locals derived this knowledge. But it is rather clear

that they were convinced that Jure Grando had emerged from the ground as something called a vampire. By secret, **stealthy** tactics and **maneuvers**, the now vampiric Grando was determined to drink the blood of good civilians. He especially liked to trouble his former wife, the poor living widow, Mrs. Grando.

Do you **balk** at believing these strange tales from another age? Can we **confer** now and discuss the case of Jure Grando? Most of the evidence, if there was any, is lost to history. The **scant** traces that remain of any Grando, or of any facts, or of any vampires, show us next to nothing.

Equally well-founded reports of vampires spread through Europe in the century after

Asanbosam

Krvopijac

Draug

in other places, there have been thousands of reports in recent decades about the bloodsucking creature called the chupacabra. It has a taste especially for goats. Needless to say, **intensive** investigations have ensued. And piercing, **strident** calls for action have been voiced in this country by chupacabra believers. They feel an urgent need to find out what is happening to the goats. The results, you ask? Alas, most chupacabras appear to be coyotes with mange.

The fascination with vampire stories will persist, just like our love of other fantasies. To enjoy a fantasy is one thing, and to enjoy a harmless fright is fine. But to believe that every shadow is like a thing alive—that is another thing, entirely.

this episode. By what **earmarks** does one know a vampire?

There are many similarities in vampire tales from around the globe. From Russia to France, **valiant** witnesses leapt forward to relate bold tales about these **frigid** monsters. (Though in France, one wit was heard complaining that the businessmen were the real bloodsuckers.) African tradition informs us of the dread asanbosam. It also thirsts for blood. The thing has hooks for feet and hangs upside-down. The Chinese once feared the jiang shi, which hops along and sucks the life energy out of its victims. The draugs in Scandinavia lingered about graves. They protect buried treasure and drink the blood of trespassers. If their appetite was strong, draugs would eat their victims too. The Bulgarian krvopijacs have only one nostril apiece. They can be **sabotaged** if wild roses are laid around their graves—that will stop them!

We needn't dip far back to old tales in the Western Hemisphere to uncover eyewitness accounts of bloodsucking creatures. In Mexico, Chile, Nicaragua, and Puerto Rico, and by now

Chupacabra

Audio

For iWords and audio passages, go to SadlierConnect.com.

Unit 12 ■ **169**

Definitions

Note the spelling, pronunciation, part(s) of speech, and definition(s) of each of the following words. Then write the appropriate form of the word in the blank space in the illustrative sentence(s) following.

1. abduct
(ab dəkt')

(v.) to kidnap, carry off by force
Some people with vivid imaginations fear that hostile aliens will come to Earth to _____abduct_____ humans.

2. balk
(bôk)

(v.) to stop short and refuse to go on; to refuse abruptly; to prevent from happening; (n.) (in baseball) an illegal motion made by a pitcher
My horse _____balked_____ when I urged it to go up the steep mountain slope.
The opposing team scored an additional run because of the pitcher's _____balk_____.

3. confer
(kən fər')

(v.) to consult, talk over, exchange opinions; to present as a gift, favor, or honor
The committee will _____confer_____ before taking any action on the proposed new contract.

4. frigid
(frij' id)

(adj.) extremely cold; lacking in warmth or feeling
Antarctica has a very _____frigid_____ climate.

5. incalculable
(in kal' kyə lə bəl)

(adj.) too great to be counted; unpredictable, uncertain
Concerned scientists worry that global warming may cause _____incalculable_____ damage to our environment.

6. intensive
(in ten' siv)

(adj.) thorough, deep; showing great effort; concentrated
It took _____intensive_____ physical therapy for the injured athlete to regain her strength and speed.

7. maneuver
(mə nü' vər)

(n.) a planned movement; a skillful plan; a scheme; (v.) to perform or carry out such a planned movement
The troops carried out a night _____maneuver_____ as part of the training mission.
It takes a steady hand to _____maneuver_____ the high-speed power drill.

8. sabotage
(sab' ə täzh)

(n.) an action taken to destroy something or to prevent it from working properly; (v.) to take such destructive action
Foreign embassies worry about _____sabotage_____.
Protesters decided to _____sabotage_____ the factory.

Synonyms and antonyms are provided at SadlierConnect.com.

9. strident
(strīd' ənt)

(*adj.*) harsh, shrill; unpleasant sounding
Her _____ **strident** _____ laughter showed harsh ridicule.

10. valiant
(val' yənt)

(*adj.*) possessing or acting with bravery or boldness
Sir Galahad was a _____ **valiant** _____ knight of King Arthur's Round Table.

Using Context

*For each item, determine whether the **boldface** word from pages 170–171 makes sense in the context of the sentence. Circle the item numbers next to the six sentences in which the words are used correctly.*

1. This is no time for sudden or dramatic moves; instead, we must take a **strident** approach to the problem.

2. You would not want to be in a situation in which you would be forced to abandon ship and try to survive in the **frigid** waters of the Atlantic Ocean.

3. Homeowners, especially those who live along the coast, must do all they can to **balk** before the hurricane hits.

4. The number of atoms in the universe must surely be **incalculable**.

5. Everyone admired the grace and **sabotage** with which the young ballerina performed the difficult role.

6. Powerful pumps on this tugboat can **abduct** water from the sea so that it can then be used to fight a fire on a ship, boat, or dock.

7. At college graduation ceremonies, representatives of the school often **confer** honorary degrees to people who have made significant contributions to society.

8. We will take an **intensive** Spanish language class before our trip to Peru this summer so that we are prepared to converse with the local residents.

9. Stunt pilots can **maneuver** planes to perform tricks with names such as *inside loop*, *outside loop*, and *barrel roll*.

10. The soldier was awarded a medal for his **valiant** service.

Choosing the Right Word

*Select the **boldface** word that better completes each sentence. You might refer to the passage on pages 168–169 to see how most of these words are used in context. Note that the choices might be related forms of the Unit words.*

1. The Labrador retriever received a medal from the fire department for its (**valiant, incalculable**) act of saving a drowning man.

2. When their pitcher committed the (**balk, sabotage**), the umpire advanced our runner from first to second base.

3. As election day gets closer, the tone of the candidates' political oratory becomes more and more (**frigid, strident**).

4. What do you think the United States should do when its representatives are (**sabotaged, abducted**) and held for ransom?

5. When we made our appeal for funds, their response was so (**incalculable, frigid**) that we realized we would have to find other ways of raising money.

6. In her floor exercise, the champion gymnast performed some of the most amazing (**sabotages, maneuvers**) I have ever seen.

7. The future is indeed (**incalculable, valiant**), but we must face it with faith and confidence.

8. Although our club is run more or less democratically, we don't have the time to (**confer, abduct**) about every minor detail.

9. When a conquering army overruns a country, the only way the people may have to strike back is by acts of (**maneuvers, sabotage**).

10. The brave defenders of the fort waged a (**strident, valiant**) battle against the enemy's troops.

11. Aunt Lorna (**conferred, balked**) when the waiter at the seafood restaurant told her that the dinner special—the "catch of the day"—was $41.00.

12. Because her condition was so poor after the operation, she was placed in the hospital's (**incalculable, intensive**) care unit.

You may wish to provide students with an explanation and example of a related form.

Completing the Sentence

Choose the word from the word bank that best completes each of the following sentences. Write the correct word or form of the word in the space provided.

abduct	confer	incalculable	maneuver	strident
balk	frigid	intensive	sabotage	valiant

1. When the winds begin to turn _____**frigid**_____ in November, our thoughts turn to our warm and sunny island off the coast of Florida.

2. The breakdown of all these machines at the same time cannot simply be a coincidence; we suspect deliberate _____**sabotage**_____.

3. The new recruits were rudely awakened from their peaceful sleep by the _____**strident**_____ voice of the sergeant barking commands.

4. Because I'm afraid of heights, I usually _____**balk**_____ at the idea of sitting in the first row of the topmost balcony in a theater.

5. No doubt our antipollution program will be expensive, but the cost of doing nothing would be simply _____**incalculable**_____.

6. In Shakespeare's words, "Cowards die many times before their deaths; the _____**valiant**_____ never taste of death but once."

7. The president will _____**confer**_____ well-deserved honors on the retiring ambassador.

8. As the day of the big game approached, our practice sessions became more and more _____**intensive**_____.

9. The millionaire has hired special guards to make sure that his valuable, prize-winning show dog, Lucy, will not be _____**abducted**_____.

10. I was amazed to see how skillfully Felicia _____**maneuvered**_____ that huge car through the heavy downtown traffic.

Encourage students to look for context clues. See page 7.

End Set A

Definitions

Note the spelling, pronunciation, part(s) of speech, and definition(s) of each of the following words. Then write the appropriate form of the word in the blank space in the illustrative sentence(s) following.

1. ambiguous
(am big′ yü əs)

(*adj.*) not clear; having two or more possible meanings
The purpose of a test is not to confuse students with _____**ambiguous**_____ questions, but to determine whether they have learned the material.

2. compact
(*v., adj.,* kəm pakt′;
n., käm′ pakt)

(*adj.*) closely and firmly packed together; small; (*v.*) to squeeze together; (*n.*) an agreement between parties; a small case containing a mirror and face powder; a small car
Computers are much more _____**compact**_____ now than they were a generation ago.
Workers at the town dump were asked to _____**compact**_____ the trash to save space.

3. earmark
(ir′ mark)

(*v.*) to set aside for a special purpose; to mark an animal's ear for identification; (*n.*) an identifying mark or feature
Let's _____**earmark**_____ the money we received for the new building fund.

4. implement
(im′ plə mənt)

(*n.*) an instrument, tool; (*v.*) to put into effect
The harrow is a farm _____**implement**_____ that is used to pulverize and smooth soil.
The highway patrol will _____**implement**_____ the new speed limit as of July 1 of this year.

5. indisputable
(in dis pyüt′ ə bəl)

(*adj.*) beyond question or argument, definitely true
With such _____**indisputable**_____ evidence, Judge Lee must rule to drop all charges against my client.

6. scant
(skant)

(*adj.*) not enough; barely enough; marked by a small or insufficient amount
Somehow, we made the _____**scant**_____ supply of food stretch for nearly a week.

7. stealthy
(stel′ thē)

(*adj.*) done in a way so as not to be seen or observed; sneaky, underhanded
The nervous robber took _____**stealthy**_____ glances at the cash register.

8. strapping
(strap′ iŋ)

(*adj.*) tall, strong, and healthy
That _____**strapping**_____ young man is a good wrestler.

Practice with synonyms and antonyms is on page 178.

9. thrive
(thrīv)

(*v.*) to grow vigorously; to grow in wealth and possessions
Angie hopes that her business will
_____**thrive**_____ in today's Internet culture.

10. titanic
(tī tan′ ik)

(*adj.*) of enormous size, strength, power, or scope
The movie plot explores the _____**titanic**_____
struggle between the forces of good and evil.

Using Context

*For each item, determine whether the **boldface** word from pages 174–175 makes sense in the context of the sentence. Circle the item numbers next to the six sentences in which the words are used correctly.*

(1.) Although the company has announced its decision to rebrand, its plan to **implement** a new corporate logo will not go into effect until next year.

2. The author suffered a series of **strapping** illnesses in childhood, which may explain why weak, sickly characters often appear in his stories.

3. I was grateful when the storm clouds finally rolled away and I could see the **ambiguous** sunlight streaming from the sky.

(4.) It is amazing that the accomplished celebrity was able to **thrive** after being raised in such a troubled environment.

(5.) The lawyer knows that all evidence of her client's innocence must be **indisputable** or the prosecutor will find a way to prove it otherwise.

6. I plan to **earmark** the issue when we're all together tomorrow, as it has now been resolved.

7. My arms felt so **titanic** after lifting the heavy object that I could hardly pick up a pencil for the rest of the day.

(8.) "Perhaps if you paid more than **scant** attention in class, your grades would be better," the teacher warned the distracted student.

(9.) The mischievous child tried to be **stealthy** as he made his way to the cookie jar, but his mother saw him and put the jar further out of reach.

(10.) I always carry with me a **compact** hairbrush that can fit in a space as small as my pocket.

Choosing the Right Word

*Select the **boldface** word that better completes each sentence. You might refer to the passage on pages 168–169 to see how most of these words are used in context. Note that the choices might be related forms of the Unit words.*

1. Of all the evergreens that tower in America's forests, none can surpass the height and girth of the (**titanic, indisputable**) California redwoods.

2. The first Pilgrim settlers signed an agreement called the "Mayflower (**Compact, Implement**)."

3. We have worked out a good plan on paper; now we must decide how we are going to (**implement, thrive**) it.

4. Since *presently* means both "right now" and "in the future," any statement containing it must be considered (**titanic, ambiguous**).

5. Creeping (**stealthily, ambiguously**) through the underbrush, the enemy came within a few yards of the stockade before the guards saw them.

6. When he says that his analysis of the problem is (**titanic, indisputable**), all he means is that he's not willing to listen to anyone else's ideas.

7. The extra money being raised by the band booster club has been (**earmarked, compacted**) to fund future band trips.

8. I don't think democracy can (**earmark, thrive**) in an atmosphere of racial and religious hatred.

9. After straining and sweating in the hot sun for an hour, we realized that we had pushed the stalled car only a(n) (**scant, indisputable**) quarter mile.

10. "It's an (**indisputable, ambiguous**) fact that the finest guitar players in rock music were from the 1970s," Brandon said.

11. Truthfulness and sincerity are the (**earmarks, compacts**) of an honest person.

12. Why is that big, (**strapping, stealthy**) fellow in the advertisement always kicking sand into the face of the 98-pound weakling?

You may wish to provide students with an explanation and example of a related form.

Completing the Sentence

Choose the word from the word bank that best completes each of the following sentences. Write the correct word or form of the word in the space provided.

ambiguous	earmark	indisputable	stealthy	thrive
compact	implement	scant	strapping	titanic

1. Each year a portion of the school budget is _____**earmarked**_____ for the purchase of new books for the library.

2. When our team saw their _____**strapping**_____ 200-pound defensive linemen, we realized that we would have a hard time running against them.

3. Since the amount of time we have to prepare for the final exams is exceedingly _____**scant**_____, we had better make the best of every hour.

4. I prefer the _____**compact**_____ edition of the dictionary because it is so much lighter and less bulky than the unabridged version.

5. For a person who loves to argue as much as Gene does, there is nothing that is really _____**indisputable**_____.

6. Even mighty warships were endangered by the _____**titanic**_____ waves that loomed like mountains above them.

7. In your training to become a dental assistant, you will become familiar with many of the _____**implements**_____ that dentists use.

8. The cactus is an example of a plant having natural adaptations that enable it to _____**thrive**_____ even in a very dry climate.

9. Why must you always be so _____**ambiguous**_____ when I want you to give me a straight yes-or-no answer?

10. At first the zebras did not notice the _____**stealthy**_____ movements of the lions inching their way closer to the harem.

Encourage students to look for context clues. See page 7.

End Set B

Unit 12 ■ *177*

Synonyms

*Choose the word or form of the word from this Unit that is the same or most nearly the same in meaning as the **boldface** word or expression in the phrase. Write that word on the line. Use a dictionary if necessary.*

1. the **inarguable** star of the team   indisputable

2. **reserve** the money for the scholarship fund   earmark

3. interpreted the **unclear** remark   ambiguous

4. haunted by the **piercing** cries   strident

5. a **robust** young athlete   strapping

6. **consult** with others before making a decision   confer

7. failed to **flourish** without sun and water   thrive

8. tried to **cripple** the communications system   sabotage

9. **exhaustive** negotiations between the employer and the union   intensive

10. the **brave** commander   valiant

11. not able to survive on **meager** wages   scant

12. an effective **tactic** used to win the case   maneuver

13. lending us **limitless** support   incalculable

14. a most **standoffish** welcome   frigid

15. **resist** because of fear   balk

Antonyms

*Choose the word or form of the word from this Unit that is most nearly opposite in meaning to the **boldface** word or expression in the phrase. Write that word on the line. Use a dictionary if necessary.*

1. decided to **abandon** the plan   implement

2. the decision to **release** the hostages   abduct

3. noticed her **conspicuous** glances   stealthy

4. drives an **oversized** car   compact

5. made a **tiny** effort   titanic

Writing: Words in Action

Answers to the prompt will vary.

What is your opinion about the existence of monsters? Why do you think some people create stories about them? Why do others believe in them? Write a brief essay supporting your views with examples, observations, and the reading (pages 168–169). Write at least three paragraphs. Use three or more words from this Unit.

Vocabulary in Context

*Some of the words you have studied in this Unit appear in **boldface** type. Read the passage below, and then circle the letter of the correct answer for each word as it is used in context.*

Let's face it: Bats aren't cuddly, not like dainty kittens or even **strapping** llamas and alpacas. Bats' squashed, **compact** features and sharp, pointed teeth—not to mention their unusual habit of flying around in the dark—scare people. However, bats, the only mammals that can fly, play an important role in nature. They help control harmful pests like mosquitoes. (Even the tiniest bats have **titanic** appetites; a brown bat, for example, can eat up to 1000 mosquitoes in just one hour!) They also perform a key role in pollination. But now bats are in grave danger, and they need our help.

Bats all over the world are being negatively affected by modernization. It has led to loss of habitat and food sources and to devastating disease. At least nine bat species in North America are on the "threatened" or "endangered" list. It's long past time we **implement** measures to save the bats. Wildlife conservationists recommend simple steps we can take, such as supplying boxes for bats to nest in and turning off glaring outdoor lights. There are plenty of other ways to get involved.

Bats have been portrayed as monsters throughout history. Old wives' tales of bats sucking blood like vampires or even attempting to **abduct** small children abound. But study bats up close and you'll discover a far different story. They are smart, highly social creatures that communicate with one another in their own bat language of buzzing and clicking sounds. Why not **confer** with your friends to see what *you* can do to save our nocturnal flying friends?

---

1. What is the meaning of **strapping** as it is used in paragraph 1?
   a. delicate   **c.** sturdy
   b. ugly   **d.** useful

2. In paragraph 1, what does the use of the word **compact** suggest about bats' faces?
   a. They are unusual.   **c.** They look angry.
   b. They are small.   **d.** They can't see.

3. What does the word **titanic** most likely mean as it is used in paragraph 1?
   a. unlimited   **c.** varied
   b. graceful   **d.** gigantic

4. The word **implement** means about the same as
   a. seek ways   **c.** go against
   b. carry out   **d.** look for

5. Which word means the same as **abduct** as it is used in paragraph 3?
   a. eat   **c.** snatch
   b. raise   **d.** share

6. **Confer** comes from the Latin word **conferre**. **Conferre** most likely means
   a. to bring together   **c.** to carry out
   b. to confess   **d.** to seek out

Vocabulary for Comprehension
Part 1

Read "An International Science Lab," which contains words in **boldface** *that appear in Units 10–12. Then answer the questions.*

An International Science Lab

"Science lab" usually means a clean, bright room in which researchers work with high-tech equipment. Antarctica, the fifth largest of Earth's seven continents,
(5) is itself an enormous, ice-cold science lab. It has no native population. Few living things can survive in its brutal climate. But scientists are attracted to the rare features of this desolate continent.

(10) Antarctica is more than 95 percent ice-covered all year long. It has had the lowest air temperature ever measured, as well as some of the highest winds. Because it has no industrial pollution, its
(15) ice and snow are pure. All that ice makes it doubtful that any settlement or economic development will ever take place in Antarctica, but many tiny outposts have sprung up since the 1950s.

(20) In that decade, twelve nations set up research stations all over Antarctica. Representatives of those nations got together to draft a **compact** devoting the continent to peaceful study. This
(25) pact went into effect in 1961. It forbids military action and nuclear weapons. It promotes a free exchange of ideas.

Antarctic scientists devise and carry out a wide range of tests. They study
(30) glaciers, weather patterns and conditions, icebergs, magnetism, volcanoes, the movement of rock plates, and animal and plant biology. They openly share their findings with the global scientific
(35) community.

Life in such a difficult place demands planning, special gear, and **grit.** Scientists must figure out how to do their research

safely and effectively. They must guard
(40) their health and well-being. Internet and satellite technologies surely help. Researchers so far from home can **confer** with the family, friends, and co-workers they left behind. They can stay up-to-date
(45) on world events. But they cannot easily come and go. Scientists often arrive before the Antarctic winter, when near-total darkness **engulfs** the area. They typically stay for six to ten long, cold,
(50) lonely months.

Dressing for the job of an Antarctic scientist is a unique challenge. An optimal number of layers in the right fabrics is needed to protect the body
(55) against wind, cold, and moisture during long, **rigorous** workdays outdoors. The scientific research stations themselves are challenging to build. The buildings must be designed to consider snow patterns,
(60) the effects of melting ice, and insulation against the **frigid** climate and fierce winds. Antarctica has no trees or other naturally found resources for construction, so materials are usually brought by ship
(65) and assembled on site. But they must be assembled quickly so that supply ships can leave before they are frozen in!

Despite the difficulties they encounter, researchers in Antarctica have made
(70) many important scientific achievements. These include the detection of massive under-ice lakes and canyons, the discovery of previously unknown species of animals, and the identification of ways
(75) Earth is changing both naturally and because of human activity.

1. What is the central idea of "An International Science Lab"?
   A) It is easy to do scientific research in Antarctica.
   B) Antarctica is almost totally covered with ice all year.
   C) Important international scientific research is conducted in Antarctica.
   D) Antarctica, the fifth-largest continent, has no native population.

2. What is the main purpose of paragraph 2 (lines 10–19)?
   A) to describe life inside the science lab
   B) to convince the reader of the importance of peaceful study
   C) to describe the rare features mentioned in the previous paragraph
   D) to inform readers on how to survive among the natives of Antarctica

3. What does the word **compact** mean as it is used in line 23?
   A) speech
   B) dense
   C) small car
   D) agreement

4. What is the meaning of **grit** as it is used in line 37?
   A) courage
   B) gravel
   C) persistence
   D) grind

5. According to line 42, what does **confer** mean?
   A) play
   B) argue
   C) consult
   D) study

6. What does the word **engulfs** most likely mean as it is used in line 48?
   A) avoids
   B) envelops
   C) divides
   D) empties

7. Which statement **best** provides an inference that is supported by paragraphs 5 and 6 (lines 36–67)?
   A) The future of Antarctica is uncertain.
   B) Antarctica is a signal of global warming.
   C) Antarctica has valuable resources.
   D) Working in Antarctica is difficult.

8. **Part A**
   What does the word **rigorous** most likely mean as it is used in line 55?
   A) full of life
   B) challenging
   C) easy
   D) foolish

   Part B
   Which text evidence provides the **best** clue to the meaning of **rigorous**?
   A) "twelve nations set up research stations all over Antarctica." (lines 20–21)
   B) "stay up-to-date on world events." (lines 44–45)
   C) "forbids military action and nuclear weapons." (lines 25–26)
   D) "study glaciers, weather patterns and conditions, icebergs, magnetism, volcanoes, the movement of rock plates, and animal and plant biology" (lines 29–33)

9. Which word means the opposite of **frigid** in line 61?
   A) freezing
   B) icy
   C) balmy
   D) relaxed

10. Why does the author **most likely** describe what Antarctic scientists wear and how scientific research stations are built?
    A) to weigh the pros and cons of research
    B) to emphasize the difficulties of working in Antarctica
    C) to share the most important scientific discoveries
    D) to reveal how a supply ship was frozen in

Vocabulary for Comprehension
Part 2

*Read these passages, which contain words in **boldface** that appear in Units 10–12. Then choose the best answer to each question based on what is stated or implied in the passage(s). You may refer to the passages as often as necessary.*

Questions 1–10 are based on the following passages.

Passage 1

Nearly 40,000 people died on our roads in 2015—and almost all road accidents are caused by human error. If American drivers were as reliable as the cars they
(5) drive, our roads would be much less dangerous than they are. Modern automobiles must conform to **intensive** codes of safety, but they can only ever be as safe as their drivers—and even the
(10) best drivers make mistakes.

Self-driving cars will manage the **titanic** task of eliminating human error by taking over the driving responsibilities. They avoid the kind of risks that human
(15) drivers often take without thinking. Their computerized guidance systems can calculate braking distances, relative speeds, **maneuverability**, and other important data more rapidly and
(20) accurately than any human driver. They base their decisions and predictions on accurate information rather than intuition and guesswork. They do not pick up lazy habits, or neglect necessary safety
(25) procedures—they refuse to move until their passengers are safely buckled up.

Self-driving cars are law-abiding. They never exceed the speed limit, and they are strictly teetotal. They do not get angry,
(30) either with their passengers or with other road users, and they are never distracted. Experts have noted a recent **meteoric** rise in the number of deaths on our roads, and attribute it to the **abominable** use of
(35) smartphones. Self-driving cars will never

endanger the lives of their passengers by texting their friends.

Passage 2

Self-driving cars promise safety. **Strident** supporters of the self-driving car
(40) movement proclaim that they will eliminate the 94 percent of road accidents that the Department of Transport identifies as the **consequence** of human error. We are told the world should get ready for the **valiant**
(45) new technology of self-driving cars—but are self-driving cars ready for the world?

When there is no longer a human driver processing the data and making the decisions, the car has to be infallible.
(50) Recently, a self-driving car was in a fatal collision with a tractor-trailer rig on a Florida highway. The car was apparently unable to detect the white truck against the bright sky. The passenger in the self-driving car
(55) seems to have been watching a movie— by encouraging human drivers to pay **scant** attention to the road, self-driving cars may be creating new hazards. The manufacturer has since advised human
(60) drivers to keep at least one hand on the steering wheel, and to be ready to take over driving duties at any time. This may be a sensible precaution, but aren't self-driving cars supposed to take over
(65) the driving duties from us?

Consumers are told that self-driving trucks will make heavy transport safer and more efficient by forming long convoys, called "platoons." These platoons would
(70) resemble freight trains riding along railroad tracks. Freight trains will always be safer and faster—and they already exist.

You may wish to ask students to write a few paragraphs that cite evidence from both passages in answer to the following prompt: What are the positive and negative aspects of self-driving cars?

1. Passage 1 claims that human error
   A) caused 40,000 road deaths in 2015.
   B) causes the majority of road deaths.
   C) is caused by guesswork and intuition.
   D) cannot be eliminated.

2. As it is used in line 7, "intensive"
   most nearly means
   A) long-lasting.
   B) thorough.
   C) exhausting.
   D) incomprehensible.

3. As it is used in line 18, "maneuverability"
   most nearly means
   A) competence in decision-making.
   B) obedience to the driver's commands.
   C) ability to adjust movement and direction.
   D) ability to stay on course.

4. As it is used in line 39, "strident"
   most nearly means
   A) loud.
   B) passionate.
   C) feverish.
   D) obstinate.

5. As it is used in line 57, "scant"
   most nearly means
   A) meager.
   B) excessive.
   C) less.
   D) casual.

6. Passage 2 claims that freight trains
   A) are more efficient than truck platoons.
   B) run on rails along our highways.
   C) will be replaced by self-driving trucks.
   D) provide jobs for truck-drivers.

7. Which of these words in Passage 2
   conveys a sense of irony about the
   claims made in Passage 1?
   A) strident (line 39)
   B) valiant (line 44)
   C) infallible (line 49)
   D) sensible (line 63)

8. Which choice provides the best evidence
   for the answer to the previous question?
   A) Lines 43–46 ("We ... world")
   B) Lines 47–49 ("When ... infallible")
   C) Lines 54–58 ("The passenger ...
      hazards")
   D) Lines 58–63 ("The manufacturer ... time")

9. In Passage 1, the author states that
   self-driving cars will eliminate human error.
   In Passage 2, the author demonstrates
   that self-driving cars are
   A) capable of human error.
   B) more dangerous than human drivers.
   C) inattentive to road conditions.
   D) not ready to take over driving.

10. Which statement best describes
    the overall relationship between
    Passage 1 and Passage 2?
    A) Passage 1 demonstrates a belief in the
       immediate effectiveness of self-driving
       car technology, and Passage 2
       demonstrates that self-driving cars
       are not yet ready for the world.
    B) Passage 1 shows how self-driving
       cars will reduce the number of road
       accidents, and Passage 2 shows
       how self-driving cars will make
       the road more dangerous.
    C) The author of Passage 1 believes that
       self-driving cars are ready to make a
       contribution to road safety, and the
       author of Passage 2 believes they will
       never help to prevent road accidents.
    D) Passage 1 is forward-thinking and
       ready to accept new technology, while
       Passage 2 rejects progress and clings
       to old technology, such as freight trains.

Synonyms

*From the word bank below, choose the word that has the same or nearly the same meaning as the **boldface** word in each sentence and write it on the line. You will not use all of the words.*

dole	memento	rend	subsequent
incalculable	nonconformist	resourceful	thrive
inevitable	null and void	rigorous	unerring
initiative	posterity	stealthy	vandalism

1. A **souvenir** of a vacation doesn't have to cost anything; it can be something as simple as a pinecone or a seashell.   _____ memento

2. It's fun to watch the kitten crouch and then move forward in a **furtive** manner to pounce on the toy mouse.   _____ stealthy

3. I wouldn't call writing your name in chalk on a sidewalk or brick wall an act of **willful destruction**.   _____ vandalism

4. In early trials, the new medication showed great promise, but in **later** ones, it proved to have unacceptable side effects.   _____ subsequent

5. As December approached, the settlers prepared for the **inescapable** arrival of the harsh New England winter.   _____ inevitable

6. If I forgot to fill in the date on one page, does that mean my entire application will be considered **canceled**?   _____ null and void

7. Anyone who wants to attend the summer program in computer science must be prepared for a **tough** course of study.   _____ rigorous

8. Many successful business owners started out by showing **leadership** at a young age.   _____ initiative

9. Her success as a fashion designer is due to her **unfailing** sense of the latest trends.   _____ unerring

10. No one could have predicted the many ways in which the disaster would **splinter** their peaceful existence.   _____ rend

11. It was interesting to see how the trainer would **ration** out small treats to keep the dogs' attention as he worked with them.   _____ dole

12. Scientists have found that animals such as crows, chimpanzees, and octopuses are **inventive** enough to use objects in their environment as tools.   _____ resourceful

Two-Word Completions

Select the pair of words that best completes the meaning of each of the following sentences.

1. The nimble little star quarterback _____ deftly around the _____ linebackers attempting to sack him.
  a. maneuvered … burly
  b. foiled … frigid
  c. engulfed … compact
  d. abducted … strapping

2. When I asked her where I could find the old book, her reply was so _____ that I had to spend an hour _____ for it.
  a. bumbling … abducting
  b. indisputable … earmarking
  c. ambiguous … rummaging
  d. intensive … prevailing

3. When we saw the breathtaking _____ on that lovely autumn morning, we did not want to miss the stunning vista and decided to _____ rather than rush.
  a. grit … compact
  b. relic … balk
  c. panorama … amble
  d. parody … maneuver

4. Kidnappers had made plans to _____ the official and hold him for ransom. Fortunately, the police were able to _____ the plot after an informant tipped them off about it.
  a. sabotage … distort
  b. parody … pry
  c. delude … balk
  d. abduct … foil

5. "Although we have devised a plan to deal with the situation," the official said, "we will not be able to _____ the plan until we receive the funds _____ by the government for the project."
  a. implement … earmarked
  b. replenish … conferred
  c. formulate … rummaged
  d. refurbish … maneuvered

6. I am always _____ by the amazing powers of observation and deduction exhibited by my favorite _____, the legendary Sherlock Holmes.
  a. dogged … relic
  b. dumbfounded … sleuth
  c. deluded … alias
  d. ingrained … foil

7. Animals such as the saber-toothed tiger and the woolly mammoth have been _____ for many thousands of years, but scientists have found the _____ of these animals of the last Ice Age.
  a. skimpy … foils
  b. indisputable … sleuths
  c. scant … earmarks
  d. extinct … relics

WORD STUDY

Denotation and Connotation

A word's dictionary definition is its **denotation**. A denotation is the word's literal meaning, and it conveys a neutral tone.

Words also have connotations. **Connotations** are the emotional associations that people make to certain words. These associations can be either positive or negative.

Consider these synonyms for the neutral word *individualist*:

> *nonconformist   maverick   eccentric   oddball*

Nonconformist and *maverick* have positive connotations, whereas *eccentric* and *oddball* are negative.

Look at these examples of words. Notice how the connotation of each word varies.

NEUTRAL	POSITIVE	NEGATIVE
restore	refurbish	overhaul
satire	parody	lampoon
cold	bracing	frigid

Expressing the Connotation

Read each sentence. Select the word in parentheses that better expresses the connotation (positive, negative, or neutral) given at the beginning of the sentence.

neutral
1. The movers had a difficult time trying to get the (**titanic, large**) piano into the small loft.

positive
2. We ate our lunch on the veranda and watched the tourists (**amble, trudge**) along the beach.

negative
3. The (**strident, loud**) screams from the fans made the security staff nervous.

positive
4. Randy saved the program from the ceremony as a (**keepsake, relic**) of the happy event.

neutral
5. The gymnast achieved (**meteoric, rapid**) fame after her Olympic debut.

positive
6. After spending the summer working out, Ted became a (**beefy, burly**) athlete.

negative
7. It was common for outlaws of the wild west to have several (**names, aliases**).

negative
8. Our cat (**balked, hesitated**) when I opened the door to let him outside, and he saw that it was raining.

Classical Roots

co, col, com, con, cor—with, together

A form of this Latin prefix appears in **consequence** (page 146), **compact** (page 174), and **confer** (page 170). Some other words in which this prefix appears are listed below.

coincidence	colleague	compute	confide
collaborate	composure	concurrent	correspond

From the list of words above, choose the one that corresponds to each of the brief definitions below. Write the word in the blank space in the illustrative sentence below the definition. Use a dictionary if necessary.

1. occurring at the same time; agreeing
The convicted felon was sentenced to _____**concurrent**_____ prison terms.

2. calmness of mind, bearing, or appearance; self-control
Even the car alarms wailing outside the auditorium did not ruffle the speaker's _____**composure**_____.

3. to tell something as a secret; to entrust a secret
I would never _____**confide**_____ such details to anyone but a close friend.

4. a fellow worker, associate
The proud retiree was honored by her longtime _____**colleagues**_____ at the library.

5. to work with others; to aid or assist an enemy of one's country
They agreed to _____**collaborate**_____ on the science project so they could pool their resources and ideas.

6. to determine by arithmetic; to calculate
The mechanic used a calculator to _____**compute**_____ the total repair bill.

7. the chance occurrence of two things at the same time or place
"What a _____**coincidence**_____ to bump into you here at the passport office!" she exclaimed.

8. to exchange letters; to be in agreement
My cousin and I decided to _____**correspond**_____ by e-mail after he moved to Montana.

Note that not all of the Unit words are used in this passage. *Atrocity, fluent, recitation, sulky,* and *supplement* are used in the passage on page 199.

*Read the following passage, taking note of the **boldface** words and their contexts. These words are among those you will be studying in Unit 13. It may help you to complete the exercises in this Unit if you refer to the way the words are used below.*

Polar Opposites
<Compare and Contrast Essay>

Although they may seem similar, the polar regions of planet Earth are really very different. They **affirm** the old adage that there are two sides to the same coin.

The astonishing climate **traits** of both the Arctic and Antarctica are **stupefying**. Temperatures of −60°F are not unusual. If the harsh winds and vast ice sheets do not **deter** visitors, these strangers will find the elements **disquieting** at the very least. During polar winters, the sun never rises, while during the summers, it never sets. For centuries, explorers had to give careful thought to how to **cope** with these forces of nature. It was essential to **adhere** closely to a more rigorous program of safety precautions than explorers used in more temperate lands.

The Arctic is a region of immense diversity. Although the terrain seems forbidding, many animals **prowl** the land, including polar bears, caribou, wolves, foxes, hares, and weasels. Migrant birds visit from as far away as Central and South America. Possibly the most famous of these birds is the arctic tern. This summer visitor traverses thousands of miles every year, from Antarctica to the Arctic! The ocean **surges** with abundant marine life, especially when warm currents move around some of the Arctic coasts. Surprisingly, vegetation is widespread. Algae, lichens, and dwarf shrubs persist, even in areas of permanent ice.

The Arctic is also home to a broad range of native peoples. For example, the Inuit and

The arctic fox has a thick coat and furred paws to allow for survival in an extremely cold climate.

The emperor penguin, indigenous to Antarctica, is the largest species of penguins.

Aleuts reside in northern North America and Greenland. The Eurasian Arctic is home to the Sami, sometimes called the Lapps, as well as to the Nenets (Samoyed) and the Evenks (Tungus). To suppose that these peoples view their environment as hostile would be a **misapprehension**. According to anthropologists, many Arctic residents are **optimists**. They perceive their surroundings as benevolent and **empowering**, offering an abundant livelihood.

By contrast with the Arctic, which is made up of portions of several continents, Antarctica is a true continent, the fifth largest on Earth. Its landmass covers 5.5 million square miles and lies almost wholly beneath a vast ice sheet. The ice measures 7 million cubic miles—that's about 90 percent of all the ice on Earth. In 1983, the lowest recorded temperature on Earth was measured at an Antarctic research center, Vostok Station: –128.6°F.

Unlike the Arctic, the interior of Antarctica may boast only of invertebrate microfauna, such as nematodes and ciliate protozoans. Seals and birds live on the edges of the land. Probably the most spectacular resident of Antarctica is the emperor penguin, a flightless bird standing between three and four feet tall.

Antarctica is the only continent on Earth without a native human population. Although the North and South Poles were first reached at roughly the same time in the early 1900s, the Arctic and Antarctic regions have had different exploration histories. Study of Antarctica **lagged** for some time, largely because trade routes from North America and Europe to the East seemed much more appealing in the far north.

The 1950s, however, witnessed two important events for Antarctica. First was the development of the tourist industry. Second was the Antarctic Treaty, a breakthrough in international diplomacy. This treaty preserved Antarctica from corrupt or **unscrupulous** exploitation that would **mangle** the environment. The agreement set aside the continent as a scientific preserve.

Despite differences between these two polar regions, both have been an equal source of fascination and inspiration for people throughout the centuries.

Audio

For iWords and audio passages, go to SadlierConnect.com.

Definitions

Note the spelling, pronunciation, part(s) of speech, and definition(s) of each of the following words. Then write the appropriate form of the word in the blank space in the illustrative sentence(s) following.

1. affirm
(ə fərm′)

(v.) to declare to be true, state positively; to confirm
Unexpected kindness from a stranger during a time of need can _____**affirm**_____ one's faith in human nature.

2. deter
(di tər′)

(v.) to discourage, scare off, or prevent through fear or doubt
Traffic jams won't _____**deter**_____ us from coming to your birthday party.

3. empower
(em paủ′ ər)

(v.) to give power or authority to; to enable; to permit
Signing this legal paper will _____**empower**_____ me to set up my own bank account.

4. fluent
(flü′ ənt)

(adj.) speaking or writing easily and smoothly, flowing gracefully
Susannah can speak _____**fluent**_____ Japanese, French, and Russian.

5. mangle
(maŋ′ gəl)

(v.) to injure very seriously by cutting, tearing, crushing, etc.; to bring to ruin
Workers could _____**mangle**_____ their hands in this equipment if they don't pay attention to what they're doing.

6. misapprehension
(mis ap ri hen′ shən)

(n.) a wrong idea, misunderstanding
A lingering _____**misapprehension**_____ may cause ill will between friends.

7. recitation
(res′ ə tā′ shən)

(n.) a reading in public of something that is memorized; a memorized poem or piece of prose that is read aloud
Kent was not nervous at all when he gave his Walt Whitman _____**recitation**_____ at the school assembly.

8. supplement
(səp′ lə ment)

(n.) something added to complete a thing or make up for a lack; a section added to a book or document; (v.) to provide such an addition or completion
The sports _____**supplement**_____ is my favorite part of this magazine.
Many people _____**supplement**_____ their regular diet by taking daily vitamins.

Synonyms and antonyms are provided at SadlierConnect.com.

9. surge
(sərj)

(*v.*) to have a heavy, violent, swelling motion (like waves);
(*n.*) a powerful forward rush

Runners who train hard and who have good stamina
often _____**surge**_____ ahead of the pack.
A sudden _____**surge**_____ of electrical
current could make a computer crash.

10. unscrupulous
(ən skrü' pyə ləs)

(*adj.*) dishonest; not guided or controlled by moral principles
Avoid dealing with _____**unscrupulous**_____ merchants
whenever possible.

Using Context

*For each item, determine whether the **boldface** word from pages 190–191
makes sense in the context of the sentence. Circle the item numbers
next to the six sentences in which the words are used correctly.*

1. There is no "off" switch; the only way to **empower** the refrigerator is to
disconnect the plug from the wall outlet.

2. After an interview, you should always send a note to **affirm** your interest in
the position and to thank the interviewer for his or her time.

3. Does the hospital have a generator as a **supplement** in case there is a
power failure in the regular electrical supply lines?

4. If you brake suddenly when you drive, the driver behind you can **mangle**
the rear of your car if he or she does not stop in time.

5. The lost hikers were finally able to find their way back to camp, thanks to
the **fluent** light of the full moon.

6. We were greatly relieved to learn that the report that our local fire station
might close was based on complete rumor and **misapprehension**.

7. Those old class photographs are so faded that the students in them are
almost **unscrupulous**.

8. Even though the new student knew who I was, I had no **recitation** of meeting
her and was unable to address her by her name.

9. During a hurricane or other powerful storm, a dangerous **surge** of ocean
water may hit land along the shoreline.

10. The presence of a cat in a house or apartment is usually enough to **deter**
mice from trying to settle in.

Choosing the Right Word

*Select the **boldface** word that better completes each sentence. You might refer to the passage on pages 188–189 to see how most of these words are used in context. Note that the choices might be related forms of the Unit words.*

1. Everything that I have learned about Theodore Roosevelt from history books (**mangles, affirms**) my reverence for this great president.

2. Shortly after World War II, Japan began the great economic (**surge, misapprehension**) that put it among the world's top industrial nations.

3. Jonathan was furious when his (**fluent, unscrupulous**) boss stole his ideas for an advertising campaign.

4. Ms. Edwards is having us listen to professional speakers to help prepare us for our poetry (**recitations, supplements**).

5. Even though some animals are ferocious and attack livestock, we should not be (**mangled, deterred**) from protecting their dwindling populations.

6. Who (**deterred, empowered**) you to speak for everyone in our class?

7. All those smooth words and vague promises are not going to (**affirm, deter**) us from doing what we know is needed to improve conditions.

8. My yoga class helped improve my breathing and (**supplemented, affirmed**) my training for running the marathon.

9. I agree fully with what the previous speaker has said, but I should like to (**empower, supplement**) his ideas with a few remarks of my own.

10. I would love to be half as (**fluent, unscrupulous**) in Spanish as José is in English.

11. It is far better to know you are ignorant of something than to act on the basis of wrong information and (**misapprehensions, recitations**).

12. When I saw the (**supplemental, mangled**) vehicle, I thought for sure that the driver had to be seriously injured; amazingly, though, he walked away from the wreck.

You may wish to provide students with an explanation and example of a related form.

Completing the Sentence

Choose the word from the word bank that best completes each of the following sentences. Write the correct word or form of the word in the space provided.

affirm	empower	mangle	recitation	surge
deter	fluent	misapprehension	supplement	unscrupulous

1. If you think that I would go to a party without being invited, you are under a complete **misapprehension**.

2. The witness solemnly **affirmed** that the evidence she was about to give was true.

3. As the young girl began her **recitation**, her mouth became dry and her voice began to crack.

4. In spite of all his talents, he will never gain high public office because so many voters feel that he is **unscrupulous** and cannot be trusted.

5. Do you think that it is possible to become **fluent** in a foreign language without actually living in a country where it is spoken?

6. As soon as the doors were opened, the shoppers, eager for the advertised bargains, **surged** into the store in great waves.

7. The unfavorable weather reports did not **deter** us from holding the picnic that we had planned for so long.

8. Since she has a large family, she finds it necessary to **supplement** her income by working at a second job at night and on weekends.

9. The Constitution **empowers** the president to name the people who will fill many of the most important positions in the government.

10. He is so careless in handling his textbooks that by the end of the term he has practically **mangled** all of them.

Encourage students to look for context clues. See page 7.

Definitions

Note the spelling, pronunciation, part(s) of speech, and definition(s) of each of the following words. Then write the appropriate form of the word in the blank space in the illustrative sentence(s) following.

1. adhere
(ad hēr')

(*v.*) to stick to, remain attached; to be devoted or loyal as a follower or supporter

Things will work out better if we _____**adhere**_____ to our original plan.

2. atrocity
(ə träs' ət ē)

(*n.*) an extremely wicked, brutal, or cruel act; something very bad or unpleasant

The Nazis took great pains to keep detailed records of each kind of _____**atrocity**_____ they committed.

3. cope
(kōp)

(*v.*) to struggle successfully against; to prove to be a match for, deal with satisfactorily; (*n.*) a long religious cloak; a canopy

Education and experience provide us with the skills we need to _____**cope**_____ with difficult situations.

We exchanged wedding vows under a blue _____**cope**_____.

4. disquieting
(dis kwī' ət iŋ)

(*adj.*) causing uneasiness or worry

A _____**disquieting**_____ incident at school put all the teachers and students on edge.

5. lag
(lag)

(*v.*) to move slowly or fall behind; to bring up the rear; (*n.*) a falling behind; the amount by which someone or something is behind; an interval

Please try not to _____**lag**_____ behind the others.

There is a three-hour _____**lag**_____ from the time I send you an e-mail until you receive it.

6. optimist
(äp' tə mist)

(*n.*) one who expects things to turn out for the best; someone who looks on the bright side of things

An _____**optimist**_____ holds a rosy view of life.

7. prowl
(praûl)

(*v.*) to roam about stealthily in search of something

A panther can _____**prowl**_____ freely at night because its dark fur prevents it from being seen.

8. stupefy
(stü' pə fī)

(*v.*) to make stupid, dull, or groggy; to surprise or astonish

The vet used a powerful tranquilizer to _____**stupefy**_____ the animal.

Practice with synonyms and antonyms is on page 198.

9. **sulky**
   (səl′ kē)

(*adj.*) in a bad or nasty mood, resentful; gloomy

A _____**sulky**_____ child does not make a very good playmate.

10. **trait**
    (trāt)

(*n.*) a quality or characteristic (especially of personality); a distinguishing feature

Your most appealing _____**trait**_____ is your unfailing sense of humor.

Using Context

*For each item, determine whether the **boldface** word from pages 194–195 makes sense in the context of the sentence. Circle the item numbers next to the six sentences in which the words are used correctly.*

1. I am going to distribute a student questionnaire to **cope** some ideas for planning this year's school dance.

2. Knowing that the local criminals had been caught had a **disquieting** effect on everyone in the community.

3. The normally happy-go-lucky girl was acting so **sulky** that she seemed to be an entirely different person!

4. Although your best **trait** *is* your sense of humor, I think a quality like "work ethic" would be more appropriate to include on your job application.

5. If any student fails to **adhere** to the strict rules of the boarding school, he or she will be expelled.

6. I tried to **stupefy** my friend from going into the room where his surprise party was being set up, but my distraction did not work and he entered anyway.

7. I tried my best to not **lag** behind the other hikers, but the mountain was much steeper than I was used to, and I was having trouble keeping up.

8. She tends to be an **optimist** in most situations, but sometimes she likes to plan for any potential negative outcomes.

9. I watched the cat **prowl** around the yard, looking for her next unsuspecting prey.

10. While many of the parents at the kindergarten dance recital tried to take it seriously, some of them couldn't help but giggle at the cute **atrocity** of the children forgetting their steps.

Choosing the Right Word

*Select the **boldface** word that better completes each sentence. You might refer to the passage on pages 188–189 to see how most of these words are used in context. Note that the choices might be related forms of the Unit words.*

1. Which stylistic (**traits**, atrocities) of Van Gogh's paintings do you find most enthralling?

2. Jackals and other scavengers now (**prowl**, lag) through the ruins of what was once a great city.

3. There is no one (**trait**, optimist) that makes him so likable; it is the overall effect of his personality.

4. My best friend took one look at the statue I fashioned from stray pieces of junk and exclaimed, "That's not a sculpture; it's a(n) (lag, **atrocity**)!"

5. When everything went wrong for Stan, and he saw no way out of his troubles, he muttered to himself, "I just can't (adhere, **cope**)!"

6. My definition of a(n) (**optimist**, trait) is someone who looks at an almost empty bottle of juice and says, "This bottle is one-quarter full."

7. A loud groan went through the class when we got the (sulky, **disquieting**) news that there would be a full-period test later in the week.

8. Have all these years of peace and good living (disquieted, **stupefied**) us to such an extent that we are not even prepared to defend ourselves?

9. The City Council has approved funds for a new playground, but we expect a (**lag**, trait) of several months before construction begins.

10. Come what may, I will (**adhere**, prowl) to the great ideas and ideals for which our ancestors suffered so much.

11. The worst way to deal with disappointments is to become (disquieting, **sulky**); the best way is to smile and make up your mind to try again.

12. I have always wished I had the personality to (adhere, **cope**) with very stressful situations, but the fact is I fall to pieces instead!

You may wish to provide students with an explanation and example of a related form.

Completing the Sentence

Choose the word from the word bank that best completes each of the following sentences. Write the correct word or form of the word in the space provided.

adhere	cope	lag	prowl	sulky
atrocity	disquieting	optimist	stupefy	trait

1. As the robber _____**prowled**_____ the streets looking for victims, he was unaware that undercover police officers were watching his every move.

2. We were so _____**stupefied**_____ by the bad news that for a few moments we just sat there without moving or speaking.

3. In World War I, soldiers in the trenches endured one _____**atrocity**_____ after another, such as contaminated food and water, diseases, and gangrene.

4. If you are having so much trouble with a program of four major courses, how do you expect to _____**cope**_____ with a fifth course?

5. Now that the job has been completed, I have finally become skillful in hanging the paper so that it _____**adheres**_____ firmly to the wall.

6. It is hard to be a(n) _____**optimist**_____ when nothing works out for you.

7. Naturally we were upset when we received the _____**disquieting**_____ news that our uncle had been taken to the hospital.

8. When he gets in one of those _____**sulky**_____ moods, he is as unreasonable and unpleasant as a cranky child.

9. In spite of our best efforts, collections for the Community Fund this year have _____**lagged**_____ far behind last year's figures.

10. Throughout her long and noble career, her outstanding _____**trait**_____ has been her deep love for her fellow human beings.

Encourage students to look for context clues. See page 7.

Synonyms

*Choose the word or form of the word from this Unit that is the same or most nearly the same in meaning as the **boldface** word or expression in the phrase. Write that word on the line. Use a dictionary if necessary.*

1. his dramatic **delivery** of the poem — recitation
2. hikers who **trail** behind the group — lag
3. unsure how to **manage** without her help — cope
4. had a **misconception** about him — misapprehension
5. **able to speak easily** on the topic of electricity — fluent
6. knocked down by the **rush** of the fans — surge
7. **authorized** to take the lead on the project — empowered
8. an **addition** to the regular menu — supplement
9. jailed for **corrupt** practices — unscrupulous
10. **stunned** by the news — stupefied
11. **damaged** the lock on the bicycle — mangled
12. **skulk** around the neighborhood — prowl
13. **hold fast** to the plan — adhere
14. a letter containing some **troubling** news — disquieting
15. the most unique **attribute** of the breed — trait

Antonyms

*Choose the word or form of the word from this Unit that is most nearly opposite in meaning to the **boldface** word or expression in the phrase. Write that word on the line. Use a dictionary if necessary.*

1. known for her **sunny** disposition — sulky
2. **deny** his claim to the throne — affirm
3. witnessed a **caring act** — atrocity
4. attempted to **spur on** their mission — deter
5. was a hopeless **pessimist** — optimist

Writing: Words in Action

Answers to the prompt will vary.

Using details from the passage (pages 188–189), compare and contrast the Arctic and Antarctica. In your conclusion, state which polar region you would rather visit and explain why. Include at least two details from the passage, and use three or more words from this Unit.

Vocabulary in Context

*Some of the words you have studied in this Unit appear in **boldface** type. Read the passage below, and then circle the letter of the correct answer for each word as it is used in context.*

Golf lovers who don't wish to **adhere** to their regular routine might want to travel north—far, far north, above the Arctic Circle. The midnight sun is a natural phenomenon that occurs only in the polar regions. In the Lofoten Islands in northern Norway, for example, the sun never sets from late May to late July. That's 24 hours of natural light each day—plenty of time to tee off!

Imagine playing golf at 2 a.m. against a dramatic backdrop of snowcapped mountains and sparkling, green-blue sea. Visitors could no doubt give a **recitation** of the many benefits of endless days spent under the Arctic light. Some might say they have more time to play golf, hike, or explore the quaint fishing villages and the fascinating Lofotr Viking Museum. Others might claim they have more energy just being out in so much light. Of course, those adventurous folks up playing golf or sightseeing in the middle of the night should probably **supplement** their sleep with plenty of naps. There's always the chance of becoming **sulky** from inadequate rest.

Many citizens of Norway are **fluent** in many languages and can give advice on the best places to see in the Lofoten region. If golf is your game, you might want to stick to visiting in the summer months. Arctic winters are brutal. In midwinter, the sun barely rises. Heavy snow falls, and it's frigidly cold. Just the thought of living through all those long, dark, cold days is an **atrocity** for most people from milder climates. Let's leave that to the Vikings!

---

1. **Adhere** comes from the Latin word **adhaerere. Adhaerere** most likely means
   a. to plan
   (b.) to stick to
   c. to imitate
   d. to give up

2. What is the meaning of **recitation** as it is used in paragraph 2?
   (a.) presentation
   b. sample
   c. proposal
   d. challenge

3. What is the meaning of **supplement** as it is used in paragraph 2?
   a. subtract from
   b. indulge in
   (c.) add to
   d. try out

4. The word **sulky** means about the same as
   a. hopeful
   b. cheerful
   c. energetic
   (d.) gloomy

5. Which word means the same as **fluent** as it is used in paragraph 3?
   (a.) articulate
   b. simple
   c. impressive
   d. reserved

6. What does the word **atrocity** most likely mean as it is used in paragraph 3?
   a. a challenge
   (b.) a monstrosity
   c. a problem
   d. an answer

UNIT 14

Note that not all of the Unit words are used in this passage. *Abstain, enumerate, extort, replica,* and *self-seeking* are used in the passage on page 211.

*Read the following passage, taking note of the **boldface** words and their contexts. These words are among those you will be studying in Unit 14. It may help you to complete the exercises in this Unit if you refer to the way the words are used below.*

Madam C. J. Walker and Her Wonderful Remedy
<Biographical Sketch>

Pioneering entrepreneur Madam C. J. Walker was likely both the first woman and first African American self-made millionaire. She achieved her fortune by creating, marketing, and selling a hair tonic for African American women. She **transformed** her life and reached her **exalted** status through hard work, determination, and courage. As she liked to say, "I got my start by giving myself a start."

Madam Walker's real name was Sarah Breedlove. She was born in 1867 into a **glum** world of poverty and hardship. Her parents were newly freed slaves who worked the cotton fields on a Louisiana plantation. They left her an orphan at age seven.

Sarah Breedlove's early life was full of sadness, trouble, change, and **upheaval**. Seeking **sanctuary** from an abusive brother-in-law, she married as a 14-year-old and became a mother as a 17-year-old. She went from picking cotton to washing clothes for $1.50 a day. Despite her lack of formal education and money, she was not content to remain an obedient and **submissive** wife or employee to a tough **taskmaster**. She had other ideas.

To treat her hair loss and a scalp problem caused by poor nutrition, she began mixing homemade hair-care recipes. She hit upon a scalp conditioner and healing formula and dubbed it Madam C. J. Walker's Wonderful Hair Grower. (She used her third husband's name,

C. J. Walker, **appending** "Madam" as well for sparkle.) She turned her remedy into a booming business.

Knowing that he who hesitates is lost, Madam Walker quickly took her product on the road. She traveled for years, selling her hair and beauty products successfully door-to-door to a **responsive** and eager audience. Hotels refused to **accommodate** African Americans, so she often stayed instead with local African American parishioners.

After years of struggle, business was so good she was able to hire and train sales agents. They were all African American women seeking a better life. In 1910, Madam Walker moved to Indianapolis and **amalgamated** her different business ventures into The Madam C. J. Walker Manufacturing Company. The Walker compound consisted of a factory, beauty school and salon, and training center for her growing sales force.

A **tally** of Madam C. J. Walker's many accomplishments shows she was not just a successful businesswoman. She was also a philanthropist and arts patron. She used her influence and fortune to help others. She gave large sums to charities and orphanages.

Madam Walker was vocal about social injustice. She spoke out against racist attitudes at a time when it was risky to do so. She petitioned Congress and the President to support federal anti-lynching laws. And she showed her **allegiance** to the National Association for the Advancement of Colored People (NAACP), pledging $5,000 to its anti-lynching campaign. It was the largest single donation the civil rights organization had ever received.

In 1998, the United States Postal Service issued a stamp **commemorating** Madam Walker and her extraordinary accomplishments. Her New York mansion is a National Historic Landmark, as is the former Walker Company building in Indianapolis, which now houses the Madame Walker Theatre Center. There is a street in Manhattan honoring Madam Walker and her daughter, A'Lelia, who was a famous Manhattan society figure.

Harvard Business School recognized Madam Walker as one of the great American business leaders of the twentieth century. It would not be unrealistic or **far-fetched** to say the rags-to-riches story of the little girl who dreamed big has inspired generations.

Audio

For iWords and audio passages, go to SadlierConnect.com.

Beauty mogul Madam C.J. Walker at the wheel of her Model T Ford

Madam C.J. Walker's Wonderful Hair Grower sparked a beauty empire.

Definitions

Note the spelling, pronunciation, part(s) of speech, and definition(s) of each of the following words. Then write the appropriate form of the word in the blank space in the illustrative sentence(s) following.

1. **abstain**
   (ab stān')

   (*v.*) to stay away from doing something by one's own choice
   I find it hard to _____**abstain**_____ from these tempting and delicious desserts.

2. **allegiance**
   (ə lēj' əns)

   (*n.*) the loyalty or obligation owed to a government, nation, or cause
   At a festive yet solemn ceremony, fifty new citizens swore _____**allegiance**_____ to their adopted nation.

3. **append**
   (ə pend')

   (*v.*) to attach, add, or tack on as a supplement or extra item
   We were dismayed when our teacher decided to _____**append**_____ an additional assignment to our already huge load of homework.

4. **enumerate**
   (i nü' mə rāt)

   (*v.*) to count; to name one by one, list
   These booklets _____**enumerate**_____ and compare all the high-tech features that new televisions can offer.

5. **extort**
   (ek stôrt')

   (*v.*) to obtain by violence, misuse of authority, or threats
   The kidnappers tried to _____**extort**_____ a huge sum of money in return for releasing their prisoners unharmed.

6. **glum**
   (gləm)

   (*adj.*) depressed, gloomy
   The losing team wore _____**glum**_____ expressions on their faces as the final buzzer sounded.

7. **replica**
   (rep' lə kə)

   (*n.*) a copy, close reproduction
   We visited a life-size _____**replica**_____ of the *Mayflower*, the Pilgrim ship docked near Plymouth, Massachusetts.

8. **self-seeking**
   (self sēk' iŋ)

   (*adj.*) selfishly ambitious
   That _____**self-seeking**_____ politician will promise just about anything to win a few more votes.

Synonyms and antonyms are provided at SadlierConnect.com.

9. **tally**
(tal' ē)

(*v.*) to count up; to keep score; to make entries for reckoning; to correspond or agree; (*n.*) a total or score

They will _____ **tally** _____ the votes after 9:00 P.M.

Our teacher keeps an accurate _____ **tally** _____ of all of our absences.

10. **upheaval**
(əp hēv' əl)

(*n.*) a sudden, violent upward movement; great disorder or radical change

The sudden change in leadership caused dramatic social and economic _____ **upheaval** _____.

Using Context

*For each item, determine whether the **boldface** word from pages 202–203 makes sense in the context of the sentence. Circle the item numbers next to the six sentences in which the words are used correctly.*

(**1.**) In his speech at the awards ceremony, the director said, "Because there are so many people who helped to make this film a success, I don't have time to **enumerate** all of them."

2. The honey was so thick and **glum** that it was almost impossible to squeeze it out of the plastic bottle.

3. Stalactites are pointy rock formations that **append** like icicles from the ceiling of a cave.

(**4.**) First we will **tally** the number of tickets sold; then we will multiply that number by 10, the cost in dollars of each ticket, to see how much money we have raised so far.

5. Most people will need to read this poem several times to be able to properly **extort** its meaning.

(**6.**) It's good manners for audience members to **abstain** from talking while viewing a movie at a cinema or a play in a theater.

(**7.**) The group of knights raised their swords and solemnly swore their **allegiance** to the king and queen.

(**8.**) Is that a real dinosaur skeleton in the lobby of the museum, or is it a **replica**?

9. We sent her an email as well as a card to congratulate her on her **upheaval** to vice-president of the company.

(**10.**) The **self-seeking** captain clearly cared more about the success of his voyage than the safety and well-being of his crew.

Choosing the Right Word

*Select the **boldface** word that better completes each sentence. You might refer to the passage on pages 200–201 to see how most of these words are used in context. Note that the choices might be related forms of the Unit words.*

1. Only seven members of the Security Council voted on the resolution; the others (**abstained, tallied**).

2. The mayor had to choose between (**allegiance, tally**) to his political party and his judgment of what was best for the city.

3. Ms. Wilentz is the kind of manager who does not try to (**extort, abstain**) cooperation from the people under her, but earns it by being a real leader.

4. Instead of working so hard to prepare (**replicas, allegiances**) of famous works of art, why don't you try to create something original?

5. My trainer wants me to (**abstain, enumerate**) from eating highly processed foods, especially those made with sugar and wheat.

6. If you look so (**self-seeking, glum**) just because you can't go to the party, how are you going to react when something really bad happens?

7. He enjoys (**abstaining, enumerating**) all the factors that enabled him to rise from poverty to great wealth, but he always omits the important element of luck.

8. I could tell from the players' (**self-seeking, glum**) expressions that the team was losing the game.

9. I didn't have time to write a letter to Lucy, but I (**appended, enumerated**) a few sentences to my sister's letter, expressing my congratulations.

10. Unless the poor people of the country see some hope of improving their lives, there will probably soon be a great social (**allegiance, upheaval**).

11. Experience has taught me that people who constantly boast about their unselfishness are often secretly quite (**glum, self-seeking**).

12. The detective's suspicion was aroused when the suspect's story failed to (**tally, extort**) with the known facts of the case.

You may wish to provide students with an explanation and example of a related form.

Completing the Sentence

Choose the word from the word bank that best completes each of the following sentences. Write the correct word or form of the word in the space provided.

abstain	append	extort	replica	tally
allegiance	enumerate	glum	self-seeking	upheaval

1. Though an injured hand kept Larry from actually bowling, he took part in the tournament by keeping a careful **tally** of the scores.

2. Remember that the Pledge of **Allegiance** is not a formula to be repeated mechanically but a summary of our sacred duty to our country.

3. We learned in our science class how **upheaval** of Earth's crust has resulted in the formation of mountains.

4. When we visited New York City, we bought a small **replica** of the Statue of Liberty as a memento of our trip.

5. I love basketball games, but I have decided to **abstain** from attending them until I can get my grades up to where they should be.

6. I know that Mother has given you all kinds of instructions before you leave for camp, but let me **append** some extra advice of my own.

7. When Ben Franklin said, "God helps those who help themselves," he did not mean that the most important thing in life is to be **self-seeking**.

8. Imagine how **glum** we felt when a sudden wave of warm weather melted all the snow and ruined our plans for a winter carnival!

9. The driving instructor **enumerated** carefully the bad habits and practices that are likely to lead to accidents.

10. Is there anything more despicable than trying to **extort** money from innocent people by threatening them with bodily harm?

Encourage students to look for context clues. See page 7.

End Set A

Unit 14 ■ *205*

Definitions

Note the spelling, pronunciation, part(s) of speech, and definition(s) of each of the following words. Then write the appropriate form of the word in the blank space in the illustrative sentence(s) following.

1. **accommodate**
   (ə käm′ ə dāt)

   (*v.*) to do a favor or service for, help out; to provide for, supply with; to have space for; to make fit or suitable

   That van is the ideal vehicle for carpooling because it can __accommodate__ nine passengers.

2. **amalgamate**
   (ə mal′ gə māt)

   (*v.*) to unite; to combine elements into a unified whole

   Two small companies will __amalgamate__ into one large corporation on June 1.

3. **commemorate**
   (kə mem′ ə rāt)

   (*v.*) to preserve, honor, or celebrate the memory of

   Each May we __commemorate__ Grandpa's life by lighting a special candle for him that burns for 24 hours.

4. **exalt**
   (eg zôlt′)

   (*v.*) to make high in rank, power, character, or quality; to fill with pride, joy, or noble feeling; to praise, honor

   Let us now __exalt__ the heroes for their courage and character in the face of all this adversity.

5. **far-fetched**
   (fär fecht′)

   (*adj.*) strained or improbable (in the sense of not being logical or believable), going far afield from a topic

   No one will believe the __far-fetched__ excuse you just gave!

6. **responsive**
   (ri spän′ siv)

   (*adj.*) answering or replying; reacting readily to requests, suggestions, etc.; showing interest and understanding

   The host of the charming inn was __responsive__ to our every wish.

7. **sanctuary**
   (saŋk′ chə wer ē)

   (*n.*) a sacred or holy place; refuge or protection from capture or punishment; a place of refuge or protection

   The exhausted refugees found __sanctuary__ in a local church.

8. **submissive**
   (səb mis′ iv)

   (*adj.*) humbly obedient; tending to give in to authority, obeying without protest

   In some cultures, boys and men still expect girls and women to behave in a totally __submissive__ manner.

Practice with synonyms and antonyms is on page 210.

206 ■ *Unit 14*

9. taskmaster
(task' mas tər)

(*n.*) one whose job it is to assign work to others; one who uses his or her power to make people work very hard

The crusty old boss was a harsh _____taskmaster_____ but also an efficient manager.

10. transform
(trans fôrm')

(*v.*) to change completely in appearance or form; to make into something else

A heavy rain could _____transform_____ the parched yellow fields into a lush green landscape again.

Using Context

*For each item, determine whether the **boldface** word from pages 206–207 makes sense in the context of the sentence. Circle the item numbers next to the six sentences in which the words are used correctly.*

1. When we realized how similar our projects were, we decided to **commemorate** our efforts and work on one project together.

(2.) A makeover or new haircut can give a person a fresh look, but it will not **transform** him or her into a different person.

3. I thought the lead in the play was quite good, but the critics continued to **exalt** the actress and suggest that she had no talent whatsoever.

4. The expression on the interviewer's face was **submissive**, showing that he was not impressed by my summary of my employment experience.

(5.) My sister was not particularly **responsive** to my suggestion that she do my chores for the rest of the month.

(6.) When I had to make a last-minute trip, I was grateful to find that the single hotel at my destination was able to **accommodate** me.

(7.) The people who had to evacuate their homes were glad to find **sanctuary** in a community center out of harm's way.

8. He is such a negative person that he can find a way to **amalgamate** even in the best of circumstances.

(9.) A new manager was brought in to be a **taskmaster** for the unmotivated workforce, pushing them to be more productive every day.

(10.) Your paper was well written, but the comparison of a classic novel to a modern reality show was too **far-fetched** to get your point across.

Choosing the Right Word

*Select the **boldface** word that better completes each sentence. You might refer to the passage on pages 200–201 to see how most of these words are used in context. Note that the choices might be related forms of the Unit words.*

1. In Robert Louis Stevenson's classic story, a chemical potion (**exalts**, **transforms**) the good Dr. Jekyll into the evil Mr. Hyde.

2. Because she sets extremely high standards for herself and is always pushing herself to do better, she is her own most severe (**taskmaster**, **sanctuary**).

3. The new hotel is spacious enough to (**accommodate**, **exalt**) large groups of people attending conventions and banquets.

4. When he felt low, he found that singing (**exalted**, **amalgamated**) his spirits.

5. Isn't it a little (**far-fetched**, **submissive**) to suggest that the pollution of our environment is mainly caused by creatures from outer space?

6. On the weekends, my parents are (**taskmasters**, **sanctuaries**), handing out lists of chores for all the children to do.

7. Each member of the basketball team was awarded a trophy to (**transform**, **commemorate**) the championship season.

8. Nina is not very (**submissive**, **responsive**) to the idea of hiking up Mt. Kilimanjaro for her honeymoon.

9. The United States has a long history of providing (**taskmasters**, **sanctuary**) to those fleeing persecution abroad.

10. We cannot have a peaceful and just society so long as any one group is required to be (**responsive**, **submissive**) to another.

11. After a complete makeover, the scruffy young man was (**exalted**, **transformed**) into a distinguished-looking gentleman.

12. Financiers are planning to (**accommodate**, **amalgamate**) various businesses in the United States and England into one huge multinational corporation.

You may wish to provide students with an explanation and example of a related form.

Completing the Sentence

Choose the word from the word bank that best completes each of the following sentences. Write the correct word or form of the word in the space provided.

accommodate	commemorate	far-fetched	sanctuary	taskmaster
amalgamate	exalt	responsive	submissive	transform

1. I enjoyed the first part of the detective story, but the surprise ending was so **far-fetched** that I couldn't accept it.

2. On Memorial Day, Americans gather in ceremonies across the country to **commemorate** the nation's war dead.

3. Can you see why it was logical for various labor unions in the clothing and textile industries to **amalgamate** into a single organization?

4. In just a few years, she was **transformed** from an awkward tomboy into a charming young woman.

5. Anne usually seems to be quiet and **submissive**, but she has a way of flaring up when she feels that anyone is being unfair to her.

6. Under the U.S. Constitution, officials are never **exalted** to a point where they are more important or more powerful than the law.

7. Every entertainer likes a(n) **responsive** audience that shows it appreciates and enjoys a performance.

8. A portion of the forest has been set aside as a bird **sanctuary** for the protection of endangered species in the area.

9. I would like to **accommodate** you, but I don't think it is right to allow you to copy my homework.

10. Good employees don't need a(n) **taskmaster** to keep them working.

Encourage students to look for context clues. See page 7.

Synonyms

*Choose the word or form of the word from this Unit that is the same or most nearly the same in meaning as the **boldface** word or expression in the phrase. Write that word on the line. Use a dictionary if necessary.*

1. fear of displeasing the **overseer**   taskmaster
2. a space big enough to **house** our belongings   accommodate
3. **acclaimed** as a standard of beauty   exalted
4. was **receptive** to our every wish   responsive
5. has clearly proven his **devotion**   allegiance
6. the **disruption** of the political party   upheaval
7. **memorialize** the veterans   commemorate
8. keep an accurate **record**   tally
9. an **arrogant** and opportunistic person   self-seeking
10. an **imitation** of the painting   replica
11. **alter** the room for the festivities   transform
12. **attach** her comments to the report   append
13. as **itemized** on the packing slip   enumerated
14. lit candles in the quiet **place of worship**   sanctuary
15. chose to **refrain** from voting   abstain

Antonyms

*Choose the word or form of the word from this Unit that is most nearly opposite in meaning to the **boldface** word or expression in the phrase. Write that word on the line. Use a dictionary if necessary.*

1. was **cheerful** after the tournament   glum
2. told a **believable** tale   far-fetched
3. known for being a **rebellious** stallion   submissive
4. a reputation for **donating** money   extorting
5. **separate** the ingredients   amalgamate

Writing: Words in Action

Answers to the prompt will vary.

Suppose you are a sales representative. You want to persuade your company to sell Madam C. J. Walker's beauty products. Write a persuasive proposal stating why the products would enhance company sales. Use at least two details from the passage (pages 200–201) and three or more words from this Unit.

Vocabulary in Context

*Some of the words you have studied in this Unit appear in **boldface** type. Read the passage below, and then circle the letter of the correct answer for each word as it is used in context.*

Most shampoo users can **enumerate** the reasons why they love shampoo. It leaves their hair squeaky clean, soft, and shiny. It smells great. But just who came up with the idea?

German inventor Hans Schwarzkopf concocted powdered shampoo in the early 1900s. Then in the late 1920s he introduced liquid shampoo, a **replica** of the shampoo we use today. But the first shampoo can be traced to 16th-century India. Brews of fruit pulp, flower petals, herbs, and oils were massaged into the scalp to purify hair. In fact, the word *shampoo* comes from a Hindi word that means "to massage."

For thousands of years, people all over the world used soaps made from animal fats, wood ash, and plants to clean their bodies and—sometimes—their hair. In truth, though, although they would apply sweet-smelling tonics and **append** fancy hair ornaments, most never bothered to clean their hair at all, except on special occasions!

British colonial traders brought the Indian method of cleaning hair to Europe. In the late 1700s, **self-seeking** Indian businessman Dean Mahomet traveled to London and introduced Indian hair massage to English society, making his fortune. The idea of shampooing hair gradually caught on. People washed their hair more frequently, although most still used harsh soaps in bar form. The twentieth century saw the rise of many fancy shampoo brands. Shampoo became a billion-dollar industry. These days, the "no-poo" anti-shampoo movement has gained ground. Some people are choosing to **abstain** from using shampoo altogether. But you'd have to **extort** most shampoo lovers to go without their beloved brands!

---

1. What is the meaning of **enumerate** as it is used in paragraph 1?
a. demonstrate   c. spread
b. list   d. invent

2. What is the meaning of **replica** as it is used in paragraph 2?
a. partial idea   c. close reproduction
b. perfect experiment   d. complete opposite

3. **Append** comes from the Latin word **appendere**. **Appendere** most likely means
a. to try   c. to create
b. to substitute   d. to hang

4. The word **self-seeking** means about the same as
a. opportunistic   c. fearless
b. adventurous   d. shy

5. Which word means the same as **abstain** as it is used in paragraph 4?
a. attempt   c. avoid
b. want   d. sample

6. What does the word **extort** most likely mean as it is used in paragraph 4?
a. oppose   c. require
b. coerce   d. encourage

See pages T29–T31 for assessment options.

UNIT 15

Note that not all of the Unit words are used in this passage. *Confiscate, pantomime, pessimist,* and *wistful* are used in the passage on page 223.

*Read the following passage, taking note of the **boldface** words and their contexts. These words are among those you will be studying in Unit 15. It may help you to complete the exercises in this Unit if you refer to the way the words are used below.*

Running With the Big Dogs
<Magazine Article>

Throughout history, humans have depended on working guard dogs to protect and herd their animal flocks. For centuries, these dogs have served as **beacons** of protection. A well-trained guard dog is probably the most sensible **precaution** a shepherd or rancher can take to protect his herds against dangerous **encounters** with wolves or bears. The size, strength, and speed of three breeds shed some light on their ability to **retaliate** fiercely against attackers.

First is the Great Pyrenees. This truly massive breed takes its name from the Pyrenees—mountains located between France and Spain. Comparative **data** show that this is one of the largest of the flock guardians. A Great Pyrenees may stand as high as 32 inches and weigh up to 130 pounds. The medium-long, snow-white coat is sometimes shaded with gray or tan. The Great Pyrenees's coat blends in with a flock of sheep or goats and functions as a **sham**. Would-be attackers often do not suspect that the large white shape among the herd animals is really a protector of **epic** courage and strength. A Pyrenees will stop at nothing to **chasten**, or even kill, any invader threatening his flock.

It does not **detract** from the Pyrenees's awesome reputation to note that it is easily trained and especially patient with children. This makes the Pyrenees a **wholesome** household pet. The breed combines safety, affection, and beauty.

Like the Great Pyrenees, the Komondor sheepdog of Hungary enjoys the benefit of camouflage. A Komondor's white coat is doubly protective because it is corded from head to tail. The breed's tangled and woolly coat perfectly enables it to **prosecute** its mission of guarding a flock. Potential predators do not suspect the strength that lurks beneath those ropy cords. In addition, the Komondor's seemingly **uncouth**

Great Pyrenees guard sheep and goats.

jacket guards it against the fangs and claws of **berserk** enemies. Finally, a Komondor's coat superbly insulates it against harsh weather.

A Komondor is only slightly smaller than a Great Pyrenees. Males stand up to 28 inches high and may weigh 100 pounds or more. With a large head and a long, agile stride, the Komondor is truly a majestic animal.

Farther east in Europe, the Turkish Kangal Dog offers a third canine example of outstanding strength and courage. Largely unknown outside Turkey, the Kangal is prized in its homeland as a national treasure. The

28 inches tall

The Komondor
dog and a
Leicester sheep

photograph below **underscores** several typical characteristics of the breed. Like a Pyrenees and a Komondor, a Kangal blends in with the herd. This dog is short-coated and almost always exhibits a black mask and ears. The legs are large-boned and well-muscled, and the tail is curled. The breed's homeland is the rugged steppe, or prairie, of east-central Turkey. Unlike the Great Pyrenees and the Komondor, coated in **celestial** white, the Kangal usually sports a gray or tan-colored coat. The very appearance of a Kangal projects authority. Any illusions that attackers of the herd may harbor will surely be **punctured** if a Kangal is on duty.

Readers can find out more about each of these breeds. Nationally recognized breed associations are located throughout the country.

Inez P. Farquar is a regular contributor to Dog Days *magazine. When she's not playing fetch with her two terriers, Ms. Farquar volunteers at her local animal shelter.*

The Turkish Kangal
Dog guarding goats

Audio

For iWords and
audio passages, go to
SadlierConnect.com.

Definitions

Note the spelling, pronunciation, part(s) of speech, and definition(s) of each of the following words. Then write the appropriate form of the word in the blank space in the illustrative sentence(s) following.

---

1. berserk
(bər sərk')

(*adj., adv.*) violently and destructively enraged
A _____**berserk**_____ man terrified the crowd of subway riders.
The wounded lion went _____**berserk**_____ in his cage.

---

2. chasten
(chā' sən)

(*v.*) to punish (in order to bring about improvement in behavior, attitude, etc.); to restrain, moderate
Dad knows how to _____**chasten**_____ the stubborn child with a firm but soothing voice.

---

3. detract
(di trakt')

(*v.*) to take away from; reduce in value or reputation
Nothing can _____**detract**_____ from your beauty!

---

4. encounter
(en kaun' tər)

(*n.*) a meeting (especially one that is unplanned); a meeting of enemies, battle; (*v.*) to meet or come upon
Remember our _____**encounter**_____ with that skunk?
We might _____**encounter**_____ other curious animals.

---

5. pantomime
(pan' tə mīm)

(*n.*) a play or story performed without words by actors using only gestures; (*v.*) to express in this way
The performer included a short _____**pantomime**_____.
We _____**pantomime**_____ when we're unable to speak.

---

6. precaution
(pri kô' shən)

(*n.*) care taken beforehand; a step or action taken to prevent something from happening
I advise you to take every _____**precaution**_____ necessary to prevent a household fire.

---

7. puncture
(pəŋk' chər)

(*n.*) a small hole made by a sharp object; (*v.*) to make such a hole, pierce
The _____**puncture**_____ caused the balloon to explode.
I winced as the thorn _____**punctured**_____ my skin.

---

8. sham
(sham)

(*adj.*) fake, not genuine; (*n.*) something false pretending to be genuine; a pretender; a decorated pillow covering; (*v.*) to pretend
The play includes a _____**sham**_____ fight scene.
Her claim that she's a princess is a _____**sham**_____.
Don't _____**sham**_____ an illness in order to miss a day of school.

Synonyms and antonyms are provided at SadlierConnect.com.

9. uncouth
(ən küth′)

(*adj.*) unrefined, crude; awkward or clumsy

Although the quality of his work was good, his
_____**uncouth**_____ attitude cost him the job.

10. wistful
(wist′ fəl)

(*adj.*) full of melancholy yearning or longing, sad, pensive

Her _____**wistful**_____ look made me sad.

Using Context

*For each item, determine whether the **boldface** word from pages 214–215 makes sense in the context of the sentence. Circle the item numbers next to the six sentences in which the words are used correctly.*

1. It would be impossible to **encounter** the damage that a large-scale oil spill could cause to the area's fragile ecosystem.

(2.) Performers in classic ballets such as *Sleeping Beauty* and *The Nutcracker* must be skilled not only in dance but also in the art of **pantomime**.

(3.) The band's lead singer stopped in the middle of a song to **chasten** some members of the audience and remind them that flash photography was not permitted.

(4.) The product, which comes with claims that it can instantly cure a cold or the flu, is clearly a **sham**.

5. Because he seemed completely sincere and **uncouth**, the witness made a positive impression on the jury.

(6.) Some of the seaside town's residents strongly oppose construction of the new hotel because it would **detract** from their view of the water.

7. Some people dislike the sharp, **wistful** taste of raw mustard greens, while others find it assertive and pleasing.

8. The fallen tree on the road is a **precaution** that should be reported right away.

(9.) In one scene in the movie, a robot goes **berserk** and attacks the captain and crew of the spaceship.

(10.) You can repair the **puncture** in the air mattress with this patch and this glue.

Choosing the Right Word

*Select the **boldface** word that better completes each sentence. You might refer to the passage on pages 212–213 to see how most of these words are used in context. Note that the choices might be related forms of the Unit words.*

1. My grandmother becomes (**wistful**, **detracted**) when she recalls her childhood in the Swiss Alps.

2. Her writing style is a little (**wistful**, **uncouth**), but what it lacks in polish and refinement is more than made up for by its wonderful humor.

3. Parents who fail to (**chasten**, **detract**) their children for rude, impolite behavior may regret their lenient attitude later.

4. As I watched through the soundproof hospital window, the skaters on the pond seemed to be carrying out a colorful (**pantomime**, **sham**).

5. I knew that it would be difficult to raise funds for the recycling program, but I never expected to (**chasten**, **encounter**) so many tough problems.

6. I, for one, was extremely offended by the teen's (**wistful**, **uncouth**) behavior and foul language.

7. For some strange reason, the photocopier suddenly went (**berserk**, **wistful**) and started spewing vast quantities of paper all over the floor.

8. Many a perfectly healthy employee has been known to (**puncture**, **sham**) illness to avoid going to work.

9. My first (**encounter**, **precaution**) with the new neighbors was amicable, and I believed we were all going to become good friends.

10. The news that I had been dropped from the football squad (**detracted**, **punctured**) my dream of becoming a great gridiron hero.

11. It does not (**chasten**, **detract**) in the least from his reputation as a great player to say that all the team members deserve equal credit.

12. Although I do not get seasick, I am going to take some anti-motion sickness medication just as a (**precaution**, **puncture**).

You may wish to provide students with an explanation and example of a related form.

Completing the Sentence

Choose the word from the word bank that best completes each of the following sentences. Write the correct word or form of the word in the space provided.

berserk	detract	pantomime	puncture	uncouth
chasten	encounter	precaution	sham	wistful

1. Nothing can _____ **detract** _____ from the fact that he stood by us in our hour of greatest need.

2. With a(n) _____ **wistful** _____ expression on his face, the prisoner looked through his cell window at the patch of sky that meant freedom to him.

3. Late that afternoon, one of the inmates went _____ **berserk** _____ and totally wrecked the infirmary.

4. In the old days, whippings and other forms of physical punishment were used to _____ **chasten** _____ student misbehavior, even in college.

5. Before we use the blowtorch in our industrial arts class, we are required to take the _____ **precaution** _____ of wearing goggles.

6. Although he could speak no English, he made us understand by the use of _____ **pantomime** _____ that he was extremely thirsty.

7. Little did I realize when I _____ **encountered** _____ that old man on a lonely beach that this chance meeting would change my life.

8. Freedom of speech is a(n) _____ **sham** _____ and a mockery if it does not apply to people whose opinions are very unpopular.

9. So there I was with a(n) _____ **puncture** _____ in one of my rear tires, on a lonely road, on a dark night, and during a violent rainstorm!

10. In polite society, it is considered _____ **uncouth** _____ to balance peas on your knife at the dinner table.

Encourage students to look for context clues. See page 7.

End Set A

Definitions

Note the spelling, pronunciation, part(s) of speech, and definition(s) of each of the following words. Then write the appropriate form of the word in the blank space in the illustrative sentence(s) following.

1. beacon
(bē′ kən)

(*n.*) a light or other signal that warns and guides; a lighthouse; anything that guides or inspires

Sailors returning to port on a dark night search for the glow of a familiar ____**beacon**____.

2. celestial
(sə les′ chəl)

(*adj.*) having to do with the sky or heavens; heavenly; yielding great bliss or happiness

The sun is the brightest ____**celestial**____ body in our solar system.

3. confiscate
(kän′ fə skāt)

(*v.*) to seize by authority; to take and keep

The police will ____**confiscate**____ that car.

4. data
(dā′ tə)

(*pl. n.*) information; facts, figures, statistics

For math class, we collected ____**data**____ on the Internet sites students visited during the past week.

5. epic
(ep′ ik)

(*n.*) a long narrative poem (or other literary composition) about the deeds of heroes; an event or movement of great sweep; (*adj.*) on a grand scale, vast, titanic

Beowulf, the English ____**epic**____, was written around the year 700.

It describes ____**epic**____ struggles between the forces of good and evil.

6. pessimist
(pes′ ə mist)

(*n.*) one who believes or expects the worst; prophet of doom

A ____**pessimist**____ sees a glass as half empty.

7. prosecute
(präs′ ə kyüt)

(*v.*) to bring before a court of law for trial; to carry out

She was told she would not be ____**prosecuted**____ if she restored the money.

8. retaliate
(ri tal′ ē āt)

(*v.*) to get revenge; to strike back for an injury

I would ____**retaliate**____ for that cheap insult, but I fear it may only make matters worse.

Practice with synonyms and antonyms is on page 222.

218 ■ *Unit 15*

9. underscore
(ən' dər skôr)

(*v.*) to draw a line under; to put special emphasis on;
(*n.*) a line drawn under something

The dire situation in the hospital's emergency room _____**underscores**_____ the importance of having enough doctors and nurses available.

The word with the _____**underscore**_____ is in Spanish.

10. wholesome
(hōl' səm)

(*adj.*) healthy; morally and socially sound and good; helping to bring about or preserve good health

He always eats _____**wholesome**_____ foods.

Using Context

*For each item, determine whether the **boldface** word from pages 218–219 makes sense in the context of the sentence. Circle the item numbers next to the six sentences in which the words are used correctly.*

1. Reading a variety of materials on different subjects is a good way to **confiscate** a broad vocabulary.

(2.) The best way to **underscore** your opinion on something is to use real-life examples that will help prove your point.

(3.) Before you write your paper, make sure you have sufficient **data** to support your claims on the topic.

(4.) The new movie tells the **epic** story of a soldier's journey from his enlistment to his experience during World War II.

5. After spending a long day around many people, I need to **retaliate** to my bedroom to get some rest.

(6.) Even though she has faced many struggles throughout her life, she is not a **pessimist** and always hopes for the best.

7. I was willing to give horseback riding a try until I saw the **celestial** horse before me and was petrified to get on this huge creature's back.

8. His **wholesome** diet consists mainly of fast food and sweets, so I have been encouraging him to eat better.

(9.) When the hiker realized she was completely lost on the trail, she looked around for a **beacon** that would lead her back to the entrance.

(10.) The attorney was determined to **prosecute** the criminal but had to find enough evidence to prove the suspect's guilt.

Choosing the Right Word

*Select the **boldface** word that better completes each sentence. You might refer to the passage on pages 212–213 to see how most of these words are used in context. Note that the choices might be related forms of the Unit words.*

1. Laura Ingalls Wilder wrote a series of children's books that describe the (**celestial, epic**) story of Western migration.

2. The report that he sent to the president of the company (**underscored, retaliated**) the need for better planning and more careful use of funds.

3. During the long years of defeat, Lincoln searched for a general who would (**prosecute, underscore**) the war fearlessly until the Union was saved.

4. She had such a (**celestial, epic**) expression on her face that I thought she'd seen a vision of heaven.

5. If you try to smuggle goods into this country without paying the customs duties, the inspectors may (**retaliate, confiscate**) the goods and fine you.

6. The trouble with being a(n) (**underscore, pessimist**) is that you are so taken up with what is going wrong that you are unaware of what is going right.

7. The youth center was a (**pessimist, beacon**) to young people seeking help and guidance.

8. Before we can plan properly for the upcoming school year, we must have accurate (**beacons, data**) on the results of last year's programs.

9. Marie is not really pretty, but her sparkling personality and (**celestial, wholesome**) charm make her very attractive.

10. Is it right to (**retaliate, confiscate**) against an evil act by performing evil acts of one's own?

11. When I want a(n) (**epic, wholesome**) snack, I eat a handful of almonds.

12. There is an old saying, that a (**underscore, pessimist**) suffers twice—once when anticipating a calamity, and again when it happens.

You may wish to provide students with an explanation and example of a related form.

Completing the Sentence

Choose the word from the word bank that best completes each of the following sentences. Write the correct word or form of the word in the space provided.

beacon	confiscate	epic	prosecute	underscore
celestial	data	pessimist	retaliate	wholesome

1. Now that we have gathered a vast number of ____**data**____, it is up to us to draw some useful conclusions from all this information.

2. My definition of a(n) ____**pessimist**____ is someone who worries about the hole in the doughnut and forgets about the cake surrounding it.

3. When she said she would "turn the other cheek," she simply meant that she would not ____**retaliate**____ for the injury done to her.

4. After the war, all the property that had been ____**confiscated**____ by the government was turned back to its former owners.

5. Though many people doubted that the new program would do any real good, I thought it was a very ____**wholesome**____ development.

6. Isn't it remarkable that a(n) ____**epic**____ poem such as *The Iliad*, written almost 3,000 years ago, still has interest for readers today?

7. The workbook directions instruct the user to ____**underscore**____ the subject of each sentence in red and the predicate in blue.

8. In ancient times, people gazed at the sky and studied the planets and other ____**celestial**____ bodies to predict the future.

9. The police have done their job in arresting the suspect; now it is up to the district attorney to ____**prosecute**____ him and prove his guilt.

10. Over the years, a great many ships have been saved from destruction by that tall ____**beacon**____ standing on the rocky coast.

Encourage students to look for context clues. See page 7.

End Set B

Synonyms

*Choose the word or form of the word from this Unit that is the same or most nearly the same in meaning as the **boldface** word or expression in the phrase. Write that word on the line. Use a dictionary if necessary.*

1. might **seize** our property _____ confiscate
2. with a strong desire to **avenge** _____ retaliate
3. **safeguards** built into the system _____ precautions
4. photographed the sun and other **stellar** bodies _____ celestial
5. should **emphasize** its safety features _____ underscore
6. **draw away** the reader's attention from the plot _____ detract
7. **put on trial** for burglary _____ prosecute
8. a convincing, yet **phony** excuse _____ sham
9. **nourishing** fruits and vegetables _____ wholesome
10. a **beam** of light _____ beacon
11. a small **pinprick** in the leather _____ puncture
12. enjoyed reading the Greek **saga** _____ epic
13. conveyed his ideas through **the use of gestures** _____ pantomime
14. sure to certify the **figures** _____ data
15. a crowd that is **out of control** _____ berserk

Antonyms

*Choose the word or form of the word from this Unit that is most nearly opposite in meaning to the **boldface** word or expression in the phrase. Write that word on the line. Use a dictionary if necessary.*

1. the family's **cheerful** gathering _____ wistful
2. **idealists** who always share their views _____ pessimists
3. **praised** the demonstrators for their conduct _____ chastened
4. surprised by her **refined** behavior _____ uncouth
5. **avoided** bad weather _____ encountered

Writing: Words in Action

Answers to the prompt will vary.

Suppose that you are a herder who must choose one of the three dog breeds discussed in the passage (pages 212–213) to protect your herd. You must convince your family that your choice is correct. Write a letter supporting your choice. Use at least two details from the passage and three or more words from this Unit.

Vocabulary in Context

*Some of the words you have studied in this Unit appear in **boldface** type. Read the passage below, and then circle the letter of the correct answer for each word as it is used in context.*

If we cast a **wistful** look back at Hollywood history, canine stars loom large. No one can **confiscate** the larger-than-life reputations of these dogs of yore: Rin Tin Tin, Toto, and Lassie. Although these animals may not have been speaking actors, their gestures and expressions could **pantomime** a huge range of emotions. When film and television were young, the canines were **epic** actors in stories that touched us deeply.

Rin Tin Tin was a German shepherd who first starred in the film *Where the North Begins* (1923). The real "Rinty" was discovered by an American serviceman named Lee Duncan in World War I. Rin Tin Tin became legendary for loyalty and courage. He was even nominated for an Oscar for Best Actor in 1929.

Even in the eyes of a **pessimist,** *The Wizard of Oz* (1939) might be one of Hollywood's most inspirational movies. Dorothy, the protagonist of the film, has a faithful companion in Toto, a loveable Cairn terrier who plays an important role in the story. Interesting fact: Toto, a male in the story, was actually played by Terry, a female terrier. She was paid $125 a week, an astronomical salary by the standards of the day.

And now we come to Lassie, possibly the most famous film canine of all time. Lassie was the lead character in *Lassie Come Home* (1943) and then in an extended series of films and TV series. A female Rough Collie, Lassie was the symbol of **wholesome** values: courage, honor, and loyalty. In the series, she regularly risked her life to save her human friends from danger.

---

1. What is the meaning of **wistful** as it is used in paragraph 1?
- **a.** cheerful
- **b.** pensive
- **c.** jubilant
- **d.** resigned

2. What is the meaning of **confiscate** as it is used in paragraph 1?
- **a.** seize
- **b.** reinstate
- **c.** merge
- **d.** invigorate

3. The word **pantomime** means about the same as
- **a.** conceal
- **b.** fuse
- **c.** describe
- **d.** show

4. The word **epic** means about the same as
- **a.** sensitive
- **b.** heroic
- **c.** ingenious
- **d.** amiable

5. Which word means the same as **pessimist** as it is used in paragraph 3?
- **a.** hero
- **b.** hypocrite
- **c.** killjoy
- **d.** Pollyanna

6. What does the word **wholesome** most likely mean as it is used in paragraph 4?
- **a.** baneful
- **b.** injurious
- **c.** abstract
- **d.** beneficial

See pages T29–T31 for assessment options.

Vocabulary for Comprehension
Part 1

*Read "Goya: A Victim of His Art?", which contains words in **boldface** that appear in Units 13–15. Then answer the questions.*

"Goya: A Victim of His Art?"

The masterful Spanish painter Francisco de Goya (1746–1828) **coped** with strange bouts of illness at various times in his life. Might his illness have explained the
(5) dramatic changes in his work? His early paintings were gentle and bright. His graceful portraits were lovely. But over time, his work grew dark, **wistful**, and moody. He began to paint angry,
(10) pessimistic scenes in thick, dark colors. Art historians have long debated the reasons for this shift in Goya's style. Could it have been his health?

Modern science has evidence to
(15) suggest that Goya may have had a severe case of lead poisoning. High levels of lead in the bloodstream can cause muscle and joint pains, headaches, hearing loss, dizziness, mental distress,
(20) nausea, deranged conduct, personality changes, and finally, death. This list **tallies** with the list of symptoms that Goya suffered.

Goya's **disquieting** symptoms forced him to take breaks from painting. When
(25) he felt well enough to return to painting, he would rush back to his studio. There he would grind pigments again and paint enthusiastically to make up for the **lag** in his output.
(30) Like most artists of the past, Goya made his paints himself. Grinding the pigments put him at risk of inhaling lead dust and getting it in his eyes, mouth, and ears and on his skin. Goya also

(35) sometimes applied lead-based pigments to his canvas using only his fingers, so he could have absorbed the lead through his skin, as well.

Goya was known to use an unusual
(40) amount of a pigment called *lead white*. This pigment commonly consisted of two forms of lead combined simply with vinegar. Many of the great masters used lead white because it was durable,
(45) dried quickly, and maintained a fresh appearance. Although other artists risked lead poisoning, few used as much lead white as Goya did. Lead white gave Goya's works their characteristic pearly
(50) glow. But it also made him sick.

Lead poisoning is not unheard of among the great artists of the past. In fact, lead poisoning is a suspected cause of the illness of famous artist Vincent
(55) Van Gogh (1853–1890). Another highly regarded painter, Candido Portinari (1903–1962), was diagnosed with lead poisoning seven years before his death. Unfortunately for Goya, modern medical
(60) understanding of the toxic effects of lead did not emerge until the late 1800s.

It no longer seems **far-fetched** to think that Goya's physical condition changed his artistic vision. One can only wonder
(65) how modern medical knowledge might have prevented his illness and allowed him to express his later genius.

1. What does the word **coped** mean as it is used in line 2?
   A) avoided
   B) discovered
   C) dealt with
   D) suffered from

2. What does the word **wistful** most likely mean as it is used in line 8?
   A) colorful
   B) bright
   C) full of secrets
   D) full of sadness

3. Why does the author **most likely** include the two rhetorical questions in lines 4–5 and line 13?
   A) to set the focus for the entire passage
   B) to later refute these questions with the facts
   C) to challenge the reader
   D) to explain the structure of the passage

4. **Part A**
   What is the meaning of **tallies** as it appears in line 21?
   A) agrees
   B) totals
   C) merges
   D) degrades

   Part B
   Which sentence from "Goya: A Victim of His Art?" provides the **best** clue to the meaning of the word **tallies**?
   A) "early paintings were gentle" (lines 5–6)
   B) "graceful portraits were lovely" (line 7)
   C) "reasons for this shift in Goya's style" (line 12)
   D) "evidence to suggest" (lines 14–15)

5. As used in line 23, what does the word **disquieting** suggest about Goya's symptoms?
   A) They were surprising.
   B) They were disturbing.
   C) They were unusual.
   D) They were hard to describe.

6. What does the word **lag** in line 29 suggest about Goya ?
   A) He quickly produced a glut of paintings while he was ill.
   B) He happily took a break from painting.
   C) He fell behind in his painting and worked hard to make up for lost time.
   D) He showed signs of lead poisoning but ignored them.

7. What is the author's **most likely** reason for including lines 39–50?
   A) to describe lead-based pigments in detail
   B) to list symptoms of lead poisoning
   C) to praise other great artists who used lead-based pigments
   D) to strengthen the argument that Goya's symptoms were those of severe lead poisoning

8. Which word means the opposite of **far-fetched** as used in line 62?
   A) improbable
   B) sympathetic
   C) plausible
   D) shocking

9. Which of the following **best** outlines the structure of this passage?
   A) Goya's biography, lead poisoning
   B) lead-based pigments, lead poisoning
   C) Goya's later work, lead poisoning, Goya's symptoms
   D) changes in Goya's work, symptoms, lead-based pigments, lead poisoning

10. Which statement about the author's point of view is **best** supported by "Goya: A Victim of His Art"?
    A) The author believes that Goya is Spain's greatest genius.
    B) The author suspects that severe lead poisoning caused great changes in Goya's work.
    C) The author is horrified by Goya's many physical symptoms.
    D) The author thinks that Goya's later paintings are superior to his early work.

Vocabulary for Comprehension
Part 2

*Read these passages, which contain words in **boldface** that appear in Units 13–15. Then choose the best answer to each question based on what is stated or implied in the passage(s). You may refer to the passages as often as necessary.*

Questions 1–10 are based on the following passage.

Although some people believe that the term "modern" in modern architecture relates to a contemporary period of design, that is a **misapprehension**.
(5) Modern refers to a specific **trait** of architecture that was dominant from the mid-nineteenth century to the 1970s. Modern architecture emphasizes shape, form, light, and transparency rather than
(10) ornate embellishments. Industrial metals like steel, concrete, and glass give modern architecture its distinctive look. The style is defined by clean lines and minimalist interiors. Modern architects
(15) let the design speak for itself. Therefore, they do not add **supplements** to enhance the design. Many modern designs have angular roof lines and vaulted ceilings and their blueprints have fewer walls
(20) and create open living spaces. Modern architecture also asserts that design should be **submissive** to nature rather than dominating it.

The architect most commonly
(25) associated with modernism is Frank Lloyd Wright. Early in his career, Wright worked with Louis Sullivan. Sullivan was an American architect known as "the father of skyscrapers." Sullivan dreamed of
(30) identifying a uniquely American style of architecture. Through his **encounters** with Sullivan, Wright was later able to **transform** this dream into reality. In 1893, Wright designed the Winslow House in
(35) River Forest, Illinois. The house had expansive, open interior spaces, and it

represented Wright's style, which would later be known as "organic architecture."

In 1915, the Japanese emperor
(40) commissioned Wright to design the Imperial Hotel in Tokyo. Wright created a modernist masterpiece while taking several **precautions** to ensure that the building was earthquake proof. After the
(45) Great Kanto earthquake of 1923 decimated the city, Wright's Imperial Hotel was the only large building to survive the earthquake. In the mid-1930s, Wright was commissioned to build a house for a
(50) family in Pennsylvania. This home, called Fallingwater, is distinguished by its several balconies and terraces built on top of a waterfall. This home is one of Wright's most notable works, and it remains a
(55) national landmark.

In 1934, Wright began the project that would consume the next 16 years of his life: designing the Guggenheim Museum in New York City. After 700 sketches and
(60) 6 working drawings for the building, Wright achieved his goal. Visitors to this building are **stupefied** by its white cylindrical exterior and all of the other geometric shapes that comprise the
(65) internal structure. There was some artistic **upheaval** after the building was designed. These artists believed that the exterior of the building should not overpower the art inside it. Nonetheless, the Guggenheim
(70) Museum still stands, decades after Wright's death, as a modernist marvel and an architectural **beacon** for all who see it.

1. As it is used in line 4, "misapprehension" most nearly means
A) miscalculation.
B) misgiving.
C) misfortune.
D) misunderstanding.

2. The author includes lines 8–23 to
A) distinguish modern architecture from previous forms of architecture.
B) describe some of the important features of modern architecture.
C) name some of the significant buildings that use modern architecture.
D) reveal the philosophy that guides modern architecture.

3. As it is used in line 22, "submissive" most nearly means
A) subservient.
B) subterranean.
C) substitute.
D) subversive.

4. Why does a passage about modernism have information about Frank Lloyd Wright?
A) Wright identified a uniquely American style of architecture.
B) Wright worked with "the father of skyscrapers."
C) Wright is a famous modernist architect.
D) Wright's style was "organic architecture."

5. Which choice provides the best evidence for the answer to the previous question?
A) Lines 24–26 ("The architect ... Wright")
B) Lines 27–29 ("Sullivan ... skyscrapers'")
C) Lines 29–31 ("Sullivan ... architecture")
D) Lines 35–38 ("The ... architecture'")

6. What is the meaning of the word "encounters" as it is used in line 31?
A) meetings
B) fights
C) auditions
D) sidesteps

7. What is the meaning of the word "precautions" as it is used in line 43?
A) steps to postpone an inevitable event
B) steps without adequate preparation
C) steps to prevent something from happening
D) steps following written instructions

8. The author implies that it took Wright 16 years to design the Guggenheim Museum because
A) it was a complex project that involved 700 sketches and 6 working drawings.
B) designing a cylindrical exterior had never been accomplished previously.
C) he was ambivalent about the geometrical interior of the building.
D) he was concerned about the artistic upheaval that his designs received.

9. Why did some artists oppose the design of the Guggenheim Museum?
A) They did not like the white cylindrical exterior of the building.
B) They did not understand the geometric shapes inside the building.
C) They believed that a museum's exterior should not overshadow the art inside.
D) They argued that this design did not adequately represent modern architecture.

10. What is the main idea of the passage?
A) Wright transformed modernism into an architectural movement.
B) Modernism's influence on Wright was evident in his designs.
C) Wright designed several buildings, including the Imperial Hotel, Fallingwater, and the Guggenheim.
D) Designing the Guggenheim Museum was Wright's highest achievement.

Synonyms

*From the word bank below, choose the word that has the same or nearly the same meaning as the **boldface** word in each sentence and write it on the line. You will not use all of the words.*

adhere	cope	fluent	sanctuary
affirm	data	glum	self-seeking
allegiance	exalt	recitation	surge
commemorate	far-fetched	responsive	unscrupulous

1. Although my current situation is not ideal, I will **make do** with it while seeking out greater opportunities.

   _____ cope _____

2. The best authors are **open to** constructive criticism because they want to use the feedback to improve their writing.

   _____ responsive _____

3. She told a story so **unlikely** that I first marveled at her ability to create such a fiction before scolding her for lying.

   _____ far-fetched _____

4. He claims to be able to speak **eloquent** French after studying the language for only one year.

   _____ fluent _____

5. When she heard her classmate take credit for the work she had done, a sudden **flood** of outrage overwhelmed her.

   _____ surge _____

6. Even when it's difficult, I always **hold fast** to my personal rule of being kind to everyone I meet.

   _____ adhere _____

7. The town decided to **memorialize** the former mayor's life by having a celebration in his favorite park every year on his birthday.

   _____ commemorate _____

8. The **dejected** look on her face told me that she had not passed her driving test yet again.

   _____ glum _____

9. You can admire your favorite celebrities, but there is no reason to **elevate** them to superhuman status because of their fame.

   _____ exalt _____

10. I wonder if the ability to review businesses online makes **crooked** salespeople think twice before trying to dupe their patrons.

    _____ unscrupulous _____

11. I would not be nervous about giving a **performance** of a poem that someone else wrote, but reading my own work is extremely frightening to me.

    _____ recitation _____

12. He described himself as simply "ambitious," but we could all see that he was **opportunistic** enough to badmouth others to get ahead at work.

    _____ self-seeking _____

Two-Word Completions

Select the pair of words that best completes the meaning of each of the following sentences.

1. "The only way we are going to _____ people from texting while driving a car," the speaker observed, "is to impose stiff penalties on such behavior and _____ offenders to the full extent of the law."
  a. exalt … puncture
  b. deter … prosecute
  c. empower … accommodate
  d. detract … chasten

2. The young, newly discovered actor has such _____ good looks that adding any makeup would _____ from her natural beauty.
  a. wholesome … detract
  b. empowering … abstain
  c. sulky … transform
  d. uncouth … append

3. In the opening of *The Iliad*, Homer's famous _____ poem about the Trojan War, the hero, Achilles, who has not been accorded the proper reward for his brave deeds, is _____ moodily in his tent.
  a. disquieting … shamming
  b. celestial … prowling
  c. berserk … lagging
  d. epic … sulking

4. It's difficult to _____ all the reasons I like him, especially because he has exhibited so many excellent _____.
  a. puncture … beacons
  b. amalgamate … lags
  c. enumerate … traits
  d. pantomime … epics

5. The _____ who had been lurking very suspiciously around the neighborhood was caught in the act of breaking into our house. The police _____ the set of burglar's tools that he had with him as evidence to back up the charges against him.
  a. pessimist … enumerated
  b. sham … mangled
  c. optimist … underscored
  d. prowler … confiscated

6. To say our new boss is a(n) _____ is one thing. But you are wrong to say that you believe she is making us work very hard to _____ for past wrongs that were done to her.
  a. pessimist … extort
  b. taskmaster … retaliate
  c. sham … prosecute
  d. atrocity … mangle

7. There's a wise old saying that a(n) _____ will see a partially filled glass of water as half full, while a _____ will see the same glass of water as half empty.
  a. optimist … pessimist
  b. taskmaster … sham
  c. trait … beacon
  d. replica … tally

WORD STUDY

Idioms

In the passage "Madam C.J. Walker and Her Wonderful Remedy" (see pages 200–201), the writer says that Madam Walker "took her product on the road." The writer means that Madam Walker traveled from one place to another to sell her product.

"On the road" is an **idiom**. Idioms are words, phrases, or expressions based on colorful comparisons. Their meanings should not be taken literally. People usually learn idioms by hearing and using them in everyday speech. Idioms are unique to every language. When you learn a new idiom and its meaning, you are also learning how different cultures, communities, and generations see the world.

Choosing the Right Idiom

*Read each sentence. Use context clues to figure out the meaning of each idiom in **boldface** print. Then write the letter of the definition for the idiom in the sentence.*

1. Tim tried to explain his tardiness to the teacher, but she did not fall for his **old song and dance**. ___e___

2. **A little bird told me** that Gwen was getting braces next week. ___c___

3. We just got a new boss, so this is not the time to **make any waves**. ___i___

4. "No matter how much money I save from what I earn babysitting," Alison complained, "it just seems to be **a drop in the bucket**." ___h___

5. Garret is still **finding his feet** in his new job as a grocery store cashier. ___j___

6. I know I was angry at James for a while, but that is all **water under the bridge** now. ___d___

7. I don't mean to **rain on your parade**, but I heard the concert was cancelled. ___a___

8. Marie is very health conscious; **once in a blue moon**, though, she'll eat something sugary. ___f___

9. I can't worry about the game tonight," Sam said. "I've got **bigger fish to fry**." ___g___

10. I couldn't **believe my ears** when I heard you were moving. ___b___

a. spoil your fun

b. believe what I'm hearing

c. A secret source I can't reveal gave me the information

d. a past event that is no longer important

e. excuses or lies

f. very infrequently

g. more important business to attend to

h. a very small amount

i. cause trouble; draw attention to yourself

j. getting comfortable in

Classical Roots
pre—before

This Latin prefix appears in **precaution** (page 214). Some other words in which this prefix appears are listed below.

prearrange	prefer	preliminary	preoccupy
precise	prehistoric	premature	preside

From the list of words above, choose the one that corresponds to each of the brief definitions below. Write the word in the blank space in the illustrative sentence below the definition. Use a dictionary if necessary.

1. belonging to the period before written history
The museum has a fascinating new exhibit that explains how scientists identify and classify the bones of _____**prehistoric**_____ animals.

2. very definite or clear, exact; very careful; strict
The doctor left _____**precise**_____ instructions on how to clean the wound.

3. to like better, choose over something else; to put forward, press
Although many customers _____**prefer**_____ to order healthy appetizers and main courses, restaurant owners report an increased interest in rich desserts.

4. to have authority over, oversee
Tomorrow is the first opportunity our principal will have to _____**preside**_____ at the community school board meeting.

5. unexpectedly early in development; coming too soon
The expectant mother was alerted to the possibility of a _____**premature**_____ birth, so she took extra good care of herself.

6. coming before the main business or action; introductory; something that comes before the main event, a curtain-raiser
Although the young boxer lost the _____**preliminary**_____ bout, knowledgeable fans could readily see that he had promise.

7. to absorb one's attention completely or at the expense of other things
She was so _____**preoccupied**_____ with the novel that she forgot to return my phone call.

8. to arrange ahead of time
One important task of a travel agent is to _____**prearrange**_____ transportation and accommodations so that the client can focus on enjoying the trip.

Synonyms

Select the two words or expressions that are most nearly the same in meaning.

1. **a.** keepsake   **b.** memento   **c.** pacifist   **d.** oracle
2. **a.** engulf   **b.** maneuver   **c.** manipulate   **d.** liberate
3. **a.** synopsis   **b.** allegiance   **c.** consequence   **d.** fidelity
4. **a.** gloat   **b.** supplement   **c.** infuriate   **d.** relish
5. **a.** cascade   **b.** queue   **c.** deluge   **d.** enigma
6. **a.** rigorous   **b.** contemporary   **c.** compliant   **d.** submissive
7. **a.** stupefy   **b.** compact   **c.** waylay   **d.** compress
8. **a.** numb   **b.** celestial   **c.** nimble   **d.** limber
9. **a.** meteoric   **b.** immense   **c.** titanic   **d.** stealthy
10. **a.** empower   **b.** pry   **c.** accommodate   **d.** authorize
11. **a.** billow   **b.** surge   **c.** confer   **d.** induce
12. **a.** ravenous   **b.** famished   **c.** outright   **d.** sheepish
13. **a.** immerse   **b.** besiege   **c.** douse   **d.** prowl
14. **a.** encounter   **b.** vacate   **c.** confront   **d.** tally
15. **a.** balk   **b.** saunter   **c.** replenish   **d.** amble

Antonyms

Select the two words or expressions that are most nearly opposite in meaning.

16. **a.** acute   **b.** bumbling   **c.** optional   **d.** taut
17. **a.** immobile   **b.** jovial   **c.** smug   **d.** glum
18. **a.** motivate   **b.** cringe   **c.** bluster   **d.** deter
19. **a.** innovation   **b.** trait   **c.** replica   **d.** sham
20. **a.** optimist   **b.** responsive   **c.** incalculable   **d.** pessimist
21. **a.** maximum   **b.** giddy   **c.** mortal   **d.** minimum
22. **a.** append   **b.** confiscate   **c.** detract   **d.** enumerate
23. **a.** acquit   **b.** wither   **c.** thrive   **d.** depict
24. **a.** ruffle   **b.** dole   **c.** vow   **d.** prevaricate
25. **a.** expend   **b.** retrieve   **c.** denounce   **d.** idolize

Two-Word Completions

Select the pair of words that best completes the meaning of each of the following sentences.

26. It is a bad idea to _____ breakfast in the morning, because you will probably find yourself _____ and tired later in the day.

   a. dissect … strapping
   c. rummage through … sulky
   b. skimp on … sluggish
   d. cede … inflammatory

27. Taking the _____ to make friends with new students at school can really help them _____ the changes happening in their lives.

   a. illusion … tarry
   c. terrain … abstain from
   b. onset … repent
   d. initiative … cope with

28. Doesn't it make you a(n) _____ to expect that she pay you back right away when it often takes you a month to _____ someone?

   a. atrocity … refurbish
   c. hypocrite … reimburse
   b. nonconformist … prosecute
   d. sage … constrain

29. The new principal has begun _____ stricter rules about the use of _____ materials in school.

   a. foiling … resourceful
   c. designating … wholesome
   b. commemorating … burly
   d. implementing … illicit

30. The _____ look on her face made me think she was lost in a _____ about happier times and better places.

   a. impassable … remorse
   c. wistful … reverie
   b. gainful … extinct
   d. perishable … petty

31. Though not normally _____, he can be quite stubborn when he thinks his judgment is _____.

   a. headstrong … indisputable
   c. rotund … logical
   b. dogged… global
   d. strident … strapping

32. Some people really enjoy a brisk wind and _____ winter air, but I prefer the _____ breezes and warm air of late spring.

   a. adverse… fluent
   c. boisterous … inept
   b. frigid… serene
   d. partisan … amiable

Supplying Words in Context

To complete each sentence, select the best word from among the choices given. Not all words in the word bank will be used. You may modify the word form as necessary.

arid	delude	facet	refute
beacon	devastate	maze	retaliate
culprit	encompass	prevail	subordinate
debut	epic	puncture	variable

33. Now that the two candidates have finished their long, hard campaigns, it is up to the voters to say which one will _____**prevail**_____.

34. You are just _____**deluding**_____ yourself if you think you can do well in school without study.

35. The story of the men who first climbed to the top of Mount Everest is a(n) _____**epic**_____ of human courage and strength.

36. His arguments were so soundly based and so well presented that no one could _____**refute**_____ them.

37. Only a tiny _____**puncture**_____ in the skin showed where the doctor had made the injection.

38. Parents will always _____**subordinate**_____ their own interests to the well being of their children.

dispatch	fray	pantomime	sleuth
dumbfounded	groundless	pathetic	taskmaster
eerie	instantaneous	rendezvous	unerring
far-fetched	misrepresent	sabotage	valiant

39. What a(n) _____**eerie**_____ feeling it gave us to listen to ghost stories as we sat around the flickering campfire!

40. In silent movies, actors had to express ideas and emotions by means of _____**pantomime**_____.

41. Coach Robinson is a strict _____**taskmaster**_____, who expects instant obedience and 100 percent effort from all his players.

42. She is so shrewd that her judgments of people are almost _____**unerring**_____.

43. My long-awaited _____**rendezvous**_____ with Eileen turned out to be a disappointment when she got sick and could not make it.

44. I cannot believe that these repeated breakdowns of the machinery are no more than "accidents"; I suspect _____**sabotage**_____.

Word Associations

*Select the word or expression that best completes the meaning of the sentence or answers the question, with particular reference to the meaning of the word in **boldface** type.*

45. A school course dealing with **vocations** will help you
    a. become a good dancer
    b. plan for a career
    c. develop your speaking ability
    d. become a "math shark"

46. If you receive news that is **disquieting** you will probably be
    a. upset
    b. pleased
    c. calm
    d. delighted

47. Which of the following would be a **chastening** experience?
    a. going to a party
    b. winning a scholarship
    c. doing poorly on this exam
    d. spending the day at the beach

48. A person who **abducts** another will probably
    a. be arrested for kidnapping
    b. receive a prize
    c. go to the hospital
    d. get picked for a team

49. You would seek **sanctuary** if you were
    a. in the dark
    b. rich
    c. hungry
    d. being pursued

50. A basketball player who lacks **stamina** would be likely to
    a. argue with the referee
    b. show a lack of team spirit
    c. tire quickly
    d. miss foul shots

51. A habit that is deeply **ingrained** is
    a. easy to get rid of
    b. of no great importance
    c. a bad one
    d. hard to change

52. A study program might properly be called **intensive** if it
    a. calls for hours of hard work
    b. will help you get a summer job
    c. is a lot of fun
    d. is open to everyone

53. A student who is lost in a **reverie**
    a. is well prepared for final exams
    b. is daydreaming
    c. has a toothache
    d. has taken a wrong turn

54. A person who **reminisces** a great deal might be criticized for
    a. using foul language
    b. borrowing money
    c. living in the past
    d. insulting other people

55. A person who is wearing **manacles** is probably a
    a. teacher
    b. judge
    c. prisoner
    d. model

56. You will **affirm** your mastery of the words taught in this book if you
    a. score 100% on this Final Test
    b. never use them in class
    c. spell them incorrectly
    d. forget what they mean

Choosing the Right Meaning

Read each sentence carefully. Then select the item that best completes the statement below the sentence.

57. As punishment for failing the exam, his father **restricted** his after-school activities.
The word **restricted** most nearly means
a. ended **b.** limited **c.** widened **d.** guided

58. The report provided the **data** I needed to finish my research paper.
The word **data** most nearly means
a. money **b.** equipment **c.** information **d.** assistance

59. The teacher corrected the **misapprehension** that the rule "I before E except after C" applies in all cases.
The word **misapprehension** most nearly means
a. formula **b.** examination **c.** misunderstanding **d.** plan

60. He spent so much time **dawdling** over which movie to see that by the time he made a decision, both films had already started.
The word **dawdling** most nearly means
a. fighting **b.** napping **c.** working **d.** loafing

61. The **inevitable** result of procrastination is a lot of stress the night before an exam.
The word **inevitable** most nearly means
a. unavoidable **b.** sudden **c.** unexpected **d.** regrettable

62. Her dream is to turn her talent as a skilled **mimic** into a career as an actress.
The word **mimic** most nearly means
a. imitator **b.** athlete **c.** politician **d.** speaker

63. After our ill-fated first meeting I had many **misgivings** about the new team member, but I've found I like her very much after taking time to get to know her.
The word **misgivings** most nearly means
a. victories **b.** presents **c.** doubts **d.** setbacks

64. Although she usually acted meek, during tough times she showed more **grit** than anyone else.
The word **grit** most nearly means
a. restlessness **b.** judgment **c.** fear **d.** courage

65. Those who had been following the case closely thought the "not guilty" verdict a **parody** of justice.
The word **parody** most nearly means
a. fear **b.** mockery **c.** example **d.** cause

The following is a list of all the words taught in the Units of this book. The number after each entry indicates the page on which the word is defined.